"Kathleen Ness has written a must-read for anyone considering education, school psychology, and social advocacy. From her upbringing in rural America to her work in public schools, Kathleen's experiences provide readers with an in-depth understanding of the current educational system and calls to action for the future".

—**Dr. Natasha Olson**, *Nationally Certified School Psychologist*

"Never before have students and school personnel so deeply needed skills to build their sense of belonging and safety at school. This book gives practical guidance and strong helpful research for school psychologists and those who work alongside them to advocate at every level to meet these needs".

—**Sally A. Baas**, *Ed.D., Professor Joshua Vossler Emeritas of Education at Concordia University, St. Paul, Director of Southeast Asian Teacher Program, and Faculty Senate Chair of Hmong Culture and Language Program*

"Read this book. Kathleen Ness has eloquently laid out how important and easy it is to advocate for the things we care about. Ms. Ness reminds us that our voices matter. In her words and her actions, she inspires us all to stand up and speak out for change".

—**Jos G. Linn**, *Manager of Grass Roots Impact, RESULTS*

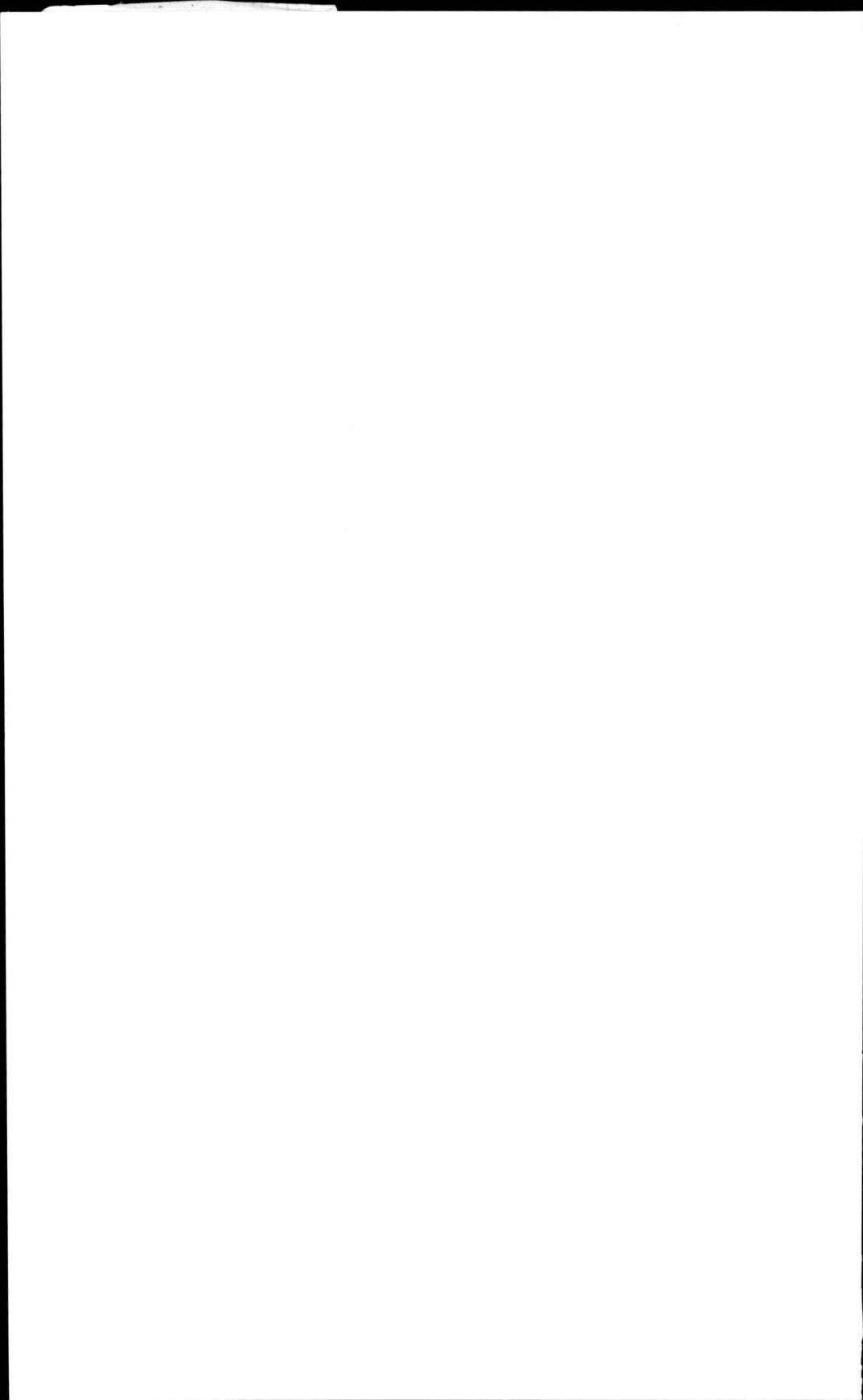

School Psychologists as Advocates for Social Justice

School Psychologists as Advocates for Social Justice explores how school psychologists promote and protect the educational rights of children, using the author's extensive experience as illustration.

The roles of school psychologists have expanded from strictly assessment to advising school districts on how to improve school climate, helping schools face tragedy, and counseling students dealing with trauma. Combined with pertinent research, personal narratives describe challenges the author faced while a teacher and later as a school psychology practitioner and illustrate how necessary advocacy is in addressing the academic, behavioral, and emotional needs of students. Careful consideration is given to equity issues of disability, racism, Islamophobia, and bilingualism in schools.

Combining informative personal experience with research, emphasizing the importance of children's rights within the school community, and encouraging effective advocacy with legislative leaders, this book is a necessity for both new and seasoned school psychologists.

Kathleen Ness, N.C.S.P., retired, also holds a Master of Arts in the Teaching of English. She advocates for children, schools, and families through NASP and with RESULTS.

School Psychologists as Advocates for Social Justice

Kathleen Ness

Routledge
Taylor & Francis Group

NEW YORK AND LONDON

Designed cover image: Getty Image

First published 2023
by Routledge
605 Third Avenue, New York, NY 10158

and by Routledge
4 Park Square, Milton Park, Abingdon, Oxon, OX14 4RN

Routledge is an imprint of the Taylor & Francis Group, an informa business

Library of Congress Cataloging-in-Publication Data
Names: Ness, Kathleen, author.
Title: School psychologists as advocates for social justice / Kathleen Ness.
Description: 1 Edition. | New York : Routledge, 2023. | Includes bibliographical references and index. |
Identifiers: LCCN 2022034007 (print) | LCCN 2022034008 (ebook) | ISBN 9781032390871 (Hardback) | ISBN 9781032390864 (Paperback) | ISBN 9781003348344 (eBook)
Subjects: LCSH: School psychologists—United States. | School psychology—United States—Case studies. | School psychologists—Training of—United States.
Classification: LCC LB3013.6 .N37 2023 (print) | LCC LB3013.6 (ebook) | DDC 371.7/13—dc23/eng/20220722
LC record available at https://lccn.loc.gov/2022034007
LC ebook record available at https://lccn.loc.gov/2022034008

ISBN. 978-1-032-39087-1 (hbk)
ISBN: 978-1-032-39086-4 (pbk)
ISBN: 978-1-003-34834-4 (ebk)

DOI: 10.4324/9781003348344

Typeset in New Baskerville
by Apex CoVantage, LLC

To Tim, for everything

Contents

About the Author

Kathleen Ness began her career teaching diverse populations in the American South and Pakistan. This experience helped prepare her for her second occupation, as a rural school psychologist, first in a special education cooperative in North Dakota, followed by three decades in a Minnesota co-op. Children with disabilities, the children of Somali immigrants, and Indigenous and Hispanic students gave her further lessons in diversity. Her passion for civic advocacy grew out of witnessing the harm of shrinking resources on schools and of poverty in the lives of children. Once she retired, she joined RESULTS, a nonpartisan advocacy organization, and in this book, she shares what she has learned about how to be an effective advocate. Kathleen is a Nationally Certified School Psychologist (retired) and holds a Master of Arts in the Teaching of English. She lives in Grand Forks, North Dakota, with her husband, Timothy Ness.

Acknowledgments

Thank you to Amanda Savage, Editor, Mental Health at Routledge/Taylor & Francis Group, for supporting my project, and to her Editorial Assistant, Katya Porter, for shepherding me through the publication process and making this book possible.

I wrote this book upon the encouragement of my final school psychology intern, Dr. Natasha Olson, who felt the stories from my experience as a teacher and school psychologist were timely enough that they should be shared with others, beyond just the students I supervised. I am grateful for Natasha's insights as a current practitioner and her faith in the value of my efforts.

My husband, Tim Ness, also urged me to describe my experiences and volunteered his editorial skills and countless hours of his time. I appreciate his expertise and the loving devotion he gave to my project. My son, Josh, has been a godsend as a technical expert, coaching me on computer skills and advising me on publishing and research practices. His example as a published book author inspired me to try my hand. A special thank you to Christina Heady, for her technical assistance, also.

I am grateful beyond measure to Jolene Mikkelson, who shared her professional expertise as an occupational therapist and her personal experience with raising a son with a disability. Her comments added a depth to my chapter on relationships with parents that would have been impossible otherwise.

I owe a debt to the Minnesota School Psychology Legislative Committee, which brought me up to date on social justice issues affecting schools and provided a living example of ongoing advocacy for schools and the children they serve. Dr. Sally Bass and Marilyn Liefgren urged me on, with Marilyn sharing insights from her own research on social justice. I thank Sara Howe for her phrase, "sleuth psychologist". The youngest members of the committee especially inspired me, as they took on the responsibility of their new career as practitioners and, at the same time, devoted time to advocacy.

I must also express thanks for the support from friends, all of whom were teachers at some point in their lives. Pat Danielson, Rosemary Hoverson, Phyllis Kalliokowski, and Karen Wills Cunningham offered encouragement and were willing readers and listeners. Karen also introduced me to RESULTS, the advocacy organization that has shaped my retirement and is featured in this book.

I must extend a heartfelt thank-you to Marti Vanderpan, who accompanied me for decades as a fellow rural itinerant school psychologist and who partnered with me in several of the most challenging experiences I write about. A burden shared is a burden divided. Gary Jones, my director for many years, supported me while I pursued nontraditional activities such as incorporating sand tray world play into my practice. Without his backing, I would have been less effective in my role, and not nearly as joyful.

Thank you to Dr. Sonya Brandt, Dr. Lisa Stewart, and Bridgette Campoverde for their support at the proposal stage of the book.

RESULTS, the nonprofit civic action anti-poverty organization I joined in retirement, deserves my deepest gratitude. Jos Lin, a grassroots organizer for RESULTS, cheered on all my successes with letter writing and speaking with the office staff of my members of Congress, as well as providing four educational webinars for the Minnesota School Psychology Association. I thank him for his editing and encouragement, all the while schooling me in civic advocacy. His contribution made the book complete.

I must acknowledge the inspiration of my parents' example. Rognvaldur and Nettie Johnson were fine role models of compassion for others, particularly in their concern for people with disabilities.

Finally, I wish to express my appreciation to all the students, their parents, teachers, paras, administrators, janitors, school secretaries, special education teachers, speech clinicians, school counselors, school social workers, school nurses, occupational therapists, physical therapists, and school psychologists—everybody comprising my school and special education co-op communities—for putting me to the test and, in the course of it, teaching me what I could not have learned without them. I hope in the telling of my stories I have not misspoken.

Chapter 1

Introduction

If I were asked to sum up the mission of school psychology in one word, my answer would be advocacy. As advocates, school psychologists support policies which assure that children are treated fairly. Such policies have implications not only for learning, but also for physical, mental, and behavioral health. At its basis, the profession exists to help kids overcome barriers which interfere with their ability to thrive.

This is a book filled with anecdotes and narratives from my life as a teacher and school psychologist, set against the significant legal and historical developments that have had an impact on our nation's schools in the last 50 years, and so affected my work. The emergence of the disability rights movement and the advances and setbacks of the civil rights movement over the past century helped to shape our schools, and my experience serves as one example.

From the beginning of my teaching experience at age 21 to the moment I retired as a school psychologist 44 years later, the quest for educational justice was an overriding theme on a national scale, and so filtered down into my daily practice. As a result, I would find myself at the vortex of tensions between the old way of doing things and the mandate to uphold educational rights in school as enacted into law, most notably the 1975 Individuals with Disabilities Education Act. The expansion of the profession of school psychology parallels the growth of children's rights, and school psychologists serve to promote and defend them. Advocating for equitable treatment of children in school who might otherwise be underserved was central to my role.

As a teacher I worked in such settings as an all-Black elementary school at the beginning of racial integration in the American South, a private American school in Pakistan during the proclamation of jihad against America by the Ayatollah Khomeini, and a migrant school for the children of Hispanic farm laborers in North Dakota. Gaining experience with diverse populations helped to prepare me for my second career, as an itinerant rural school psychologist for special education cooperatives in North Dakota and Minnesota. With the ongoing relentless economic

DOI:10.4324/9781003348344-1

decline of many rural communities, I also witnessed the impact of shrinking resources on schools and of poverty in the lives of children and their families.

The list of challenges facing schools at the present time is daunting: the increase in childhood depression, anxiety, suicidality, and homelessness; the increase in bullying related to race, religion, ethnicity, and gender; inadequate funding resulting from budget cuts, attrition from teaching, school psychology, and other specialties; fear of school mass shootings; and, amid it all, adapting to a pandemic. Sustaining adequate special education services in school and promoting a positive school climate for everyone under these conditions requires tremendous strength and dedication from school personnel, and more resources than are generally available.

In addition, one must advocate within an environment that isn't always sympathetic, so upholding children's educational rights can take a toll. Furthermore, in the face of shrinking school budgets, school personnel are often stretched thin. They face pressures that can be exhausting over time, and many wonder how best to cope. Stress among school professionals has risen to the point that even the most experienced wonder if they can persist until retirement age. A woman about 20 years my junior asked, "How did you do it? How did you survive?" This led to a conversation about the stress she—and all the school psychologists we knew— suffered. Because she feared she wouldn't, she wanted to know how I had made it to my mid-60s without having to quit out of sheer exhaustion, and this was before the pandemic struck.

I heard a similar sentiment from Dr. Natasha Olson, the school psychologist who succeeded me in the position I vacated through retirement and was the last graduate student intern I mentored. She felt my stories from my years first as a teacher and then as a school psychologist resonated all too well with the current challenges facing her and her cohorts, so she encouraged me to share them in writing, believing they deserved a wider audience.

Through my narratives, I highlight the racial and cultural issues that confronted me in diverse school settings. How culture intertwines with one's identity serves as a recurring theme throughout the book, and I reflect on the insights I gained along the way. Through this lens I examine the bonds, interactions, and the roles we play with parents, teachers, administrators, and other school personnel, and, most importantly, the children we encounter, all of whom can add to our stress or save us from it. Much depends on how well we navigate relationships day to day in our school communities, and cultural awareness is an important factor.

More and more, school psychologists, like others who work in schools, must find ways to protect themselves. Deliberate steps must be taken to preserve strength and peace of mind. Personal self-care by itself, however, is not enough to address the level of stress educators, including school psychologists, suffer. It is necessary but not sufficient to cultivate healthful work and personal habits that can minimize the toll of dealing with occupational pressures and absorbing the secondary trauma from witnessing the suffering of children. Public policy at all levels of government must also be addressed to preserve public education and the professions which serve it.

Policy decisions made over the decades have set the course for disproportionate funding of public schools. I give an overview of how taxation policies affect education, resulting in ample funds for schools in affluent districts and inadequate services in impoverished communities. During much of the time I wrote this, the Covid-19 pandemic was raging, wreaking havoc on the learning of millions of our children. A brief history of pandemics and their impact on school life, as well as commentary on the crisis itself, also seemed both timely and necessary.

I devote a chapter specifically to civic advocacy because I would like to see all public schools provide enough resources, including support staff personnel. Professional services need to be adequately funded through state and federal appropriations, so we must address weaknesses in public policy. A positive side effect of political action is that raising one's voice respectfully builds self-confidence and serves to strengthen resolve. The current increase in organized advocacy among school psychologists proclaiming the need for our profession gives me hope.

I must acknowledge that only my voice is represented here. I do not and cannot speak for anyone else, knowing my point of view has been shaped by my unique identity and personal history. I am a woman (she, her) of Scandinavian descent whose forebears acquired farmland in North Dakota under the Homestead Act. This Act made land available to European immigrants which was acquired from Indigenous people through fraud or under threat from the U.S. military. My background is rural, complemented by urban and foreign experiences in my youth. That said, I hope that what I have to say is universal enough that it can offer meaning to others, particularly young people embarking on their careers in schools.

Questions to guide discussion are provided at the end of the text.

Chapter 2

Why It Took Me So Long to Become a School Psychologist

In 1964, my mother, Nettie Johnson, became a night attendant on a women's ward at what was then known as the Grafton State School. The State School was a large, overcrowded residential institution with an intimidating reputation. Sometimes residents responded aggressively with staff, so my family wondered how safe she would be. Also, among the residents were those with severe physical deformities and limitations which rendered them quite helpless. Confronted with the magnitude of her responsibility to those suffering extreme disability, my mother lost a pound a day just from the stress of her first week on the job. But this was her best opportunity to earn income. My father needed surgery and couldn't work, and she was determined to provide for us.

For the 15 years she worked there, beginning when I was a sophomore in high school, and the remaining three decades thereafter until the end of her life, I listened to her recount her experiences. In my youth her stories discouraged me from considering a career in psychology because of her descriptions of conditions in the institution, but from my vantage point now, I realize she became my model of how to treat—and think about—people with disabilities. At the time I became a school psychology practitioner, I believed I was embarking on a path independent of influence from my childhood, not recognizing that I was following my mother's lead. As it turned out, any originality on my part was in the details. Her stories also set the stage for my interest in governmental and institutional policy as it affects individual lives.

The Grafton State School

The State School was built in 1904 and was intended at that time to instruct the "feeble minded", the terminology of the day, in skills related to farming. Over time it became much less of a location to train people in agricultural skills and instead became primarily a place to house people with developmental disabilities. By the time my mother took a position there, the place was overcrowded and understaffed. Compared with

DOI:10.4324/9781003348344-2

other states, North Dakota had the dubious distinction of providing the least funds per capita to provide for the residents than any other state in the union (Association for Retarded Citizens of ND v. Olson, 1982).

At the State School, my mother's duties as a night attendant consisted of tending to the needs of residents and making sure they were safe. That meant escorting people to the bathroom if they were ambulatory, helping them in and out of bed, and keeping those in diapers dry. It was common for some to be tied into their beds to prevent them from falling on the floor. This was a consideration especially for people with epilepsy, who were subject to violent seizures, and my mother often voiced worries about them. Caring for them was a grave responsibility, especially for someone with no training in healthcare.

Sometimes people were put in strait jackets and tied down to control their behavior, even to punish them. My mother objected to this practice. She immediately set about building relationships with people so they would stay in bed just because she asked it of them. She also questioned the purpose of the time-out room, which she believed was overused. It seemed to her that it all too often served as a jail, with residents isolated far longer than their misbehavior warranted.

My mother never lost her sensitivity to the helplessness she witnessed. I remember her talking about a woman whose head was so large and heavy and her body so small that she could not sit up and, consequently, spent her life in bed. My mother often commented on the suffering accompanying disability, shaking her head, and wondering out loud why some people had to be so unfortunate.

My Mother and Polio Rehabilitation

Besides her compassion for the residents, my mother also brought a bit of experience with rehabilitation to her position, thanks to a crisis within her own family decades earlier. When my mother was about 12 years old, one of her younger sisters contracted polio during an epidemic. The doctor who paid a house call ended his visit by declaring to my grandmother that her daughter would be a "helpless cripple" for the rest of her life. My grandmother, however, had other ideas.

She recruited her two oldest daughters, my mother being one of them, to help the younger one regain the ability to walk. The two older sisters helped by rubbing their sister's arms and legs and applying heat on them. As she gained strength, they supported her between them as she took her first tentative steps. On one side her arm and leg were partially paralyzed, but little by little, step by step, she regained mobility. This was an early lesson for my mother in seeing hope where one might be tempted to give in to despair. Perhaps it is why she had a habit of seeing possibilities, not just limitations.

My Mother's Approach

She did what she could to aid and comfort the residents, whether it meant making sure no one ever had to lie in bed in a urine-soaked diaper or learning how to talk to someone so restraints would be unnecessary. Her hunch proved correct. Speaking to people kindly and showing patience with them was usually sufficient. Her kindness was also her best protection against harm. Over time the residents on her wards grew to trust her. I believe my mother's best gift was her compassion. She saw everyone on her wards as human beings first and never underestimated their capacity to feel, even if they couldn't walk or speak. She became their ally, and soon lost all fear of the people she cared for.

Keeping everyone comfortable by making sure they were warm, clean, and dry throughout the night was a source of pride for her. She treated them the way she would have wanted to be treated, had her fate been theirs. The residents' affection for her was obvious. Many called her Mama, and when she came on duty for her shift several would run to her, repeating "Dontin, Dontin", their attempt to pronounce "Johnson", her last name. It was evident in how she spoke about them that she considered herself to be their protector, instilling her routine with meaning. "Poor things", she would say. "Just because they can't talk doesn't mean they don't feel".

That children could be abandoned for any reason was an injustice that offended my mother deeply. Many of the residents were left on the advice of the physician who attended their birth. Parents were told to forget the child and turn it over to the state. This was typical advice from the medical/psychological community in the mid-twentieth century. The thinking at the time was that the stress of caring for children with severe impairments would destroy family life (Nielson, 2012).

Because my mother disapproved of separating children from their parents, she made a point of reuniting a family with their daughter who had been placed in the State School shortly after birth. When my mother realized she was caring for the teenage daughter of a family she knew, she informed them, convinced they would want to know. The parents were over-joyed to hear about their child, and soon they were taking her home for visits.

Most of the residents she told me about had severe disabilities, but there were others who she swore were of normal intelligence. My mother had heard that these women had been left there as infants because they were the result of an illegitimate birth. She often commented on the injustice they had been dealt. Aggrieved by their fate, she would wonder out loud to me about what their lives would have been like had they been given the opportunity to live outside the State School. It would take almost another two decades to pass before residents such as these would be placed within their community, rather than institutionalized.

Much was asked of employees like my mother. Fortunately, many co-workers shared my mother's concern for the residents. Judging from the records of the court case brought against the State School, however, we know there were staff who deliberately engaged in cruel practices. Because the institution was severely underfunded and consequently, understaffed, great harm was done through sheer neglect (Association for Retarded Citizens of ND v. Olson, 561 F. Supp. 473 D.N.D., 1982).

The Impact on Me

Because of the trials my mother faced, I developed an awe of anyone who worked with people with disabilities. Thanks to the hair-raising tales she told, such as the story of the alleged murder of an attendant by an enraged resident, I concluded the school was a dangerous place, more of a human warehouse than an educational institution. I dismissed psychology as a profession without ever really considering it.

With 20/20 hindsight, however, I now realize that my mother's stories about the people she cared for primed me for a future connected to special education. Her narratives illustrated the basic humanity of the residents and her determination to do right by them in their plight served to inform my heart. Furthermore, I now believe my mother's acute awareness of injustice influenced me to pay close attention to how fairly children are treated.

Her example of adapting under difficult circumstances guided me throughout my career as a teacher and, later, as a school psychologist. She kept her expectations realistic, knew what her own priorities needed to be, and sought support among co-workers and friends. She did the best she could within the limits she was allowed, while trusting her own judgment to go beyond when she saw the need. Her first consideration was the well-being of the residents; she never forgot human lives were at stake.

Because she knew how much relationships mattered, my mother stood on a strong foundation. She built rapport with those in her care, which helped ensure everyone's safety. She made friends with like-minded co-workers, which strengthened her resolve. She gained the respect of her supervisors because she never failed to carry out her responsibilities, however difficult. Perhaps most importantly, her actions were invested with deep meaning; she knew the value of what she did.

My mother recognized that she needed to attend to her own needs as well as those of the people she cared for. During her work life she had a habit of calming herself by crocheting, because, she said, "It helped steady my nerves", and she bore witness by telling her stories, which discharged some of her secondary trauma and at the same time informed her listener. Had she been as well educated as Engla Schey or

Judy Heumann, two disability rights advocates who appear in the next chapter, I suspect she also would have spoken out and become an advocate. Her one regret in life, she told me, was that she "wished she had said more".

When I went off to the university at age 18, I pursued the career my father might have had, had he gone on in school beyond eighth grade. A lover of poetry, especially that of his first language, he read and recited Icelandic poems regularly. He even served as a linguistic guide for an Icelandic linguist who came to North America to study the language of the "western Icelanders", as we are called by those who live in Iceland. The scholar told me my father spoke the most beautiful Icelandic he heard among the people he visited. I had no way to judge, but my father's recitations had always touched me, and I believe they helped to inspire my interest in teaching English, my first language. Although I didn't learn Icelandic, I caught his love of words. He once told me he probably should have become a teacher. It was not a coincidence that was the career I chose.

My mother's stories were the very first influence forming my attitude toward psychology as a profession, and they frightened me away. As it turned out, my path to becoming a school psychologist began with my teaching in various settings for about a decade. I now think of that time as my apprenticeship in learning how politics shapes schools and in understanding the needs of the children they exist to serve. I had no inkling that my teaching positions would lead me to school psychology; I expected to remain a teacher in some capacity for my entire career.

My final school psychology intern, Dr. Natasha Olson, on the other hand, majored in psychology as an undergraduate and then went straight through to a doctoral degree in school psychology. By comparison, my path was oblique. When Natasha asked what drew me to our vocation, I felt I had to begin by telling what at first discouraged me from it. As scholars have observed, it is not unusual for school psychologists to join the profession "by happenstance" (Barrett et al., 2019). Research shows I am not the only one to have followed a winding road to school psychology. We didn't know where we were going until we got there. My journey is a case in point.

References

Association for Retarded Citizens of ND v. Olson, 561 F. Supp. 473 D.N.D. (1982).

Barrett, C., Heidelburg, K., & Malone, C. (2019). The NASP exposure project: Addressing workforce shortages and social justice. *Communiqué, 47*(5), 8–10.

Nielson, K. (2012). *A disability history of the United States*. Beacon Press.

Chapter 3

Claiming Disability Rights

The Union of Disability Rights and Civil Rights

By the mid-twentieth century, the civil rights movement and the disability rights movement were recognizing one another as kindred spirits on the national level. They both sought to claim full human rights for the people they represented. An important early figure in the quest for disability rights was Robert Payne, a Black man from West Virginia, who was disabled because he had been severely burned in a mining accident in 1967. Three years later, he led a wildcat strike of about 40,000 coal miners.

The United Mine Workers Union (U.M.W.A.) had become corrupt and squandered funds intended for disabled members. Payne joined with other victims of this corruption, forming the Disabled Miners and Widows of Southern West Virginia, a group which had among its members many African-American women and disabled miners. Another group formed, calling themselves Miners for Democracy, and together with Payne's organization and the Black Lung Association, they exerted enough pressure for the U.M.W.A. to reform. Because of the demographic composition of these groups, civil rights and disability rights were advocated for under the same umbrella. Judith Heumann, a leader among those with disabilities, observed, "When we were united, it was as if progress happened overnight" (Nielson, 2012). This collaboration led to President Lyndon Johnson's War on Poverty, brought into law a few years later (Heumann, 2020).

The impact of this union would also be felt in public school. Many children with disabilities would now be able to live at home and receive services in their neighborhood school, rather than being placed in an institution. In my home state of North Dakota, these developments would eventually affect the Grafton State School through dramatic restructuring, which would improve the treatment of the residents. In the 1980s, my mother's place of work would undergo tremendous change.

One of the most effective figures in the disability rights movement of the second half of the twentieth century was also a polio survivor. In 1968,

DOI:10.4324/9781003348344-3

just a few years after my mother took her position at the State School, Robert L. Burgdorf, Jr., had wanted to follow in his father's footsteps as an electrician. He had the skills to do the work, but he was refused the opportunity; he was sent away by the foreman doing the hiring for a summer assistant job with the comment, "We're not hiring any cripples here" (Shapiro, 1994, p. 107).

Twenty years later, Burgdorf was a skilled attorney and specialist in disability law. He joined forces with another powerful advocate, Justin Dart, Jr., who, like Burgdorf, was a polio survivor and a member of the National Council on the Handicapped, under the Reagan administration. They, with the support of thousands of people with disabilities, were able to guide the 1990 Americans with Disabilities Act (A.D.A.) into becoming a law, a remarkable feat (Shapiro, 1994).

The Disability Rights Independent Living Movement

Another giant of the disability rights movement was Judy Heumann. She contracted polio when she was two and became a paraplegic. Her parents were Jews who had survived the Holocaust. They refused to send her to an institution because they were suspicious of doctors who wanted disabled children sent away, knowing it had meant extermination back in Germany (Heumann, 2020, pp. xi–xiii).

Heumann grew up to become one of the most significant leaders in the Disability Rights Independent Living Movement. Her leadership in the fight for disability rights helped to shift the notion of physical disability from being considered a personal medical issue to a problem of equal access to opportunity within the community. Eventually it came to be viewed as a civil rights issue, which in due time shaped the argument used to force restructuring at the State School in Grafton. As Heumann emphasized, "we tend to think that equality is about treating everyone the same, when it's not. It's about fairness. It's about equity of access" (Heumann, 2020, p. 153).

Engla Schey, Advocate in Minnesota

Beginning decades earlier, there were efforts to counter the injustices of institutional life in many parts of the country. In Minnesota, Engla Schey, an attendant in a mental hospital, prompted the 1940's crusade to improve conditions for residents and workers in state institutions. Her own father was a resident in an asylum, having committed himself because he was suicidal. Schey desperately tried to persuade him against taking such drastic action, but he went ahead anyway, and eventually died there. Because she couldn't rescue her own father from an institution, she committed her life to reforming them (Foote, 2018).

Schey crusaded for mental health reform in her state and persuaded Unitarians from Minneapolis/St. Paul to lead the charge. As the following excerpt from her journal indicates, Schey's approach to those in her care was similar to my mother's:

> I had always maintained that the best weapon to use on any ward for protection was rapport. I had great confidence in this weapon and had no fear . . . "They know you're for them", said a doctor in another institution. He went on to say that explained why Schey was never physically attacked.
>
> (Foote, 2018, p. 61)

On a national scale, conscientious objectors during World War II (WWII) who were assigned to work in facilities for people with psychiatric and cognitive disabilities, advocated on behalf of their charges after the war ended. They exposed the brutal practices and grim conditions prevalent in the institutions where they had been assigned. In 1947 their narratives describing the places where they worked were published in a book entitled, *Out of Sight*. The book gained the attention and praise of Eleanor Roosevelt, who wrote about it in her newspaper column. Two decades later, in the 1960s, *Christmas in Purgatory* by Burton Blatt and Fred Kaplan was published. It was a book of photographs depicting horrific conditions in four state institutions in New England. After pushing for reform for about a decade, however, the authors gave up, concluding that the only alternative was to evacuate the institutions (Nielson, 2012).

Application of Fourteenth Amendment to Disability Rights

When deinstitutionalization finally occurred, it was because institutions were deemed to be in violation of the civil rights of the residents, as guaranteed by the U.S. Constitution under the Fourteenth Amendment (Association for Retarded Citizens of ND v. Olson, 1982). In September of 1980, the Association for Retarded Citizens of North Dakota sued the state of North Dakota. The Grafton State School was accused of violating the state and federal rights of its residents. A professor of disability studies at Syracuse University, Steven Taylor, testified against the institution. He had observed conditions at the State School, and he reported alarming conditions: "I came across this young man literally shackled, chained, to the wall". Mr. Taylor had observed conditions in several institutions in other states. "I had seen people in strait jackets, cloth ties, but I had never seen anybody chained" ("Researcher Recalls Conditions . . . ", 2011).

The case resulted in the state of North Dakota having to limit the use of medications, cease corporal punishment, reduce the use of physical restraints, institute proper feeding programs, conduct a skill and needs inventory on all residents, and hire an additional 125 personnel, as well as make a host of other changes. In addition, these circumstances were deemed to be "harmful in themselves, and have caused regression among the residents; for example, reduced ability to communicate, reduced ability to walk or feed one's self" (Association for Retarded Citizens of ND v. Olson, 1982).

Decades after deinstitutionalization came to North Dakota, I encountered a clinical psychologist who years before had been hired to be part of the process to restructure the developmental center after the class-action suit in the early 1980s required deep changes at the State School. When I told him about my mother's connection to the institution, he said the only reason he was able to persevere through his assignment was the example set by all the people like her. He said he began each day by telling himself that others had worked there, so he could bear it, too. He considered it to be the hardest challenge he had ever faced.

I look back in gratitude at my mother's strength adapting to his difficult setting and placing herself squarely on the side of the vulnerable. She provided example after example of combining courage with responsibility. While as a teacher I on occasion witnessed serious violations of human rights, I soon came to see that school can be an ideal environment to address inequities. Children live much of their waking lives in school, so working toward improving that environment is worth any effort. This notion became central to my thinking and action throughout my career.

Distributive, Procedural, and Relational Justice

The topic of just treatment in the context of a school setting can be demystified by considering it along "distributive, procedural, and relational" dimensions (Malone & Proctor, 2015, pp. 21–23). The relational dimension refers to how we treat people, distributive refers to how resources are allocated, and procedural refers to how decisions are made, paying attention to whether our decisions favor or disfavor members of a particular group and whether our measurement tools are culturally sound.

How my mother and Engla Schey treated residents serves as illustrations of relational social justice. Choosing to speak calmly rather than resorting to forcibly tying people down when they were agitated stands as an example. My mother did not have the authority to officially make procedural changes, but she did what she could, such as encouraging parents to connect with their children, a departure from recommended practice. She checked frequently to see if her people had wet diapers, rather than checking only at official rounds, because she knew they would sleep better if they were dry. Wards were understaffed; there was more work than one person could reasonably handle if the job were done right. My mother compensated as best she could by addressing needs, not just following established procedures.

Schey had the determination and know-how to join the effort to improve procedural and distributive effects at the state level, resulting in transformative change. Thanks in part to her efforts, procedural injustices such as tying people in strait jackets to punish them and other coercive practices were eliminated. The Minnesota state legislature increased funding, a distributive effect, so more and better-trained staff were hired, overcrowding was restricted, and in other ways conditions were improved.

A facility in Minnesota comparable to the one in which my mother worked benefited from reforms that occurred over time. When it was built in 1895, it had been named the Faribault State Hospital for the Feeble-Minded, then renamed the Faribault State Hospital for the Feeble-Minded and Epileptic Colony in 1906. By the 1960s, however, conditions at Faribault again required redress. In 1972 a lawsuit including Faribault alleged (in the language of the day) that the rights of mentally retarded residents had been violated because of "inadequate treatment". By 1973 the Faribault Public Schools had taken over the responsibility for the education of all the children from the facility. It was finally renamed the Faribault Regional Center in 1985, each renaming revealing the attitudes of the time (Foote, 2018, p. 61).

From a distributive perspective, my mother unfortunately had no influence, because the state legislature determined how much funding was allotted for the institution. In the end it took a lawsuit against the state of North Dakota to improve the level of procedural and distributive justice, which in turn, improved how people were treated individually. That would occur a decade after the reforms at Faribault.

On the national level, the work of activists like Judy Heumann cemented disability rights into federal law under the 504 provision of the Rehabilitation Act of 1973, which, among other directives, required schools to be physically accessible to students. Students also had to be given a reasonable way to get to school, so wheelchair-accessible buses were mandated. Legislation focused directly on making sure children with disabilities could become well educated was also influenced by Huemann and her cohorts. They advised the lawmakers who created Public Law 94–142, known as the Individuals with Disabilities Education Act, which was passed in 1975 (Shapiro, 1994).

These determined activists also influenced the content of the Americans with Disabilities Act of 1990, the civil rights law prohibiting discrimination on the basis of disability. Thereafter, disability rights would be considered civil rights, so people with disabilities could no longer be denied opportunity on the basis of their disability. As Colorado

Representative Patricia Schroeder said, "What we did for civil rights in the 1960s we forgot to do for people with disabilities" (Heumann, 2020, p. 171). The main argument opponents of this legislation built their case on was the "separate but equal" doctrine; the same discriminatory idea that had been applied to segregate Blacks from Whites in years past.

The Impact of Deinstitutionalization

Thanks to the deinstitutionalization that swept the country in the last decades of the twentieth century, my mother's story became a part of history. Instead of placing most people with severe disabilities in facilities like the State School, the plan was to move them into much smaller settings, such as group homes. Only those with the most severe impairments would remain in residential facilities. There was insufficient political will, however, on the national level to appropriate enough funding to create suitable housing to accommodate people with disabilities, so many were shifted to nursing homes, repeating essentially the same experience of institutional care. Even worse, others ended up homeless. A tragic irony is that the prison system has to an extent taken over where the state institutions left off. From 1980 to 2000, according to the APA, deinstitutionalization accounted for about 7% of the increase in prison population (Collier, 2014).

The upside of deinstitutionalization, for all its shortcomings, meant that a great many children were then able to remain in their own homes and attend the local school, rather than be sent away from home. This had a direct impact on what was required of school psychologists, because they needed to know how to assess these children within the school setting and assist teachers in accommodating their needs. Now the trend toward privatization adds a complication.

If children with disabilities are educated in public schools, they are guaranteed services. But not all states require private schools to provide services on-site. A child enrolled in a private school may have to be transported to a public school for specialized instruction. Also, the situation varies from state to state, with some states mandating full services on-site in private schools, while others require much less intervention. Ironically, school choice can result in restricted instructional choices for children with disabilities, an unintended consequence of federal policy.

We must also bear in mind that the current issues we deal with in schools today all have their roots in events that occurred long ago. We need to grasp the import of the history behind our laws and practices to understand why things are the way they are. School policies are often developed at the legislative level, far away from the practical, day-to-day functioning of schools and may be out of touch with the realities of children's lives.

This has been evident over the past 40 years, as lawmakers have cut taxes which in the past provided funding for public education. When I compare the current situation to the era in which I came of age, I realize my childhood was a hopeful time. We could afford to go to college without assuming a lifelong burden of debt. Public education from kindergarten through university was well-funded because the government allocated sufficient resources and progress was being made toward racial integration, a topic that will be addressed in the next chapter.

As Peter Temin comments, "Education was the key to American prosperity in the twentieth century. It is not too much to claim that we lived through an 'American century' because we had a long tradition of education that was the envy of the world". We need to revitalize that tradition, not only for the sake of our children but also for the sake of our country (Temin, 2017, p. iii).

School professionals have both a responsibility and an opportunity to influence the direction our leaders take. We have the background, insight, and experience to address the issues of the day that affect our schools and the children who attend them. How resources are distributed matters. Education is one avenue for children from impoverished backgrounds to become financially secure as adults. Because of our grasp of the history of disability rights and their connection to civil rights, up-to-date knowledge about what promotes optimal learning, and day-to-day practical experience in school communities, we have knowledge worth sharing with elected officials before they cast their votes.

References

Association for Retarded Citizens of ND v. Olson, 561 F. Supp. 473 D.N.D. (1982).

Collier, L. (2014). Incarceration nation. *Monitor on Psychology, 45*(9).

Foote, S. (2018). *The crusade for forgotten souls: Reforming Minnesota's mental institutions 1946–1954*. University of Minnesota Press.

Heumann, J. (2020). *Being Heumann: An unrepentant memoir of a disability rights activist*. Beacon Press.

Malone, C., & Proctor, S. (2015). Demystifying social justice for school psychology practice. *Communiqué, 48*(1), 21–23.

Nielson, K. (2012). *A disability history of the United States*. Beacon Press.

Researcher Recalls Conditions Once Reserved for North Dakota's Intellectually Disabled. (2011, July 11). *Grand Forks Herald*. www.grandforksherald.com/lifestyle/researcher-recalls-conditions-once-reserved-for-north-dakotas-intellectually-disabled

Shapiro, J. (1994). *No pity: People with disabilities forging a new civil rights movement*. Three Rivers Press.

Temin, P. (2017). *The vanishing middle class: Prejudice and power in a dual economy*. The MIT Press.

Chapter 4

Hard Lessons

Teaching in the South

Desegregation Arrives

At long last, the "Southern Manifesto" that several Southern congress-men issued to counter school desegregation after the 1954 *Brown v. Board of Education* Supreme Court decision could no longer hold sway. States would have to bow to federal law. Compliance with *Brown v. Board of Education* would be determined by how well schools integrated their "facilities, staff, faculty, extracurricular activities and transportation" History, Art & Archives, U.S. House of Representatives, n.d. The Southern Manifesto of 1956).

I happened to be living in a city in the American South when the order to integrate was being carried out. Because I was willing, was White, and had a bachelor's degree in hand, I was an acceptable hire to be placed in a racially segregated Black school that was following the mandate to integrate. The public school system was caught short of teachers because several resigned in protest over desegregation. Anyone like me could be hired immediately off the street.

I had a little bit of experience working in a public school before I became a full-fledged teacher, having completed a temporary job for eight weeks as a study hall supervisor. The junior high school, now newly integrated, was formerly all White. With racial integration just under way, tensions sometimes ran high, and I had as many as 75 students to supervise at a time. I replaced a woman whom students told me left to be admitted to a mental hospital. One taunted me, assuring me that I would end up in the same place. I was glad the boy had tipped his hand, alert-ing me to the challenge ahead. No matter how intimidated I might feel, it had better not show.

I could see I was in for a quick baptism into behavioral group manage-ment, but it was 1970, so just the fact that I was cast in the role of teacher gave me authority. I trusted that authority, and it kept me from being afraid. I started by doing what I could to improve the environment. Stu-dents were expected to do homework or read, but some wouldn't bring

DOI:10.4324/9781003348344-4

anything to do. Others would have already finished their assignments. I had a large magazine rack in the room which didn't have much in it, so I asked if I could have back issues of magazines from the library to give students something to read if they were idle. Knowing reading might not appeal to everyone, I also provided magic markers and paper if kids wanted to draw. And then I spent my day moving quietly around the room, watching for anyone who needed help with schoolwork. Anyone idle was immediately directed to get a magazine or was offered a paper to write or draw on.

I had youthful energy and optimism on my side, but I had a soft voice and small stature, so my physical appearance did not command respect. (As a matter of fact, one morning the janitor almost refused to let me in when I arrived because "seventh graders aren't allowed in the building so early".) I knew I looked weak, so I realized I couldn't act scared. Consequently, when trouble broke out, I would slip in between angry boys ready to land a swing and stand firm, a strategy I would never advise anyone to use now. One boy would become so alarmed he would cover his eyes and plead, "M'am, please don't do that!" I only did it a few times, and no one got hurt. Perhaps he was right; maybe I was foolish to be so bold, but what I knew was that it worked. I didn't want to relinquish my authority by summoning the assistant principal, whom they all feared, and for good reason. Just the threat of him gave the most rebellious pause, as the next incident illustrates.

Thinking Off My Feet

Eventually some boys tried to test my mettle. My desk sat in front of large, screenless windows. Right outside the windows was a flat roof extending out many feet. One day before the bell rang a group of boys came up to my desk as I sat taking attendance. Within moments they had circled my chair. Then they opened the window. It was clear what they intended to do. They were practically bursting with glee at the thought of setting me out on the roof, but as they were lifting me, I caught the eye of the ringleader. I said that I could appreciate the humor of the situation, but I wondered if the assistant principal would be equally amused. We locked eyes for a moment, I gave him a questioning look, he nodded to his prank partners, and they gently set me down. "Good choice!" I said.

I did make it through the two months, and a few weeks later, I was hired in a different school to teach fifth-grade math and handwriting in a school with an all-Black student body. After a brief interview at the district office, they instantly arranged for my temporary certification, and I found myself assigned a classroom. The school district was so desperate that all they cared was that I had a college degree of any kind. I replaced a White woman who was being allowed to return to her former school where a mid-year vacancy had just occurred. I felt uneasy upon hearing she was leaving her class with half the year left, and I wondered if her exit would make them wary of me. Given the fact that one teacher had left in midstream, I vowed to make it to summer so the students' education wouldn't be disrupted a second time.

With no deliberate planning on my part, I was about to participate in school desegregation. With a total faculty of 35 teachers, I and two other Whites represented racial integration during this school year; the entire student body would remain all Black until the beginning of the next term. Sixteen years after it was mandated to happen, the beginning of desegregation had arrived.

My Parents and Civil Rights

Perhaps I was drawn to the civil rights movement in part because I was raised by a mother who was sympathetic to it. She more than once told me a story from her days as a housekeeper for a couple of old bachelor farmers before she married my dad. On a blisteringly hot day during harvest, two itinerant Black farmhands came to the back door of the farmhouse, asking for a drink of water. What they had been provided was warm and tasted bad. She pumped fresh water from the cistern, which was cold and fresh. Then she invited them into the kitchen to drink so they wouldn't have to stand outside in the hot sun.

It disgusted her that they hadn't been provided good water in the first place, when they were working hard in the heat. She would always punctuate the end of her story by stating emphatically that they had better manners than most of the White men on the crews she encountered during harvest and haying. She would shake her head disapprovingly and comment that she didn't understand why these workers had to be treated so badly.

My parents were aware of the ongoing civil rights protests occurring during my youth, thanks to the evening news on TV. Whatever concerns they may have had, given the violence that was erupting around the country, they accepted without question my decision to teach in a Black school. When I returned home to visit the next summer, my father even went so far as to say that the most important work anyone can do is to give a child a good start in learning. This was a high compliment coming from him. He would not have wanted to give me a swelled head by telling me he was proud of me.

Confronting the Impact of Slavery

Besides serving as my introduction to teaching, the semester that ensued became my crash course on the impact of the legacy of slavery and the twentieth-century civil rights movement—and the backlash against it—on public education. As you will see, some of what I witnessed alerted me to sobering realities. A product of my time, you will also see my understanding showed only partial insight into underlying causes. But the disturbing lessons never left me. They prompted me to pursue answers to my questions about the history of slavery and its implications in contemporary America. Of special concern was the pervasive use of physical punishment in Southern schools and within African-American families, which was carried over into schools such as the one where I worked.

I was responsible for three sections of students during the course of the day, with up to 37 in a class for a total of 95 children, aged 10 to 14. There were no students with identified disabilities, since disability rights legislation had not yet come into being. I soon learned my students' math skills ranged from grade level right on down to mid-first grade or less. My classroom came equipped with desks and textbooks, but without anything supplementary except some ditto sheets, and nothing motivational—no games to take the tedium out of learning math facts, and no supplementary books for those who weren't performing at the fifth-grade level.

I quickly learned that Black schools got the cast-offs from the White schools when they were finished with them; that's why most of our textbooks were old. We had a few new textbooks, but nowhere near enough for an entire class. In general, there were few classroom supplies; teachers paid for most of the necessary materials, like paper, pencils, and other classroom tools out of their own pockets. When I mentioned my surprise at how sparse the classroom supplies were, a Black colleague told me that compared to how it used to be, this year they had never had so much— because I (meaning a White teacher) was there. Later in the semester federal funds arrived so we were all able to furnish our classrooms.

Black teachers had been expected to make do with cast-offs and not much else, but we White teachers walked in and money to properly supply a classroom accompanied us. I know for certain my Black colleagues were grateful for the comparative abundance that resulted, but how could they not resent it at the same time. That race influenced school funding was bleakly apparent in my own classroom.

Becoming a Teacher

About 10% of my students could comprehend the prescribed new math text. I considered them gifted because they had managed to stay at grade level, despite all along being denied the educational resources they deserved. The rest of the students worked out of old textbooks. I made do. I tested everyone to see where they were performing and then set about grouping them and adapting assignments for them. I ended up making up my own assignments altogether for the lowest group.

I could see immediately that a large share of their math difficulties was caused by poor reading skills, so I wanted to promote reading as much as possible. I went to used bookstores, garage sales, and the Salvation Army to acquire a paperback library for my classroom that included easy reading so that students could read to themselves once they completed their assignments before our prescribed time together was up. Their hands-own favorite was a collection of poems written by Kali Grosvenor, a Black girl about their age. *Poems by Kali* had been a gift to me from a college teacher back home, who must have been prescient when he chose it for me (Grosvenor, 1970). By the end of the year it was well worn, and because my students loved it so much, I left it in the classroom for the next year's fifth graders to enjoy.

I wanted to be realistic about what I could achieve, so I set a modest goal for my class: By May's end I wanted everyone to move forward in their mathematical understanding, and for the lowest level group to know by memory, addition math facts from one to ten. I also set a goal for myself: Survive the semester without resigning in defeat.

I vowed to myself that if I accepted the position, I would last the entire semester, because my students deserved no less. I was determined to show my students that they could count on me to not walk away. What I had to offer was a desire to become a good teacher and the belief that the children in this school had a right to just as good an education as anyone else. Unfortunately, I had no training in group management, curriculum, or child development—not to mention math, and I was quite inexperienced in dealing directly with issues of race, except for what I learned in my two-month stint at the junior high. Consequently, I faced a sharp learning curve. My five months tested nearly all of my limits, and by the end of the year when I left I did so with tremendous respect and admiration for the courageous teachers—heroes, everyone—who were devoting their lives to this school.

Corporal Punishment

What challenged me the most was the school's liberal use of corporal punishment. When I was first hired and given a tour of my classroom, I was puzzled by the presence of a heavy leather strap next to the stapler, pencils, and other paraphernalia in the teacher's desk. I asked about it, and was told that every teacher was supplied one, and could use it at his or her discretion. I couldn't imagine using it. I felt secure in my own resolve never to use force with my students, but I was not prepared for the effects I would suffer working side by side others who whipped children without compunction.

My first introduction to this practice occurred one day when one of my groups of students entered my room, very excited about the science lesson they had just left. Instead of taking their seats immediately, they clamored for my attention around my desk, everyone talking at once, each trying to be the one to tell me about the experiment. I was delighted. So seldom did I see them thoroughly enjoying school that I felt it worthwhile to spend five minutes hearing them out. I hoped their enthusiasm for their science lesson would spill over onto math that day.

So quiet I almost didn't hear the wing supervisor enter, leather strap across her shoulder. She was a large, tall woman with a look so menacing I felt scared. In an instant, with no one saying a word, the students were seated in their desks, stock-still. Without looking at me, she said, "Put out your hands!" and they obeyed, thrusting their palms open and forward to receive their punishment. All I heard was the snap of the strap as it hit each palm. No child dared to cry aloud—their eyes squeezed shut in pain and tears rolled down the cheeks of even the most pugnacious. Some opened their mouths in a silent cry. I stood, helpless, unbelieving. After striking the last child, my supervisor walked out of the room as softly as she had entered. The children saw my anguish. One, to comfort me, said, "Never you mind, M'am, she didn't hurt us bad. They just stings, is all".

I didn't know what to do. Should I resign in protest, complain, do nothing—all possible alternatives seemed useless. If I resigned, my students' learning would be disrupted yet another time. One section of the current first-grade class had been retained in its entirety because teacher turnover had been so high the children had made no progress academically over the course of the past year. No, I wouldn't quit. Perhaps complain? My students had broken a school rule by not going directly to their seats. My supervisor had a right to enforce the rule. She also had the legal right to hit them, and the support of the administration and most of the staff in doing so. My only recourse, I felt, was to make sure I did not leave my students open for such treatment another time. She must never again have any reason to visit my room.

How to guarantee that she would not invade again? It was clear she would not tolerate disorder in my classroom. I had put all my energy into figuring out how to begin to teach my students math; now I realized I also had to master classroom management, and I had better do it overnight.

Lessons in Discipline

Typical of a novice, I started out by being more tolerant than I should have been. Unsurprisingly, my students took full advantage and tested me to see where I would finally draw the line. I knew now that the line had to be drawn more tightly than I would have chosen, to protect them from further punishment such as I had just witnessed. I became more consistent in enforcing the rules and insisted on a lower level of noise. I confronted the unruly about their behavior. My classroom was still a far cry from a model of quiet decorum, but gradually, almost everyone started coming around. They realized our honeymoon had ended and it was time to adhere to the rules all the time. Even so, two boys resisted all my attempts to encourage them to comply. Their behavior was highly disruptive, and they seemed to believe it was all right to ignore me. They refused to do their work and continued to disturb the others despite all my efforts.

I was at my wits' end. They understood me well enough to know that I was not going to whip them. So long as I didn't, they felt free to do as they pleased. Other students became impatient with me. They demanded to know why I didn't whip these boys. "They be so bad, don't you care?" It was clear that I had to do something to assert my authority. I decided to threaten them with a visit from the principal. I would ask him just to talk to them, thinking that might be enough to dissuade them from their misbehavior. They ignored my threat. I knew I could not back down, so I went to the principal and invited him to my classroom to speak to them. He agreed to come.

I was expecting a few firm words and an admonition to obey class rules, but I was shocked to see him remove his belt. I had requested that he talk to them—but perhaps that was how teachers requested a beating—maybe I just didn't know the code. The boys were ordered to bend over, and the principal whipped their thighs. They whimpered, cried, then cried out in pain. Then it was over, and he left as politely as he had entered. What now? I hadn't meant for it to happen. I wanted them to comply with my requests so they could learn some math and, ironically, so we wouldn't attract the attention of the wing supervisor. To keep my wing supervisor at bay, I had invited in an even harsher authority.

Had I thought further, I would have expected what happened. The extent to which physical punishment was carried out in this school was possible because the principal approved of it. So, of course, he would also actively participate. Another hard lesson. Now I knew for certain there was no one in a position of authority for me to turn to. And it wasn't even close to May.

I needed to discuss what had happened with another teacher. I wanted to know how frequently I could expect visits from the wing supervisor and how my refusal to use corporal punishment would be viewed by the rest of the faculty. I approached the woman I rode home from school with, another White woman, and someone who was an experienced teacher. She said the degree to which corporal punishment was applied varied greatly. Several rarely, if ever, whipped, and did so with great reluctance. Some did occasionally, and a few, frequently. The assistant principal didn't hesitate but usually concentrated on the older kids. The wing supervisor was also very tough.

"She'll stay out of your room if you keep things quiet", JoAnne assured me. All I had to do was achieve the impossible, I thought. JoAnne taught second grade, and she did not use the strap. She saw no reason to with small children. Because her classroom ran smoothly, she rarely saw the administrators. But because I was a fifth-grade teacher, JoAnne said I could expect my students to have dealings with them. She said the older ones were hard to keep in line, and physical punishment seemed to be the only thing they understood. But surely there had to be a better way.

The Power of Words

Besides the constant fear of another whipping, the struggle to maintain order, and the hourly challenge of trying to motivate my students to learn some math, there were also language and racial issues to be dealt with. I had a lot to learn. We had to learn to understand each other's dialect, no small task on either end. "M'am, I need a pin". "A pin, or a pen?" I'd ask. Didn't I say pin? You know, a PIN". So I'd hand the child a stick pin. "How am I spose to write with that? That's a pin, not a pin!"

Until now, my knowledge of African-American culture had been gained from books. I was familiar with the writings of several Black authors whom I had studied in a Black American literature course, so I had read about the internalized racism that Blacks suffered, but I had never witnessed it until I heard my students using racially loaded insults to tease one another. Those with a darker complexion were invariably on the losing end of these exchanges. I decided I had to do something. I called a class meeting, and I confronted them about their name-calling.

> You call each other terrible names, and yet you proclaim to me that Black is beautiful. I'm ready to believe that—I can see for myself that you are beautiful. But you're not very convincing, going around call-ing each other the ugliest names you can think of. So, what do you want me to believe? Are you ugly, or are you beautiful? You are my teachers. If you want me to believe you're beautiful, I better not hear any more mean talk. All of you know that if I ever called any one of you such names, you'd hate me. How can it be any better for you to use them against each other?

They answered me with total silence, one of the very few occasions in our time together when no one had anything to say.

An irony of the present day is that now the "N" word under certain cir-cumstances has morphed into a term of affection, such as among team-mates supporting one another. Natasha remarked that middle school White boys are using it, with the approval of a Black staff member so long as the word is pronounced without the hard "r" at the end. Language evolves; maybe we can, too. I hope this is a sign of better times to come.

Several decades ago, the human rights activist Malcolm X had begun exhorting his fellow Black Americans to appreciate themselves according to their own standards. He realized that as a young person he, too, had "been brainwashed into believing that the black people are 'inferior'—and white people 'superior'—that they will even violate and mutilate their God-created bodies to try to look 'pretty' by White standards" (Kendi, 2016).

This truth was brought home to me by how fascinated many of the girls were with my hair. They wanted to touch it, which I allowed, and I was perplexed when they said my hair was curly but didn't consider theirs to be. Some clearly disparaged their own hair and envied mine. At the time I did not know how to address the issue other than through a general policy of trying to discourage disrespect of oneself or others. I took heart that my students read and reread *Poems by Kali*. Her joyous words describing the loveliness of people who looked like them appeared to be an inspiration (Grosvenor, 1970).

Racial tension ran high that year. A year before, in early June, there had been a full-scale riot in the school neighborhood. From time to time, a few of my students vented hostility against me, being the handiest White person and one they knew wouldn't retaliate. Usually, it took the form of innuendo: "Just wait and see what'll happen to you if we have an anniversary celebration!" I usually pretended I didn't hear such comments, but one day a student uttered a statement I felt I could not ignore.

All were seated at their desks, quietly working on their math assignment for the day. I was moving up and down the aisles, answering questions on the assignment. I had just passed Leilah at her desk. She was a 14-year-old girl whom it seemed I was constantly intercepting as she tried to stab her classmates with pencils or harm them in some other way. I don't think I had ever seen her smile. To my back, she sneered, "You White bitch!" For once the classroom was dead quiet, so everyone could hear what she had said. I turned, knelt at her desk so we were eye to eye, and said, "I heard what you called me. Everyone here heard you. I cannot allow anyone to call anyone else a nasty name. I don't call you names, and I expect you to talk to me respectfully. You will have to come with me to see the principal".

The principal, in whom I had lost faith. But I felt I could not allow a student to insult me openly and not suffer consequences, and I was convinced my word carried no weight with her. As fast as gossip traveled, I knew the entire school, including the principal, would hear of the incident, anyway. But it was with a heavy heart that I escorted Leilah down the hall. She did not protest. The principal heard my complaint, suspended Leilah, and sent her home. I was very relieved. I trusted he would not resort to physical punishment with a 14-year-old girl, and I was right. What I didn't know was that he didn't need to. That task would be accomplished at home.

The next morning a woman entered my classroom before school started. She had a heavy cloth wrapped around her neck, and as she approached me, she broke into a deep, liquid cough. She clearly was sick enough that she should have been home in bed. Her voice was hoarse as she spoke:

> I'm Leilah's mama. I don't know what's wrong with that girl. I always get along with White folk. Never had no trouble. I whup her and she still don't change. You let me know if you have any more trouble. She raised her voice. "Leilah, girl, come on in here!"

Leilah entered, shuffling her feet, eyes downcast. She didn't look up. I wanted to embrace her, as she looked so defeated. But it wasn't my place to do that, since I was the reason that she had been beaten. By taking her to the principal, I became complicit. Instead, I said, "I'm glad you're back, Leilah. I'm glad you're here".

Her mother turned and left, leaving me with the knowledge that her daughter's mouthing off to me in class was deemed a serious enough offense to warrant a whipping. What a harsh world this mother and daughter inhabited that an adolescent's nasty remark necessitated such cruel punishment to appease a teacher. That I was the teacher took my breath away.

Since coming to this school, I was confronted with examples of the advantage of being White—how much power came with that identity. Because Whites were there, money for resources followed. But power has another face. It took three hard lessons for me to recognize what power I had as a teacher to unleash harm. I had witnessed my students' palms whipped because I had allowed them to violate the rule of going to their seats immediately upon entering the classroom, I saw two boys having to submit to a beating in front of their whole class because they disobeyed me, and now Leilah was returned to me after a beating for calling me a mean name. At last, I realized how potentially dangerous I was.

I vowed never again to trust anyone but myself to deal out consequences for misbehavior in my classroom. No matter how anyone acted, my response would have to be just between the two of us. As for Leilah, she became utterly passive in my class for the rest of the year. When I spoke to her, she never responded; she would not even raise her eyes to me. The breach between us could not be bridged, and I didn't blame her.

Impact of Poverty

I wondered and worried about another fifth-grade girl. She was thin and wan, and her hair was patchy. A lackluster student, she never seemed engaged with friends, either. Her school performance was so poor I asked another fifth-grade teacher about her, so I could understand her situation better. My colleague told me she was concerned about her, too. I learned that the girl was being raised by a single parent who had other children besides and was very poor. There often wasn't enough food at home, and everyone had to go without. Our student was lethargic, I learned, because she was often hungry. Mortified that a student in my classroom was suffering from malnutrition, I asked if I could pay for her lunch. My colleague, who was Black, replied that the girl's mother would never accept a donation from me. Never from a White person. She said the mother would accept lunch money for her daughter from her, so she assured me the situation was being handled. How many other children was this teacher helping to survive? I would have liked to know, but I didn't dare ask. The value of having a teacher from the same racial, cultural and community background as her students was brought home to me with this vivid example.

Consult With the Psychologist

I often wondered what a child psychologist would make of the behavior of some of my students. Benny Lee was a case in point. Benny Lee was like a six-week-old puppy in ten-year-old boy form. If he wasn't tugging at someone he was poking, pestering, running after them, or, for variety, being chased by them, all the while keeping up a non-stop monologue.

"M'am", he'd cry, close to tears, "they's picking on me!" desperate to be rescued. Most of the time, he had picked first, but had never grasped that there was any connection between his tripping them and the punch on the shoulder he got in return. He was a continual nuisance to everybody. Fortunately for him, and perhaps the only reason he had managed to survive to age ten, was that he also had puppy charm. On top of his puny body sat the face of on an angel, with large, brown eyes so expressive it sometimes hurt to look at him. His face revealed everything, instantly. By the end of my first week Benny Lee had stolen my heart, and I think he knew it.

He was my poorest math student. I suspected he was bright enough. My guess was he was too agitated to ever sit down long enough to allow himself to grasp an abstract concept, like addition facts. That was where we started, and where we ended, but in the intervening five months he did master them. Benny Lee did no work at his own desk. If allowed he would have wandered the 90 minutes he was in my room, checking out what everyone else was doing, distracting everybody, possibly annoying at least one person enough so a fight would ensue.

After a day or two of observing his routine, I realized I had to find a way to contain him, for everyone's sake. I saw that he always circled back to my desk, especially if I happened to be there, and even if I wasn't. I brought up a chair, set it right next to mine, cleared my desk of anything remotely interesting, and moved him in. If I sat right next to him, preferably with my arm around his shoulder, he could do his math. I ran my legs off, up and down the aisles checking on my 30-odd other charges, and then every spare minute back to Benny Lee, to anchor him in his chair, and I suspect, in the universe, so that he could finally learn to add.

He behaved no differently with his other teachers. The language arts teacher crossed the hall one day to see how he was getting along in my class. We compared distractibility stories, all following the same theme. On her way out she passed by Benny Lee, and threatened, "Benny Lee, you're not getting a thing done in any of your classes. If you don't settle down soon, I'm going to tell your mama!" The ultimate threat. Some kids would beg to be whipped if only you wouldn't tell their mama. Benny Lee shot back: "How you gonna tell my mama? How you gonna tell? My mama left me when I was a bitty baby and I ain't seen her since. You can't tell my mama. I ain't got one!" He tried not to cry but he couldn't help it.

It seemed like every day there was a crisis with Benny Lee, but one event stands out above all the others. Benny Lee lingered after school one day. I had work to do, but I told him I didn't mind having him there so long as he didn't disturb me. Benny Lee agreed to control himself. But within moments he started careening up and down the aisles of desks, backward, at a rapidly accelerating pace. A "Benny Lee!" and a "Benny Lee, stop!" and a "Benny Lee, stop NOW!" fell on deaf ears. By this time, he was charging down the aisle backward, slapping his hands on the desktops as he veered toward me. Frustrated with his ignoring me and fearing he could go flying when he ran out of desks at the end of the aisle, I stuck out my arm like a railroad barricade, and he ran smack into it. He turned around, stunned. Then he howled, "You hit me! You hit me!" Soon he was crying hysterically, "Not you, M' am, not you!"

I grabbed him by the shoulders and repeated, over, and over again, until he heard me, "No! I didn't hit you. I didn't hit you. I didn't hit you!" Finally he stopped crying and snuffled. "But it hurt", he protested.

"Yes, I'm sure it did! It hurt me too! You ran right into me. Didn't you hear me tell you to stop?"

He snuffled some more. "I never thought you'd hit me, Ma'am".

"I didn't".

"No, Ma'am. I glad you didn't".

But the sad truth was, I had hurt him. Whatever the intent of my action, hurt was the result. I regretted my impulsive gesture instantly, because, at least for some moments, Benny Lee felt betrayed. I now think of the teacher, and the parent, and the principal I knew who hurt children they cared about, because they wanted to teach them a lesson. I'm sure they believed they were doing it for the children's own good, to protect them from further danger. Hadn't I just done much the same thing—just a milder form? Perhaps I wasn't so different from them. We all were trying to do what was right, and I bet they wanted to believe in their own innocence as much as I did.

I needed to know if there was ever a justification for physical punishment, if situational ethics ever applied, if it was at least sometimes not a matter of right and wrong, but a matter of cultural differences. I wanted to read about corporal punishment to see what the experts said, but my daily routine was already so full just trying to keep pace with my classes that I found no time to devote to library research. I was excited, then, when a group of psychologists from the main state university showed up to spend a day with us to discuss issues relating to the process of racial integration. I could hardly wait for our coffee break so that I could corner one of them and ask him if there was any psychological research which defended corporal punishment.

My moment finally arrived. I confessed to the psychologist that I was at odds with school policy in refraining from applying the strap. I told him I wanted to know if I was justified in holding my ground, or if I was being too rigid on the point. He assured me that he knew of no research defending the use of corporal punishment and encouraged me to stand firm. I felt stronger, knowing I had his backing, and, according to him, plenty of arguments based on empirical research to support my position. We returned to the table, rejoining the 30-some teachers and other psychologists. After order was restored, the psychologist whom I had addressed began.

"Kathy asked an interesting question during our break". No, I thought. He isn't going to repeat it out loud. Please, no. But he went on. "She asked whether the use of corporal punishment was a valid disciplinary approach". "Any impressions?" My wing supervisor gave her impression first.

"The trouble with you is", she roared at me across 20 teachers and said, "you don't have discipline!" In the long silence that followed, no one mentioned that my disciplinary skills and the validity of corporal punishment were two separate issues. We squirmed, embarrassed, and one of the psychologists lectured us about the harm physical punishment can do. In response, the assistant principal insisted it was used "only as a last resort". The rest of us were all still staring at the table. I wondered how long it would be until anyone would want to speak to me again.

Negotiating Safety

Besides teaching my classes, I also had to supervise the playground during noon recess once a week. I dreaded the chore. There was very little play equipment for the kids to use, so they were often bored. In the wide-open space with little structure of any kind, the kids often got into squabbles, sometimes fights. On playground supervision days I felt more like a referee than a teacher.

"Ma'am, come quick! Tyrone's got a broken glass 'n he's gonna cut somebody bad!" I flew over to the sixth-grade play area. Kindergarteners were clumped nearby. There was Tyrone, a boy I had seen around school and knew had a reputation for violence. He had a piece of broken glass in his hand, with which he was threatening anyone close at hand. Except for the most bravely curious, most of the other children were moving to a far corner of the playground, away from Tyrone. The student who had summoned me was one of mine. He stayed with me but kept to the rear. Tyrone looked scared, almost desperate. With my arrival on the scene, he knew he had to reckon with a teacher. I was scarcely bigger than he was, and just as frightened. I had never disarmed anyone before.

I was fortunate to have my father's example to fall back on. Like my mother, he had also worked at the residential developmental center for a time after his surgery, and I remembered him talking about a resident who was showing others a sharp knife while outside one day. The man was large and very strong, and staff feared he would do terrible damage. My father had a good relationship with the man, and so he just walked up to him and quietly told him that he could get hurt or hurt others with that knife and so should hand it over to my father. The man did so, and no further intervention was necessary. I decided to try my father's approach.

Tyrone and I studied each other. His face was stormy—angry, and ready to cry at the same time. I extended my hand. "Give me the glass, Tyrone", I demanded quietly. "You could get hurt playing with something that sharp. I don't want you or anyone else getting hurt". Tyrone's gaze moved from my face to my student's, who was still with me. "Tyrone, please give me the glass". My hand was still outstretched.

"You gonna tell Mr. Thomas! That's what you gonna do!" Mr. Thomas wore a leather strap around his neck just in case a last resort situation arose on the spur of the moment. I was almost as afraid of him as Tyrone was. If I reported this incident to Mr. Thomas, Tyrone would receive the beating of his life.

"No, Tyrone, I promise. If you hand over the glass, this remains between you and me. I won't tell".

My student piped up: "She won't tell. Don't you worry. She won't tell".

I prayed Mr. Thomas wouldn't appear on the scene by chance. "Please, Tyrone. I promise I won't tell".

He set the glass in my hand. "No more weapons on the playground, promise?"

"Yes, Ma'am". He turned and ran.

So far as I know, Mr. Thomas never heard about my encounter with Tyrone. I kept our secret, and I don't doubt that he did, too.

Dignity

James stood apart. He was a private, quiet little boy, the most serious and probably the brightest student in my class. While many of the others raced and shouted, James would only observe. He set a high standard for himself, both in personal conduct and academically, and was distraught if he failed to meet his expectations. James was among a small group of students who could handle the new math text. All I ever had to do was to give one or two examples of a new type of problem, and James could carry on independently. He seemed embarrassed that he didn't know something before it was taught, almost ashamed of his ignorance.

During our five months together, James got into trouble only once, when he got into a mild scuffle with three other boys. It was a minor incident, but it occurred in the hall, and I caught them, so I kept them after school for a few minutes to remind them that they shouldn't be roughhousing in the building. The other three were unperturbed. My mild measures did not affect their pride. Only James suffered. He bit his lip, fighting back tears of remorse.

When their time was up, I excused them and sent them home. As soon as the others had scrambled out the door, I said, "I know this won't happen again, James". "No, Ma'am". "I know you learned your lesson". I smiled as I said it. James was still fighting back his tears. I tried to comfort him. "Please don't feel so bad, James. It'll be a better day tomorrow. You go on home now".

I wondered what home was like for James. Each week I invited four children home with me after school to bake cupcakes as a math lesson and as a treat for the class the following day. Among other things, this gave me an opportunity to meet parents informally when I delivered each one to his or her doorstep. James was the last, so when his father came to the door to invite me in, I was free to stay for a visit. James's meekness contrasted sharply with his father's confidence. He was as large as James was small and as forthright as James was shy. I was ushered into the living room of the immaculately tidy house. There I was seated in front of the central attraction, a lineup of graduation portraits, six in a row, standing on top of a television set. There was room for a seventh, which would be

James's. His father pointed proudly to the portraits and told me that so far, all his children had got an education.

"James here is the youngest, and I plan for him to finish school like the others". I replied that I had no doubt James would graduate from high school, considering his many abilities. "I hope so, I do hope so", said his father. "I never had no chance to finish school myself".

I told him how well-behaved James always was and how pleased I was to have him for a student. James squirmed, never looking me in the eye. I couldn't tell whether my praise was making him miserable or pleased or both. As impressive a student as he was, I had no doubt James had the ability to graduate from high school with honors and had the intellectual potential to thrive in college, given the chance. His high intelligence and deep sensitivity equipped him well for success if the world would only treat him fairly. His father had a dream for his children, and I trust that in due time James's portrait stood seventh in line.

Church in School

A smiling woman appeared at my classroom door one day and announced that she had been invited to speak to my class. She needed only a few minutes of our time—could she please say a few words right now? By then she was inside the room, making her way to the front of the classroom. I didn't have time to object, but I wondered upon whose invitation she was there, and what she intended to say to my students. As it turned out, she was there to proselytize. She delivered a rousing hellfire and brimstone sermon, urging the children to atone for their sins, threatening them with eternal damnation if they didn't. She finished her brief speech and left.

As soon as I could I flew down the hall to my head teacher's room. His students were out at recess, so I was able to have my say. I told him that a woman had just visited my room for the purpose of converting us to her religion. I said that she should be prevented from entering any other classrooms because what she was doing was unconstitutional. Mr. Jones listened attentively. He said the administration felt it was all right for her to speak because she was nondenominational. I pointed out that just because she was not associated with a church did not mean she did not have a particular point of view. "She's a fundamentalist Christian. If we want to educate our students about religion, we should also invite a liberal Christian, a Jew, a Hindu, a Buddhist, and spokespeople for every other religious attitude we possibly can. That would be educational. What we heard is simply indoctrination". My outrage grew as I spoke. "Who invited her, anyway?" I demanded. Mr. Jones clasped his hands behind his back. "I did", he replied.

How to Get Permission

I learned many lessons about teaching, some of the best through tips from other teachers. I found myself in a quandary one day, ironically because something good had finally happened. Federal grant money started pouring in, especially for supplies. I had been hired to teach handwriting and mathematics, but I also saw a great need for instruction in the visual arts. The children needed constructive ways to express themselves, and I wanted to provide them with some materials. At the very least, I wanted to stock the room with paper, paints, and the like, so that next year's class would have something to begin with in the fall. We didn't have an art teacher, so I couldn't consult a resident expert to help me compile a shopping list. I turned to Carole, a teacher whose wiliness I respected. She smiled at my idea.

"You're catching on—every good teacher is a stock-piler". I followed her advice to the letter. She told me to make as extravagant a list as I could muster. I should go to the local school supply store and write down the specific name of anything that looked appealing. Only names, not costs. Then I was to present the list to the principal for his evaluation. Carole's hunch was that he would not want to admit to me his total ignorance in this area, and so would give me a blanket approval, because federal funds were becoming plentiful. I went directly to Carole after I met with the principal. I was beaming.

"So what did he say?"

"He perused my list, asked me how much everything would cost, to which I replied that I didn't know—and that was the truth. He drew himself up to his full height and said I should go ahead and charge everything on the list".

"Now", Carole smiled, "if the bill is enormous, he can't blame you. You can be very apologetic and sympathize with him. Just make sure you've opened all the containers".

The lesson: It is easier to get forgiveness than permission, a principle every experienced teacher understands.

My Cultural Education, Sort Of

A side benefit I expected to receive from teaching at our school was what I would learn about Black culture. As an undergraduate English major, I had enjoyed studying some African-American literature, and so I was delighted when Fine Arts Day was announced. It would be a day devoted to music, dance, and entertainments of various kinds. I imagined it to be a celebration of Black culture. I could hardly wait.

A few weeks before the event each class was assigned an activity for the program. My students were to demonstrate square dancing. Square dancing? I felt like I hadn't left North Dakota. Why should square dancing be a feature of our school's fine arts fair? Then I heard what the other numbers were: The kindergarteners would dance around a Maypole, the second graders would sing patriotic songs, and on it went. Not one drop of soul in any of it. Not one word of wisdom or beauty from any Black writer, not one example of Black music or dance; nothing at all that reflected Black experience. And so, one of the most important lessons I learned about Black culture in public school was that it was ignored, even in a school in the middle of a Black community. If I saw the irony and felt the loss, what of them? But I shouldn't have been surprised. In my elementary school populated by people of Icelandic descent, we would have had the same sort of program. There would have been nothing to reflect our heritage, either. The purpose was assimilation, not ethnic or community pride.

For my students, doesey-doeing was the activity of the day, and they became proficient at it in short order. They had a good time, but I remained disappointed. A Black teacher observed our square dancing rehearsal one day. "Mmmmmmm, mmmmmmmmm!" she laughed and clapped her hands to us in encouragement. "You got rhythm!"

What Did It All Mean?

I often wondered what the five months in my classroom had meant to my students—whether my behavior had made much sense to them. I knew there were some who suspected me of not caring because I refused to whip them into submission like some of their teachers did. It took me a while to understand how a child could dislike someone for not hitting them. I came to realize that physical punishment was typical in their families, and for many of them, the main method a parent used to insist that one's authority be respected. They knew their parents and teachers cared about them; therefore, someone who didn't hit them must not care. Of course, I knew families from my home community who relied on physical punishment; this was not a foreign concept. Many in my extended family used it. "Spare the rod and spoil the child" was a common mantra. And several states, including my home state of North Dakota, allowed it. But here it seemed all too common and severe.

One day I had reason to take heart, at least about what one student thought of me. Sarah, a large, confident girl, lingered a moment before passing to her next class. Some of the boys had been testing my limits again, pushing, coaxing, me to hit them. The hot weather made everybody more excited and irritable than usual, including me. I hoped I could finish out the year without losing my temper. Fortunately, the bell saved us, but I was frazzled. After the boys charged out of the room, Sarah said, "I know what you're trying to do, Ma'am. I'm gonna be a teacher, and when I do, I ain't gonna beat on kids". Her words filled me with such gratitude I wanted to cry, but Sarah saved the moment by playfully teasing, "Ma'am, suppose you could take me shopping sometime? I dreamed once you did. And you bought me such pretty new clothes!"

"You'll have to dream me up a new salary, first, Sarah. No teacher at this school can afford a spending spree".

She was laughing as she flew out the door.

The last day of school arrived, almost taking me by surprise when it finally came. There was much to do that final week, such as preparing report cards, getting the room in order for the next year, saying my goodbyes. Suddenly, my kids were gone, report cards in hand, eager for the freedom of summer vacation. I waved them off and wondered into whose hands they would return in the fall. I knew I would miss them, and I wished I could have taught them more.

I regretted that I left without coming to know my fellow Black teachers better. I didn't know how to build a bridge; the racial divide was too wide a chasm for me to get across. None of them attempted it either, perhaps because I didn't live with the threat of violence their neighborhood experienced, nor did I know what it was like to be discriminated against because of the color of my skin. I may not have had much materially growing up, but what I did have was opportunity and safety. We walked through the same school door each morning, but we lived in different worlds.

I thought about my own future, having been accepted into a graduate program in the teaching of English. Soon I would move far away from this school, a place I had come to think of as my crucible. I was grateful that I had lasted the semester and, truth be told, relieved the year had come to an end. But I wouldn't have missed it for the world, because of what I learned about the lives of my students and colleagues, and the insight I gained from teaching within their community. It had been a lesson in race relations and my own need for humility in the face of it that would inform my attitude toward school and teaching ever after.

Nothing in my formal education could match what I learned there; I knew I would never forget my hard lessons, the greatest of which was to begin to understand the enormity of the injustice racial inequality spawned. I realized I had witnessed how the violence meted out on slaves by their owners was carried over into the present culture, and so, into my classroom. At the time I did not fully understand why this should be.

What I did not realize was how high the stakes were. Corporal punishment was intended by parents and teachers to be a lesson that children would never forget, and therefore, prevent them from placing themselves in harm's way. Asserting authority included the right to inflict pain and, combined with biblical injunction, was in the minds of many, a duty. Harm could come from many directions: police, discriminatory laws, racist White people, drug dealers, gangs. I did not fully realize how dangerous it was to be Black in America. Adults were desperate to protect the children, desperate enough even to hurt them in the process.

In his prize-winning book *Between the World and Me*, an open letter from him to his 15-year-old son, Ta-Nehisi Coates analyzes his own childhood experiences and concludes that family violence comes out of desperate fear for the safety of the children. He relates an incident from his childhood when he was six years old. He was with his parents at a park, and he went off to a playground by himself, out of view. When his worried parents found him, his dad whipped him with his belt. Coates interprets his father's behavior as a reaction borne of both fear and love. Above all, his father was trying to protect him. This sort of parental discipline was so commonplace, Coates says, that kids joked about it often, laughing about the range of weapons parents would use, from extension cords to kitchen pots. What all the children had in common was that they were afraid of their parents. Tragically, physical punishment didn't prove to protect the children from the dangerous world outside. Coates comments, "Our parents resorted to the lash the way flagellants in the plague resorted to the scourge" (Coates, 2015, p. 17). They were desperate, and it was all they knew to do.

Dr. Stacey Patton concludes that the Africans brought to America used physical force hoping to save their children from the cruelty of their owners. After the Civil War, the same practices were continued throughout the Jim Crow era and beyond. This was done, Patton, says, to preserve their children, so they could cope with the harsh challenges they would meet in their daily lives. Patton contends that the use of corporal punishment by Black parents contributes to rather than prevents the likelihood that their children will be arrested. She goes on to point out that Black children are more likely to be killed or hurt by members of their own family than are children from other groups (Patton, 2017).

To move beyond this tragedy, trauma therapist Resmaa Menakem recommends that not only Black Americans but Whites, also, need to address the historical trauma their bodies carry, due to the cruel punishments inflicted not only on Black slaves but on Whites, throughout the course of history. Neuroscience now shows that we carry vestiges of emotional trauma in our bodies, and we need to heal from it. Acknowledging the existence of it is a powerful first step (Menakem, 2017). Much has been learned about healing from trauma and developing resilience in the face of it. As Dr. Bruce Perry, psychiatrist, suggests, our first question about children suffering emotional disturbance should not be, what is wrong with them, but rather, what happened to them (Perry & Winfrey, 2021).

The good news about disciplinary practices in our schools over the past several decades is that the incidence of corporal punishment has been declining. Across the country, most states now report the absence of corporal punishment altogether. And in Alabama, corporal punishment is still used, but, ironically, it is now higher for White students than Black. Mississippi is another interesting example. Most schools in Mississippi no longer use corporal punishment. There are a small number of districts, less than 10% of the total in the state, that account for half of the incidence. Nationwide, Black students are twice as likely to be beaten in school as are their White peers, so we are still seeing a racial discrepancy (Startz, 2022). Gradual progress has been made, but not until there are no children beaten at school can we rest easy.

At present, the profession of school psychology does not reflect the diversity we see among the children who attend public schools. I can't help but ponder what a benefit it would have been to have had an African-American psychologist available for consultation at the school where I taught. To have had someone from a background like our students guiding staff on how to discipline would have been a gift beyond measure.

I entered graduate school that autumn at a university in the Midwest. As I watched the evening news one day during the first week of classes, there on the screen appeared my former principal speaking to us. He was being interviewed about the integration of the school. They showed White students and Black students entering the school building together, everyone looking cheerful. Two of my former students sauntered in front of the TV camera, making faces. One was Sarah. The principal assured us that busing was working out just fine and that they expected racial integration to go along smoothly. On that happy note, the news shifted to another story.

I hoped his assurances would be prophetic. Could their school become a place where children could thrive, signaling progress toward greater racial and educational equity? Knowing how far we had yet to go, my hope was tempered with trepidation.

It's been half a century since my experience there. Had I been asked then to predict what schools would be like now, I suspect I would have said that racial integration would have been accomplished to the degree that segregation would be told about only in history books, not on the nightly news. It would be a sad chapter, sort of like before and after the polio vaccine, a time we would look back to as a reminder of how bad things used to be. This legacy of slavery would have long since passed. But here we are, two decades into the twenty-first century. After witnessing firsthand the significance of race and of poverty in relation to school performance nearly 50 years ago, I feel the disgrace that we haven't made far more progress. It has also become increasingly clear to me how politics, more than any other influence, shapes our public schools.

References

Coates, T. (2015). *Between the world and me.* Spiegel & Grau.

Grosvenor, K. (1970). *Poems by Kali.* Doubleday & Company.

History, Art & Archives, U.S. House of Representatives. (n.d.). *The southern manifesto of 1956.* https://history.house.gov/Historical-Highlights/1951-2000/The-Southern-Manifesto-of-1956/

Kendi, I. (2016). *Stamped from the beginning.* Bold Type Books.

Menakem, R. (2017). *My grandmother's hands: Racialized trauma and the pathway to mending our hearts and bodies.* Central Recovery Press.

Patton, S. (2017). *Spare the kids: Why whupping children won't save Black America.* Beacon Press.

Perry, B., & Winfrey, O. (2021). *What happened to you? Conversations on trauma, resilience, and healing.* Flatiron Books.

Startz, D. (2022). Corporal punishment, schools, and race: An update. *Brookings.* www.brookings.edu/blog/brown-center-chalkboard/2022/01/14/corporal-

Chapter 5

Segregation, Desegregation, Resegregation

How Laws Have Shaped Our Schools

Significant laws were created by the federal government during the mid-twentieth century and they have determined the course of our public school education. Besides enforcing racial desegregation, the watershed Elementary and Secondary Education Act (E.S.E.A.) was passed in 1965. This Act expanded the role of the federal government in education that continues to this day, now under the name of Every Student Succeeds Act (E.S.S.A.), authorized in 2015. Thanks to that Act, we ever after have taken for granted that Congress will chart the course for education in significant ways (Paul, 2016).

At the time it was passed, foreign relations as well as domestic policy influenced our government's willingness to increase funding for schools. The E.S.E.A. was an important aspect of President Lyndon B. Johnson's War on Poverty, but it also spoke to those who feared what the success of Sputnik, the Soviet satellite, might mean for the security of the United States. Worry that the Russians might overtake us spurred interest in providing resources for various educational programs that had nothing to do with winning the Cold War. One might say that those of us who received grants or loans for college tuition under the 1957 National Defense Education Act have the cosmonauts to thank (Sputnik Spurs Passage of the National Defense Education Act, October 4, 1957, n.d.).

In public schools, funds were made available through title programs to address the educational needs of children who came from low-income families, children with disabilities, and those who needed instruction in English as a second language. Although states were not forced to accept the funding, they chose to meet the requirements to qualify. In the 1980s E.S.E.A. funding was trimmed back under President Reagan but was restored in response to *A Nation at Risk*, published in 1986. This critique of American education warned that American students were slipping behind academically, compared with students from other

DOI:10.4324/9781003348344-5

countries (Federal Education Policy and the States: 1945–2009, 2009). So again, the competitiveness of world politics worked in favor of school funding.

The Sanctioning of School Psychologists

And then in 1975, the Education for All Handicapped Children Act (now Individuals with Disabilities Act, or I.D.E.A.) was passed, setting into law the requirement that students with disabilities must be offered a free appropriate public education that meets their needs (University of Kansas School of Education and Human Sciences, n.d.). From this point forward, school psychologists became essential personnel in public schools. Since then, school psychology has expanded from a "test and place" role within special education to providing individual and group counseling to address problems interfering with school performance. And when crises arise in the form of death, violence, or natural disaster, school psychologists often play a key role. They consult with parents and teachers on a regular basis and offer in-services on relevant topics to school staff. Most recently, the role has expanded to help school districts create a positive school climate (National Association of School Psychologists, n.d.).

When I reflect on my teaching experience in the South, I think wistfully of what my school would have been like had there been a serious effort to address the social/emotional needs of students. Now Natasha and her cohorts help design and serve on Response to Intervention teams, which figure out how to provide a physically and psychologically safe environment for kids in school. For learning to occur, it is now recognized that a nurturing rather than an authoritarian environment is the most beneficial (Biglan, 2015). This insight alone is a great gain and counters the notion that corporal punishment is a worthy method of discipline.

Reversing Racial Integration

According to research conducted in 2002 by the Civil Rights Project at Harvard University, racial integration of public schools in the latter part of the twentieth century was helping to provide equal educational opportunities for all. At the same time, they noted a trend toward the reversal of integration. Southern districts had both the highest levels of desegregation in the 1970s and 1980s and the highest resegregation from 1986 to 2000. Desegregation meant members of minority groups for a time had increased access to schools with good teachers, better resources, and high-achieving peers. Resegregation has been undermining that progress ever since (School Segregation on the Rise Despite Growing Diversity Among School-aged Children, 2001).

A Supreme Court ruling in 2007 found voluntary school integration plans unconstitutional, which further opened the door to the current increase of school segregation, reversing gains made toward greater integration after the 1968 decision that led to my first teaching position (Greenhouse, 2007). To assure their children a good education, White families with the means to do so have been enrolling their children in affluent neighborhood schools. But even high-income Black families are not very likely to live in these neighborhoods, so their children aren't represented in these schools, and of course neither are children of color from low-income families.

They have no choice but to attend racially segregated schools in our large cities. And because the schools are underfunded, they cannot provide the range of opportunities that children need. To be sure, there have been exemplary private Black schools fostering high achievement. The all-Black Dunbar High School in Washington, DC, whose graduates attended elite colleges during the era from 1870 to 1955 and went on to leadership positions in law and government, is a fine example (Sowell, 2020). However, most schools that Blacks attend are not provided the resources necessary for such success.

The Return to Segregation

Why is this the case? To understand how we have ended up with a division between affluent White schools and impoverished Black schools, we must look at how schools are funded and the history behind it. Public schools depend on the property value of homes in their district to gain funding through local taxes. Federal financial support is comparatively low; schools largely depend on local support. When neighborhood property values are low, so are the total taxes derived from them. That is why impoverished neighborhoods have underfunded schools.

The practice of unequal funding for public schools was brought before the Supreme Court in 1973, in *Rodriguez v. San Antonio Independent School District*. In a 5-to-4 vote, justices overruled lower courts that had determined unequal funding for schools was unconstitutional.

The path toward resegregation was assured by this decision (Kristof, 2021). A further disheartening aspect of the decision was that the ruling stated that the state of Texas was not obligated to subsidize school districts with inadequate funding (Orozco, 2020).

The Impact of De Jure Housing Practices

Because of long-standing discriminatory housing practices nationwide, Black neighborhoods have been economically depressed. These practices derived from unfair lending and real estate laws and traditions supported by our government at all levels, including the Supreme Court, which benefited White-owned banks and businesses, particularly realtors, at the expense of Black families.

Sanctioned by the federal government, it was legal for realtors to refuse to sell houses to Blacks in suburban developments after WWII, following a practice called redlining. Maps of cities were drawn with red lines around neighborhoods to distinguish where Blacks could and could not own property. The suburbs were intended for Whites only, even though many of the Black applicants to buy homes were veterans of WWII and this housing was ostensibly intended for veterans. Most Blacks were restricted to ghettos, which were far less attractive places to live and quickly became overcrowded. Ghettos often were located near industrialized and other undesirable areas of a city. As a result, property values didn't increase as they would in a White suburb. In addition, unscrupulous landlords and home loan lenders were able to charge exorbitant rates which often led to eviction or repossession.

In recent years it has come to light that our racial housing patterns nationwide are as they are because of de jure (legal) reasons, not just because of de facto (nonlegal) influences. It is a common misunderstanding that Blacks, Latinos, and people of Asian descent lived where they did by choice. Because of a shared culture and perhaps language, they just chose to live in close communities. But there was another factor that wasn't emphasized, which was that they had no other alternative. When people of color tried to buy homes where redlining didn't allow, they either were denied outright or were persecuted if they managed to complete a purchase. Such attempts were rarely successful (Rothstein, 2017).

When my own education of racial inequity in schools began 50 years ago, I was ignorant of de jure segregation and had no idea of its deep implications for school funding. Now that I know more, I am determined to support the cause of equity in education. And that means providing sufficient resources at both the state and local levels to overcome the disparities. One crucial area is fair access to home ownership. School funding is dependent on local taxes.

As Andre Perry points out, the fundamental problem with segregation is the inequitable distribution of resources that occurs when schools are segregated. He cites New York City as an example of a metropolitan area that has devised a plan to make their schools accountable for distributing resources fairly. This approach counters the trend toward resegregation, a hopeful sign (Perry, 2019).

Implications for School Psychology

The deep determination among many citizens to face the legacy of slavery suggests that positive change is afoot. School psychologists are positioned to be a force for such change, and NASP offers guidance as to how to do so. For example, NASP's 2017 infographic, "Understanding Intersectionality" educates us about the impact of discrimination on those among us with multiple identities based on their minority status. Proctor, Sherrie, et al. discuss the implications for school psychologists. As they point out, "intersectionality can be used . . . in understanding of their own intersecting identities as well as those of the students they serve", and "how the intersection of identities interacts with privilege or oppression". Recommendations for how this metaphor can be applied among school psychologists are given (Proctor et al., 2017, p. 19).

This is a way to grasp the role advantage plays in our own lives and in the lives of the children we serve, and to understand who gains and who loses, according to group memberships. Intersectionality does not deny that a member of a dominant group can be disadvantaged, or that someone in a nondominant group might be privileged. The emphasis is on the advantages or disadvantages afforded a person because of their group membership. Acting on this insight is particularly important because school psychologists are predominantly White and female, and English-only speakers, unlike a lot of the students they work with. Now about half of public-school students identify as being a member of a racial or ethnic minority group, about 10% are English language learners, and about half do not identify as female. NASP has launched an effort, the NASP Exposure Project, to address this concern and increase the number of school psychologists who match the cultural and linguistic backgrounds of American society in general (Barrett et al., 2019).

Our schools are still plagued with problems created by circumstances that came into being not just decades but hundreds of years ago. Furthermore, as a nation we are woefully uninformed about the history of slavery and discriminatory laws and practices and their impact on public education. The time has come for us to teach the policies and practices of Jim Crow with much greater honesty than has been done thus far and recognize vestiges in current practice. That by itself would be a huge step toward healing.

Promoting Educational Equity Through Public Policy

I must mention one advance, however, to counter discouragement over the state of public schools. A notable difference between teaching when I began and today is the fact that professions such as school social work, school counseling, and school psychology are represented in many school communities. Although many still don't, a lot of teachers now have access to a school psychologist and other mental health professionals who are trained to address tough issues.

Fifty years ago, the closest I got to such an encounter was an expert descending from the university in a city far away, with only five minutes to spare. There is at least some likelihood that many of today's classroom teachers have access to a school psychologist. This accessibility, all by itself, enhances the chance that teachers will have support to follow best practice in managing their classrooms, which will foster relational justice at school.

There are many injustices within our educational system waiting to be rectified. Several derive from ill-intentioned laws at the state and federal levels. Amid what can seem to be overwhelming challenges, let us remember that we can raise our voices individually and collectively with our elected officials, such as members of Congress, state legislators, and school board members. Face-to-face conversations with them and their aides and other communications that make our elected officials aware of our concerns can promote distributive justice—the fair use of public resources. The best way forward seems to be to change public policies to foster equity. A change in attitude, we hope, will follow in time.

References

Barrett, C., Heidelburg, K., & Malone, C. (2019). The NASP exposure project: Addressing workforce shortages and social justice. *Communiqué, 47*(5), 8–10.

Biglan, A. (2015). *The nurture effect: How the science of human behavior can improve our lives and our world.* New Harbinger Publications.

Greenhouse, L. (2007, June 29). Justices limit the use of race in school plans for integration. *New York Times.* www.nytimes.com/2007/06/29/washington/29scotus.html

Harvard Graduate School of Education. (2001, July 17). *School segregation on the rise despite growing diversity among school-aged children.* www.gse.harvard.edu/news/school-segregation-rise-despite-growing-diversity-among-school-aged-children

Kristof, N. (2021, May 21). If only there were a viral video of our Jim Crow education system. *New York Times.* www.nytimes.com/2021/05/21/opinion/sunday/education-racism-segregation.html

National Association of School Psychologists. (n.d.). *ESSA school climate for school psychologists.* www.nasponline.org/research-and-policy/policy-priorities/relevant-law/the-every-student-succeeds-act/essa-implementation-resources/essa-school-climate-for-school-psychologists-x35148

New York State Archives. (2009). *Federal education policy and the states, 1945–2009: A brief synopsis.* www.archives.nysed.gov/common/archives/files/ed_background-overview/essay.pdf

Orozco, C. (2020, August 4). Rodriguesv. San Antonio ISD. *Texas State Historical Association.* www.tshaonline.org/handbook/entries/rodriguez-v-san-antonio-isd

Paul, C.A. (2016). Elementary and secondary education act of 1965. *Social Welfare History Project.* https://socialwelfare.library.vcu.edu/programs/education/elementary-and-secondary-education-act-of-1965

Perry, A. (2019, February 19). Measuring diversity without holding schools accountable won't bring about integration. *The Hechinger Report.* https://hechingerreport.org/measuring-diversity-without-holding-schools-accountable-wont-bring-about-integration/

Proctor, S., Williams, B., Scherr, T., & Li, K. (2017). Intersectionality and school psychology: Implications for practice. *Communiqué, 46*(4), 19–22.

Rothstein, R. (2017). *The color of law: A forgotten history of how our government segregated America.* Liverwright Publishing Corporation.

Sowell, T. (2020). *Charter schools and their enemies.* Basic Books.

Sputnik Spurs Passage of the National Defense Education Act, October 4, 1957. (n.d.). *United States Senate.* www.senate.gov/artandhistory/history/minute/Sputnik_Spurs_Passage_of_National_Defense_Education_Act.htm

University of Kansas School of Education and Human Sciences. (n.d.). *Timeline of the Individuals with Disabilities Education Act (IDEA).* https://educationonline.ku.edu/community/idea-timeline

Chapter 6

Hard Lessons
Teaching in Pakistan

Before I returned to graduate school to become a school psychologist, I had another teaching experience that brought me to a culture different from my own. In 1979 I was hired to teach senior English and language arts and social studies to seventh and eighth graders at the American School of Lahore, Pakistan. I was working as an instructor in English when a professor at our university asked if I would be interested in applying for a position at this overseas school. His children had attended it when he was in Lahore on a Fulbright Fellowship, and he thought I might like teaching there. He would recommend me if I was interested.

At first the prospect seemed too threatening to consider. Pakistan was half the world away with an unfamiliar culture and health hazards, like malaria. But what I learned about the school and the community I would join won over my apprehensions. The prospect of working in an international setting with teachers and students from many parts of the world was irresistible. When I told my mother about the opportunity, she responded with her characteristic courage. "Go!" she said, "I never had the chance". Absolved of daughter guilt, the decision was settled in my mind. As it turned out I was hired and remained in Pakistan for 15 months. During that time, the U.S. weathered the Iran hostage crisis as well as a jihad against Americans ordered by the Ayahtollah Khomeini of Iran. But that was all in the future, so when I boarded the plane to cross the sea, my thoughts were of the exotic sites and new adventures that awaited me.

Welcome to Lahore

My first memory is of walking out of the Lahore airport into what felt like a wall of heat. As my skin bloomed sweat, I told myself that others adapt, so I will too. I glanced up and noticed several men were perched on low branches in the trees nearby. I was intrigued and mystified, wondering what their purpose was. Later I learned they were waiting for possible clients to give rides away from the airport in their motorized rickshaws or taxis. Shortly thereafter, when trying to communicate with the cook,

DOI:10.4324/9781003348344-6

I realized the head movement for "yes" in Pakistan closely resembled our American head shake for "no". These images impressed on me how far away from home I was; by actual distance, I was far enough away that if I went any farther, I'd be on my way home again.

As I was quickly learning, the cultural distance was at least as far. My cultural assumptions about what was normal were immediately being challenged, a process that continued throughout my stay. Coincidentally, I had arrived on my thirtieth birthday. As I began this new decade in my life, I was positioned to gain a new perspective on the world and my place in it.

Soon after our arrival, our principal/superintendent welcomed new teachers with a delicious dinner at her home. We were served traditional, highly spiced ethnic food—nothing I was at all accustomed to—but I enjoyed it thoroughly. I especially appreciated the conversation at the table. There was a special guest, an elderly British woman who was passing through Lahore on her trip back to England after doing linguistic research. I was fascinated by this dignified, scholarly woman, more than twice my age, who was returning from what sounded like an exciting intellectual adventure, and I was honored to be in her presence. What a good omen; I felt my future opening before me. The evening seemed a delightful introduction to the life I would lead in Pakistan.

By the middle of the night, however, I was introduced to another aspect of what Pakistan held in store. I woke up very dizzy with a severe headache, stomachache, and nausea. My forehead was burning up. Fortunately, I was able to crawl on my hands and knees to the bathroom just in time to expel my dinner from both ends of my body, and I gradually started feeling a bit better. By midmorning I felt I would recover. Evidently there had been something in the chicken curry from the night before that didn't like me.

No one else at the table got sick, but as the seasoned teacher who visited me later in the day told me, you could be eating from the same table and not get sick while everyone else would, or vice versa. It was a matter of chance. Frankly, if I could have afforded a ticket home I would have been sorely tempted to go. But that was not a possibility, so I just had to adjust. Fortunately, I never again became as sickened from food as I did that first time. I learned later that it takes about four years for an American's intestinal flora to change sufficiently to adapt to all the organisms in food on the Subcontinent. Because I was there only 15 months, I was always a little bit sick. I soon learned that Westerners had a reputation for being weaklings. Perhaps this was part of the reason. In any event, my illness was just part of the price to pay to have one of the most intense and informative experiences of my life.

I was thrilled to be living in a city whose origin was so ancient the story of its beginning was attributed to mythical demigods, reaching so far back there was no historical account. In contrast, the small North Dakota immigrant community where I grew up and my Icelandic great-grand-parents had helped settle had only existed for about a century. The risk of dysentery aside, I loved having the full range of sensory experience—being bombarded by the sights, sounds, and smells of such an unfamil-iar place and culture. Overhearing Urdu being spoken around me, the strong aroma of South Asian food cooking, the call to prayer by the mul-lah at dawn—all new to me and utterly ordinary to the local residents, who sometimes stared at me passing by on my walk to school, a novel event in their day.

At school the variety of my students' backgrounds provoked my aware-ness of how different I was to them, as well as an appreciation of the uniqueness of their backgrounds. The school was attended by students from many parts of the world, with the majority from Pakistan. Most of my students were at least bilingual and many were multilingual. Many spoke excellent English (I often thought better than mine) and could converse with me very easily. Their parents were willing to pay the high tuition for their children because they wanted them to be exposed to American teachers and an American curriculum in the hope that some-day they would attend a fine American university. Some of my students already had a specific school in mind, even though most were of junior high age. My first teaching experience, in the American South, had con-fronted me with the realities of children living in poverty. Now I would be teaching in a school that was funded well enough to provide an enriched environment for an affluent international community. The contrast was not lost on me.

The school building had been erected by a rich man as a private dwell-ing. Some years before I arrived, it was converted to a school. A high brick wall surrounded the beautiful, well-tended grounds that included an outdoor swimming pool. There wasn't enough space in the main building to fit everyone in, so several of the lower grades were housed in small, charming outer buildings. My classroom was on the second floor of the mansion, in a room with an attached balcony. I often went in to correct papers and plan lessons over the weekend, and I loved perching up there while I did my work.

My room was an enviable location, not only because of the view of the lawn. A fellow teacher pointed out what a great privilege I had been given. The classroom I had been assigned was considered the best room, since it was complete with air conditioning, and I wondered if I would be able to demonstrate I deserved it. It helped that I was teaching the two classes that the faculty agreed were the most challenging in the whole school, so they knew I would be put to the test. My slight physique caused some concern. The seventh- and eighth-grade boys had a reputation for being a handful, and I noticed worried expressions as I received many sympathetic encouragements from fellow teachers, especially from those who had taught them in earlier grades. But my classes were small; I never had more than 15 students at a time.

This low student-to-teacher ratio made my job far less difficult than it might have been, had I had large classes. As it turned out, I enjoyed these high-spirited, quick-witted boys that my colleagues were warning me about. I never for a moment felt threatened by them. They sometimes tried my patience, but my students in Lahore presented nothing I couldn't take in stride. I soon learned that many of them would be expected to assume great responsibility within the next few years, because they would head large extended families who would depend on them. I was glad they still had some time to be children.

My Students

My students were fascinating to teach, in part because they came from a wide range of diverse backgrounds. My one American male student had transferred to our school from Afghanistan, because it had become too dangerous for Americans to remain there. The ambassador had been killed and the country was deemed unsafe for civilians. This boy had witnessed the shooting of his pet dogs by soldiers who entered his family's compound. He had a reputation at the school for being hyperactive and a bit unruly—not surprising, given his experience.

Political violence was nothing strange to many of my students. My Pakistani students were old enough to be knowledgeable about the execution by hanging of their former prime minister, Zulfikar Ali Bhutto, after Muhammad Zia-ul-Haq took control of their government in a military coup in 1977. These children seemed wise beyond their years to me. In contrast, I pondered how little I understood of national or international politics when I was 12 or 13. Many of my students were fast becoming critical thinkers, realizing that politics can have a dishonest, deceptive, and dangerous aspect. They were keen to understand what the truth really was; they were already skeptical of their political leaders, far less gullible than I was at their age. They looked for ulterior motives in what national leaders had to say, realizing there could be a hidden agenda.

My European students had regular opportunities to compare and contrast conditions in their home country and Pakistan. For example, one of my students was a German girl whose time was divided between life with her father in Pakistan and her professional journalist mother in Germany. Thanks to who her parents were, I wouldn't doubt that she had a more sophisticated understanding of international politics than I did. I looked forward to what I would learn from all of these worldly wise children.

On one occasion an international event directly affected the dynamics of my classroom. I had an eighth-grade student from the country that at the time was known as Yugoslavia. Its leader, Josip Broz Tito, died, evoking tremendous grief and causing deep concern among citizens. He had held their country together, and the future looked very uncertain without him. That morning I expressed condolences to my student, and much to my dismay, tears spilled down her cheeks. I realized too late I should have spoken to her privately. One of the Pakistani boys mocked her. "Are you crying?" he asked. Hearing that taunt, she burst into tears and ran from the room. Angry that anyone would be so insensitive, I turned to him as I was leaving the room to console the girl and said that surely he could feel some sympathy, considering his former prime minister had been hanged. The boy replied, "Yes, but we didn't cry". However much I disapproved of his rudeness to his classmate, there was a toughness in his spirit that I couldn't help but admire. I felt like I was looking at someone 13 going on 50.

Some of my students were from wealthy families, and I was warned that the boys, especially, were used to being indulged. I expected my students to work hard, and sometimes some would balk. An Iranian boy told me that he was impressed that I, as well as the other teachers at our school, graded according to the quality of a student's work. He said his father, who taught at a local university, was sometimes threatened with physical harm; recently a student had placed a handgun on his father's desk when he came to talk about his grade. His dad didn't give in to the pressure, and the boy was glad that the teachers at our school took the same attitude. Only once did I feel any pressure to possibly change a grade.

I had given one of my students a grade of "C" on his report card, and his father came in to question me about the validity of the grade during parent/teacher conferences. Our conferences included the student, so the boy in question would be present for his father's visit. My superintendent warned me about the dad. She told me to expect him to be courteous but demanding of me and protective of his son. I appreciated the forewarning. The boy was a pleasant child who was not very serious about his studies, and I felt he deserved the grade I had given him. He did the minimum but didn't exert himself any further.

At our appointed time the dad entered my classroom with his son. I was struck by how young my student, small for his age, appeared in the presence of his imposing, stern-faced, well-dressed father. It occurred to me what a heavy burden his father's expectation might be. We took seats around a table, and I conducted the conversation by addressing my student directly. We talked about the various required assignments, and through his answers to what I hoped was gentle questioning, he revealed to his father how much effort he had put forth to complete the work. The truth was, not very much. After I finished what was essentially an interview, the father said he could see that I had done my best to motivate and educate his son. He realized that the boy had not taken full advantage of what I had offered, and he thanked me for my efforts.

Afterward, I felt sorry for them both. The dad wanted his son to succeed in the same way he had. No doubt there was a lot at stake if the boy never became very ambitious. I could also see that the son wanted to please his father but wasn't quite up to the task. I hoped the boy's mediocre academic performance would not create a rift in their relationship.

One day one of my best students lingered at my desk to ask me a question before she left for her next class. She began by saying she didn't understand me. I asked why, and she replied that I was nice to my students, but I also made them work hard. I asked again what she didn't understand, and she said that in her experience there were two kinds of teachers: nice ones and mean ones. The nice ones were nice because they didn't want to upset their students. It was easier for them if they just didn't demand too much and kept their students happy. The ones who wanted their students to learn a lot were crabby and mean sometimes, scaring the students into working hard. But she said I was both demanding and nice. "How come?" I replied that I was demanding because I was hired to teach, and if my students weren't learning I wasn't doing my job. And I was nice to them because I liked them. "But sometimes we are really bad!" she said. "No", I said. "Sometimes students may misbehave, but that's just because they are kids. No one has ever been mean to me". She took a moment to think about what I'd said. "Now I get it", she smiled and said.

Like the girl just mentioned, most of my female students aspired to become doctors or other professionals. They had an especially strong sense of social responsibility that seemed far beyond their years. They were aware they were enjoying a privileged education and realized they should serve others as a result. One of my senior girls adored animals and wanted to become a veterinarian. Her parents vetoed that choice, however, because there were too many children needing medical care in Pakistan. People had to be the priority. By the time she graduated she acquiesced to their judgment.

On the other hand, I had one eighth-grade student whose sole aspiration was to marry, which she knew she would do when she was just a little bit older. She was very happy with the prospect. The girl was able to attend our school because her father was an employee, and it was the policy of the school to give free tuition to the children of all white-collar workers. Her family could never have afforded the education otherwise. I expressed concern for her to my principal, who told me that at least the fact that she had learned quite a bit of English would probably mean she would marry someone who could provide financial security, since knowing English would enhance her value as a bride. I was taken aback by this information, but glad to be becoming educated into the realities of my students' lives.

My high school seniors liked to discuss marriage with me, impressing upon me how strange American marriage practices seemed to them.

They all liked the idea of arranged marriage because they said they couldn't imagine submitting to the "meat market" scene they believed was typical of the United States. For example, they could not conceive of going to a bar and meeting a stranger who later would become their mate. The possibility was unthinkable. One girl said she was content with having her parents select her husband for her because she trusted them to choose a fine man. She emphasized that they would never force her to marry a man she didn't like; she would have veto power over any of their choices. Given my American experience, I found their point of view quite intriguing and surprising—at first. The more examples I saw convinced me they had a point.

One senior boy insisted that his grandparents were utterly devoted to one another and had been since their wedding day. "My grandparents are living proof that being in an arranged marriage doesn't mean you can't fall in love with your partner", he said. He was emphatic about wanting Americans to know that.

As I mentioned previously, some of my students were the children of a marriage between a European and a Pakistani. In one case I had a female student, an eighth grader, who was behaving in a way that would have not drawn attention had she been living with her mother in Europe. But she was in Pakistan with her father, and he objected strongly when he discovered she had written a note to a boy. She was defiant, and my principal told me she feared that the father would withdraw her from school and marry her off to avoid any public shame over his daughter's actions, a shocking prospect to my American sensibilities. I asked my principal if she could come and live with me for a while. My principal informed me that that would be a good way for me to end up inside a Pakistani prison. Fortunately, as it turned out, the father and daughter were reconciled, so she was allowed to continue in school with us.

My Colleagues

I admired my fellow teachers from the first moment. The faculty was almost as international as the student body, and I enjoyed getting to know teachers from Pakistan as well as from Europe, Canada, and Central America in addition to my fellow Americans.

I was particularly impressed with the confidence Pakistani female teachers displayed. Any stereotypes about Muslim women quickly faded. In general, they were much more highly cultivated than we, their American counterparts. Usually they were from wealthy families; we Americans were not. It was true, of course, that they lived within certain societal constraints that we didn't. But in their own homes and in their own minds they were freer than many Americans, I came to see. Their families had supported their education, sometimes to the point that they had studied in the United States or England and had gained advanced degrees. One of my female colleagues was finishing up a Ph.D. at the University of North Carolina, an enviable achievement. In general, they seemed confident and strong, ready to take on the world. And when the jihad occurred, they stepped up, providing refuge and advice for our protection. The more I learned about them the more impressed I became with their courage and determination and the level of family support they received for their education and independent actions.

Because of the political situation, our school was vulnerable. This was brought home to me one of the first days I was at school. My principal, an American married to a Pakistani, called me in to confer about how to handle a photograph in my social studies textbook. There was a picture depicting Mohammed, which, she said, would inflame conservative Muslims to the point our school might be burned to the ground. But she said that if I felt strongly about freedom of expression and the fact that I was representing American values she would allow the picture to remain. I thought it over and asked for the scissors to remove the potentially offending picture. I decided that if anyone wanted to see the photo, we could provide it through another means. Having the school burned to the ground with the likelihood of children meeting their deaths was not a risk I was willing to take. Later, when other American buildings were burned, I was glad for my conservative decision.

It fascinated me how my colleagues lived up to their national stereotypes. The French teacher was passionate, the British were restrained, and so forth. I wondered what impression we Americans made on them, whether we also behaved predictably. Sure enough, eventually comments made to me by my colleagues indicated that we also fit a mold. We Americans were seen as people of action. If we were dissatisfied, we organized and planned. We were impatient and accustomed to getting results. For example, when one of our teachers came close to suffocating in an allergic reaction to medication, we insisted on developing a crisis plan to get people to the hospital. And after our jihad experience, we developed an evacuation plan. We did not accept conditions we didn't like if we could figure out how to change them. We were also seen as inventive. For example, one of our American teachers was also an actress, and she had students writing and filming their own commercials. We weren't very bound by tradition, so just because something hadn't been done before was no reason not to try it.

A Lesson in How We View Each Other

One of my favorite memories of teaching in Pakistan is of a class in which I had my students tell me what Americans are like. I was teaching the concept of what a stereotype is, and I thought it would be interesting to begin by asking my seventh graders to describe Americans to me. When I gave the assignment, their eyes grew large, and they shifted uncomfortably in their desks. I quickly assured them that I realized they wouldn't be talking about me, so I would not take their descriptions to heart. I stood at the blackboard and asked that they call out words or phrases that described Americans. I even turned my back to them so they could see I wasn't paying particular attention to who said what.

"Everyone is rich, they practice odd religions, have strange courtship and wedding practices, show disrespect toward women, smell funny, eat strange food, are warlike, and violent" are some of the descriptors I remember best. I thanked them for their honesty, and then I asked them what they thought Americans would say about them. They had no idea, and no one even ventured a guess. So I told them what the list would be like. I said it would be the same list, except that "everyone is poor" would be substituted for "everyone is rich". "We aren't poor!" My class exclaimed, practically in unison. "I know that", I said. "But most Americans don't".

Then I went down their list and told them stories about specific Americans who didn't fit their stereotypes. For example, I told them about a woman, now elderly, who as a girl quit school at the end of eighth grade. She assisted her mother in raising younger brothers and sisters, and when she did leave home, she left to be what was essentially an indentured servant. She went to work for a neighboring farmer for the winter to pay off a load of grain so her father could plant again in the spring. My class didn't believe me. "In America? No!" I said I knew the story was true because the girl I described was my own mother. We went on to acknowledge that what we see on TV about people may not hold true for everyone. American movies were very popular in Pakistan and the view of Americans presented on film shaped many of their opinions.

Mutually Exotic

One of my students, an eighth-grade girl, took a deep interest in my appearance, I think because she was at an age where she was becoming acutely aware of her own. One day she paused on her way out of class to tell me that she admired my eyes; she thought the color was so exotic. I almost laughed, since I have bluish, greenish eyes, typical of those of us descended from a mixture of northern Europeans. Back home the last thing I would expect anyone to comment on is my eye color. I asked her how many people from North Dakota she would guess had eyes like mine. She thought there must be very few. When I told her how common my eye color was, she was very surprised. If you want exotic, I said, *your* eyes fit the category very well. Now it was her turn to be surprised. "Mine?" she exclaimed. "Everyone has eyes like mine!" To which I replied, "Everyone here. Not everyone where I come from". She could scarcely believe it. And then we laughed together about our exotic eyes. Our differences made us seem beautiful and exotic to each other, while we were dismissive of ourselves.

The International Becomes Personal

When the Ayahtollah Khomeini proclaimed a jihad against America in November of 1979, official Americans except for essential personnel were evacuated from Pakistan, but the teachers at the Lahore school were not considered "official", so we waved goodbye to our American students and many of their parents. They were flown back to the United States immediately because of the imminent danger from jihadists who would want to take kill Americans. Within short order, the American Library and the American Commissary in Lahore were burned to the ground. It was clear Americans were in grave danger, so we teachers went into hiding to stay out of harm's way. Fellow teachers from school offered protection without hesitation. I will always be grateful to these kind people who risked their own security to protect us. Some of us were housed in quarters vacated by the official Americans who departed. We heard later that the Pakistani soldiers who guarded us did not have live ammunition. Fortunately, no one came looking for us.

One incident I remember very clearly was a trip back to my house with my next-door neighbor to gather supplies in case we left the country. Our group naively believed women could do this more safely than men, assuming women would receive better treatment if caught. (With 20/20 hindsight, I have to say this was a foolish idea, but we accepted it at the time.) A fellow teacher and I were driven in a school van to our compound to gather necessary items. Our driver waited in the driveway for us. Just after I entered my house, I happened to glance out the large plate glass windows in the front room, only to see a young man on a motorcycle at our front gate talking excitedly to our driver. It was clear this was not a friendly conversation. The thought occurred to me that I just might be looking at my assassin. But after a few moments he roared off.

Our driver came running to my fellow teacher and me, insisting we leave *now!* He opened the back door to the van and my colleague quickly climbed in. The driver then grabbed the back of my collar and the waistband of my pants and practically threw me in after her. We covered ourselves with a blanket so we could not be seen. After we were underway my irrepressible colleague chirped ironically, "Isn't it fun being Jewish?" Being of the generation we were, we were steeped in stories of what happened in Germany and Eastern Europe during WWII during the Holocaust. No, I have to say, it wasn't fun being "Jewish". It was a profound lesson how, in a moment, one can go from being a person to becoming a symbol, and one's life is suddenly worth nothing.

The president of the school board—one of those who got on the plane—left behind funds for us to flee to the U.S. Embassy in New Delhi, India, should we wish to leave. All seven of us Americans traveled to India together. There we watched and waited for about a week, until the jihad was called off. The situation was threatening; we knew that in Lahore the American Library and the American consulate commissary were in ashes. Also, we learned that two Americans had been killed in Islamabad, where rioters attacked and burned the American Embassy, "incited by the false claim that the U.S. had seized the Grand Mosque in Mecca" (Special report no. 88. Soviet "active measures": Forgery, disinformation, political operations, 1981).

We teachers agreed that we had to act in unison. Either we all left for the United States or we would all go back to Lahore. We knew that the school would suffer a very serious blow if we left, since parents sent their children to the school largely because we were there. After a week we concluded from the reports we had received that Pakistan had returned to being safe enough for us to return. The Ayahtollah had called off the jihad because it was clear the United States had not seized the Grand Mosque. It looked like the crisis had passed. We didn't want to abandon our students, nor did we relish the thought of being unemployed back in the States, so we went back, and the school was reopened.

After we returned, we dealt with the anxiety that another jihad would occur which could include an attack on the school. We asked for a crisis plan, one that specified exactly how we would quickly evacuate the building and get to safety. This was put into place. In retrospect, I have no confidence our plan would have worked very effectively, but it served to somewhat settle our nerves. For the remainder of the academic year, the school was in a constant, low-grade state of anxiety, both because of the uncertain political situation and because of the shock of losing several students overnight. Those who remained became closer, knowing how fragile the existence of our school was. We hoped the others would return before too many months passed. As it turned out, we completed the school year without them.

While at the American Embassy in New Delhi, I had the privilege of hearing a lecture by a child psychiatrist who worked for the U.S. State Department in South Asia. He talked with teachers about how children respond to the trauma of an international incident, such as a jihad. What impressed me most was that he emphasized how children had far fewer opportunities to tell their story of what happened to them, compared with their parents. I thought of my eighth grader who had been evacuated to Lahore from Afghanistan, and his tendency to act out physically. In a nutshell, the psychiatrist said parents had cocktail parties; kids did not, emphasizing that the adults had several opportunities to listen to one another. They told their stories again and again, which aided healing. In stark contrast, kids usually didn't have others to share with in this way, and so sometimes suffered trauma effects longer than their parents did. When I returned to my classroom, I made a point to give my students opportunities to tell about their experiences.

When we returned and school reopened, we came back to a student body traumatized by the event. One Pakistani high school student asserted that civilian Americans should die for the crimes she believed the United States had committed in the Middle East and South Asia. It was unsettling to consider she might think even her teachers deserved that fate. Fortunately for us, she eventually was able to separate her thinking about private citizens from the government they happened to live under and decided that civilians did not deserve a death penalty. On the other hand, one of our colleagues, a retired colonel, took to wearing a large coat much of the time, even when it was quite warm. We suspected he was concealing a weapon beneath it in case we would need protection.

My Mentors

Threatening as the environment had become, in most ways the school remained an oasis to me, a beautiful little place usually full of goodwill and opportunity. It was unnerving to consider how vulnerable it was to political events far beyond our control, but supportive relationships within the school community sustained me. Two people, both middle-aged American women married to Pakistanis, had my back.

One was my principal, who served as a teaching mentor. My master's degree in the teaching of English qualified me to teach grades seven through 14, but I only had experience teaching English at the college level. I had student-taught seniors for several weeks in high school, but I had no experience with junior high students. Fortunately, my principal was sympathetic to me as a beginner and welcomed my questions. She brought many years of teaching experience at various levels to her position as principal/superintendent, so she was a fine resource. I loved having her visit my class to observe me. Her comments and suggestions about my handling of my junior high students and the curriculum were invariably helpful.

I asked her in enough times, however, that other teachers noticed how frequently the principal was entering my classroom. One day a colleague asked if I was struggling. I replied that I thought things were going along well enough. She said she asked because she had seen the principal going into my room a lot recently. I told her I asked her to come. "You *asked* her?" She was dumbfounded. I explained that the principal gave me helpful suggestions, and I enjoyed having her stop by. Our principal had a stern demeanor, but I had found her easy to get along with. Evidently, not everyone welcomed her as a guest.

The other person who mentored me was the elementary art teacher. Coincidentally, she had also grown up in North Dakota, so we had instant rapport. We had already met before I went to Pakistan because she had come back to visit her mother in our home state. I still carry the image of her of when we first met.

She was tall and looked wonderfully dignified in the traditional embroidered Pakistani camise she wore. I was deeply impressed by this worldly woman who had a background like mine and had successfully merged two worlds. She was 15 years older than I and had gone to Pakistan with her husband about 25 years earlier. They had met at an American university where he was working on a law degree, and she was studying art history. She told me she had just graduated from college with a B.A. degree and felt she was ready to meet the world when she married her husband and moved to Pakistan. By the time I met her, she had two adult children off in the world beyond Pakistan, and two attending our school, both of whom were my students.

We built a habit of eating dinner together the evening of the last day of the school week, and we would review our lives, at school and otherwise, together. Her husband was a politician, so she had a lot of insight into how the government worked and what the likely truth was behind political events. I enjoyed hearing her use fluent Urdu to communicate with the people in her household. She was deeply knowledgeable about Pakistani life and culture, having spent several years living in a village after she first arrived.

She had an easy laugh, and her stories riveted my attention. Married life there required that she speak Urdu, live in a joint family, cook over a wood fire, bathe with a jug beside a tub, and learn to perform many other tasks for which she had no preparation. I think she saw her younger self in me. She took me under her wing because, she said, I seemed "sweet, innocent and naïve", and therefore, was probably "a lady on thin ice", in need of protection and advice for how to manage my life at school and in Pakistan.

I was fortunate beyond measure that she became my resident mentor. It saved me from having to learn everything by trial and error. She often filled me in on the background information I needed to gain a good understanding of the culture of our school and of Pakistan, in general. For example, she educated me to the fact that Americans living in Lahore should hire servants, because they needed the work. This was especially important for Christians, she said, because they had more difficulty than Muslims in finding homes to work in.

Her deep understanding based on years of experience provided reassurance for me as I encountered unfamiliar situations. However different people seemed, she would emphasize that underneath our veneer of culture, we share a common humanity, which, in essential ways, makes us more alike than different. This was the main lesson she learned over her years in Pakistan, and I took it to heart.

I suspect one can feel at home almost anywhere; it just depends on how much imagination one brings to a place. I met a Canadian teacher who was working in Islamabad, and she told me she had just spent some years in Saudi Arabia. She missed being there, she said, because the sand dunes reminded her of undulating fields of golden ripe grain back home in the plains of Canada, north of where I grew up. The imaginative connection of a familiar image from her place of origin linked her to a faraway location that on the surface might have seemed strange and foreign. But she had an open heart, and through her imagination, she found a way home.

New Eyes

As many travelers to faraway places discover, a voyage is an education not only about the places visited but about one's own perceptions. My experience in Pakistan taught me to see the world differently than I had. Just as my time teaching in an urban Black neighborhood awakened me to hard truths within my own country, my time working in a Muslim country educated me to see my and my country's relationship to the world with greater nuance. Again, I found myself in a minority among people at school, but because I was White, that was an advantage. I gained a glimpse of the lingering effects of the caste system that had been the law of the land in India, of which Pakistan had been a part. I couldn't help but notice that the darkest among us often performed the lowliest tasks, much like the situation in my own country. It was also a lesson in the impact of British colonization—most obvious in the excellent command of English of all educated Pakistanis, and the close connection many had with England, including intermarriage in their family. Once again, I found that the quickest way to learn about one's own culture is to be immersed in a different one. It was a constant exercise in compare and contrast.

I learned about international relations on the Subcontinent, especially the highly volatile relationship between India and Pakistan, which was illustrated vividly on my first flight to India from Lahore. After take-off, the plane gained altitude with such a sharp incline that we passengers felt like we were on a rocket ship. Our principal turned around in her seat to patiently explain what was happening. "It's necessary for Pakistani planes to be above a certain altitude when crossing the India-Pakistan border to avoid getting shot down", she said. "We are only about twenty miles from the border at take-off, so we have to rise very quickly".

The danger of a plane being shot down was the least of it. India had nuclear weapons, and although the news wasn't yet official, everyone—including my junior high students—knew Pakistan did, too. India and Pakistan were arch enemies. I pondered what it would feel like if Canada had the bomb and had their missiles aimed toward the United States. I was reminded of what it felt like during the Cuban missile crisis of 1962, when I was the age of many of my students. My parents were discussing the likelihood of bombs being sent our way. This was of particular interest because we lived just a few miles from a missile silo. My heart froze when I heard my dad tell my mother that if war started, we wouldn't even know it. Of course not, I realized. We would be at ground zero. Fortunately, the Cuban crisis came and went. The Pakistan-India tensions, however, remain to this day. I was beginning to understand why my students were so politically sophisticated.

Living in Pakistan gave me a good lesson in religious and political forces at work in the Muslim world. I learned the two meanings of jihad—both the spiritual aspect that my colleagues subscribed to and the militant interpretation. It was also an education in international conflict involving superpowers. Right outside of Lahore was a large refugee camp, inhabited by Afghans fleeing their country during their war with the Soviet Union. I came to learn about the involvement of the United States, which, along with several other countries, was assisting Afghanistan against the Russian invasion, and so became deeply entangled in the geopolitical conflicts of South Asia. As it turned out, this was only the beginning of our endless wars in that part of the world. By 2001, we had had a long history of military intervention there, years before Al Qaeda took direct action against us on our own soil.

As an American professional abroad in Pakistan, I was offered special privileges. American teachers were welcomed by the diplomatic community; for example, we were given access to the consulate swimming pool and were invited to social occasions. We also enjoyed the generous hospitality of Pakistanis who invited American visitors to weddings and treated us with special regard. It was a fascinating experience to gain a glimpse into the world of wealthy South Asian families, who were living a life very different from what I had ever experienced.

But there was another side to life in Pakistan. I was confronted with the discrepancy between the lives of the rich and the poor every day on my walk to school. People living in poverty were constantly visible, their meager existence juxtaposed against the luxury and comfort the rich took for granted. The school's servants lived nearby, and I would see them doing their daily tasks. There was very little litter on the streets because every item was recycled to another purpose. Almost nothing got thrown away. They lived in tiny cement houses and conducted much of their life outside. Their possessions and opportunities were few.

The same was true of the people who worked in my house. The watchman lived on the property where I did, and his dwelling was as humble as that of the school servants. I was very uncomfortable having servants, a typical American reaction. But not employing them would undermine the local economy, as my art teacher mentor had explained. Not hiring servants meant denying people a living, so I did my best to be a fair and kind *memsaab*, the woman in authority. Seeing the extremes of the rich and the impoverished, I wondered how such a disparity could ever be overcome; it would require a massive shift in public policy to remedy. Still, it puzzled me why more wasn't being done to close the gap.

It was no wonder that many of the compounds had protective high brick walls, as did our school grounds. In some instances, such walls were topped off with shards of glass, and paid guards stood at the gates. I remember hoping the United States would never see such a wealth gap that we, too, would have homeless people living on the street, and the affluent would sequester themselves behind protective barriers. Of course, now we do, and always have had people living in extreme poverty; I just wasn't aware, because they didn't live in my neighborhood.

The topic of inequality came up in my eighth-grade social studies class when we studied slavery and the Civil War. During our discussion, a student asked why all the slaves didn't just rebel. I assured him that there were several rebellions, and many slaves did their best to escape. But consider what the consequences were if they failed. Execution would be the likely outcome. He seemed unconvinced; it appeared he thought it was simply a matter of courage. To give him some context, I asked him why his servants hadn't rebelled. His family's servants weren't enslaved, but how much opportunity did they have to dramatically alter their lives? Shocked by the question, he had no reply. I pointed out that people endure difficult circumstances when it looks like there is no reasonable alternative.

My faith in the value of a good education was fortified by the many well-educated people I encountered. They were open-minded and well informed; we Americans had no reason to feel superior. I especially valued meeting the strong Muslim women at our school. They were tough in the face of a moral challenge, as were the men, stepping up to provide protection by inviting us to their homes and providing transportation. Had jihadists caught them doing this they could have paid a price.

More than anything, I left convinced that a multicultural experience in school is deeply enriching. I was impressed daily with how sophisticated our students were about politics and how much they could learn from one another, because so many came from widely dissimilar backgrounds. Our school to me felt like a little United Nations. It gave me hope. Students with different traditions sat side by side, and it was a joy to discuss their differences and similarities with them. We didn't have to think exactly alike to share concerns for one another and the world. Every day brought opportunities for exercises in perspective taking.

Welcome Home

Returning to the United States was almost as great a culture shock as going to Pakistan had been. I missed the intense stimulation of new scents, sounds and circumstances that I had experienced daily in Lahore: The wafting of aromas from meals being prepared outside as I walked to school, the sight of people wearing their traditional dress as they passed along the street in front of my house, the sound of the call to prayer at dawn—all contributed to a rich experience. It was a comfort to be home, but at the same time, I felt a loss. One of my aunts sent me a post card to tell me she was glad I was back in "God's country", expressing no interest in my experience. Even many of my well-educated relatives and friends showed no curiosity. Some of these people may have been treated by a doctor from Pakistan, because immigrants with medical degrees often served small rural communities. But so far as they were concerned, the Muslim world was a place to fear, not wonder about or take an interest in. Then 9/11 happened, and it got even scarier.

When militant jihad came to America in 2001 in the form of planes smashing into buildings, my son was a graduate teaching assistant at an American university. He called me to talk about what he should say to his students the next day. He feared many would be very angry, to the point of hating Muslims. I advised him to describe the Pakistan I experienced. I asked that he tell his students it was true that two decades earlier jihadist Muslims had threatened and even killed Americans, but it was also true that ordinary Muslims had protected us, risking their own security. Also, over the past several years militant Islamists had done great harm to innocent Muslims around the world; we were not their only target.

Ever since I had returned home 20 years earlier, I wondered if an attack would come. When it did, it grieved me that, in general, Americans seemed to have little notion of why such an event could unfold. The time had now arrived for Americans to educate ourselves about South Asia and our relations there. We needed to learn the history of our involvement in South Asia and the Middle East so we could distinguish between those who meant us harm from those who did not and to see what role the United States played. Casting all Muslims as the enemy only revealed our ignorance. Fortunately, ignorance can be overcome. It became clear to me that a thorough understanding of our own multifaceted history, including the impact of our international actions, needed to be a part of every American's education. Otherwise, it is too easy to demonize many who mean us no harm.

Reference

United States Department of State. (1981). *Special report no. 88. Soviet "active measures": Forgery, disinformation, political operations.* www.hsdl.org/?view&did=807615

Chapter 7

Beyond 9/11

Confronting Islamophobia

The overwhelming majority of Muslims already living in this country or coming to it are upstanding people, sharing in basic American values. In the aftermath of the war in Afghanistan in 2021, many newcomers had even worked as allies to the United States, and so had risked their lives on our behalf. These people have no interest in imposing sharia laws on our system of justice, nor are they plotting to explode a suicide bomb. But particularly after 9/11, the fear of both got hold of the imagination of many of our citizens, and we are paying a high price in the form of hate crimes being committed against the innocent. Harassment in school has also increased, to the point where a Muslim young man in Texas was suspended from school and arrested for bringing a homemade clock to school after his teacher feared it might be a bomb. The charges against him were dropped and his parents filed suit against the school district for discriminating based on race and religion (Iyer, 2018).

The case was dismissed, but the concerns it raised are very much alive. Amani Al-Khatahtbeh's memoir, for example, gives firsthand insight into what it was like to be a young Muslim child growing up in the United States after 9/11. Her example of courage and defiance of stereotypical treatment educates us about what a determined individual can accomplish. Her experience also teaches us how far we have left to go before we deserve to consider ourselves a society that respects cultural differences. "I'm not really sure I understood what was going on when 9/11 happened, but I was old enough to feel the world shift on its axis that day and change everything forever" was how she described her reaction as a fourth grader (Al-Khatahtbet, 2016, p. 2). I think of a young Muslim friend of mine living in a small Minnesota community who was harassed by angry classmates telling her to "Go back to where you came from"! She and her family were faithfully law-abiding and eager to become useful participants in the American way of life. I was mortified that this innocent girl had to bear the brunt of such prejudice. Sadly, incidents

DOI:10.4324/9781003348344-7

such as this have become commonplace in schools around the country. More than ever, school psychologists need to know how to foster cultural awareness and tolerance.

Perhaps this behavior reflects the fears that arise when a community has to adjust quickly to a large number of newcomers without understanding enough about them. According to the Pew Research Center, Minnesota has a history of taking in proportionately large numbers of immigrants. For example, in fiscal 2005, the state took in 124 refugees per 100,000 state residents. Other states also have accepted comparatively high numbers. In fiscal 2016, my home state of North Dakota along with Nebraska and Idaho settled the most refugees per 100,000 residents, with North Dakota accepting 71 (Radford & Connor, 2016).

There have been and continue to be significant challenges as our country learns how to respond. For example, the Minnesota chapter of the Council on American-Islamic Relations filed a civil rights complaint against the St. Cloud school district in 2011 on behalf of the district's Somali students that included reference to religious harassment. Since then, the St. Cloud schools allow prayer time, have lunch menus with pork-free options, and have developed sports uniforms for girls who wear hijab. An international club at the technical senior high has been created that allows English language learners to express their pride in their cultural heritage. The district is trying to hire Somali-speaking teachers, a huge challenge because of the limited number of qualified personnel. To address this need, St. Cloud State University is teaming with the district to train more Somalis as public school teachers. The settlement ending the federal civil rights investigation requires the school district to report all allegations of harassment (Mitchell, 2016).

Concern about racial and religious tensions is ongoing. For example, at the national level, the U.S. Department of Education provides guidance to handle discriminatory treatment in school as part of their "Newcomer Toolkit", available online (Newcomer Toolkit, 2017).

The plight of the bullied Muslim student has not gone unnoticed. In 2016, President Obama proclaimed January 16 to be "Religious Freedom Day". The U.S. Department of Justice launched a community engagement plan to combat religious discrimination involving stakeholders from around the country, which included addressing religious discrimination in education. Problems identified included religion-based bullying and harassment, access to reasonable religious accommodation, need for increased training in understanding biases, and need for better federal guidance on Title VI of the Civil Rights Act of 1964 (United States Department of Justice, 2016). The U.S. Department of Education took steps to further the cause, including a new website on religious discrimination, with links to other governmental entities to address problems (United States Department of Education, 2017).

Advocates have recommended passage of the Safe Schools Improvement Act (S.S.I.A.), which would amend the Elementary and Secondary Act of 1965 to prohibit bullying and harassment based on a student's religion, race, color, national origin, sex, disability, sexual orientation, or gender. To date, the 117th Congress has not acted on either of this proposed legislation. S.S.I.A. was introduced in the House of Representatives by Reps. Linda Sánchez (D-CA), John Katko (R-NY), and Mark Takano on July 9, 2021, and in the Senate by Senator Bob Casey (D-PA) on July 21, 2021 (Safe Schools Improvement Act of 2021, H.R. 4402, 117 Cong., 2021–2022).

Muslims in the United States

Muslims living in our country represent a wide range of backgrounds. We do not have to travel overseas to discover that all Muslims are not alike, given the numbers of them, both immigrants and citizens, living in the United States at this time. Besides immigrants, we also have American converts to Islam, as well as children born here to immigrants and citizens. According to the Pew Research Center, the number of Muslims in the United States is increasing, having grown from 2.75 million in 2011 to 3.45 million in 2017. By 2050, they will likely comprise 2.1% of our population (8.1 million), almost double the percentage currently. That can mean there will be a corresponding increase in children enrolled in school (Mohamed, 2018).

Uninformed school psychologists need to gain a basic understanding of religious beliefs and cultural and ethnic norms to work effectively with Muslims in school. Muslims practice their religion by observing the five main rituals, which are called the Pillars of Islam. First, there is the declaration of belief, the *shahadah*, which is the acknowledgment of belief in one God with Mohammed as His Messenger. The second pillar requires the practice of performing five prayers each day. The third, *zakat*, is the practice of donating to charity at least once a year. The fourth is fasting during the month of Ramadan, and the fifth is the *hajj*, the pilgrimage to Mecca, the holy city. (Pillars of Islam, 2016) Muslims in the United States originate from many countries, but the two largest groups, each representing about a quarter of the total, are the South Asians (from Pakistan, India, and Bangladesh) and the Arabs (from Egypt, Lebanon, and Palestine) (Pew Research Center, 2011). Regardless of the place of origin, all Muslims typically have a strong sense of duty to family, to the extent that family matters more than oneself. They also share a respect for community and education, they value modesty about sexuality, and they are fatalistic: What is meant to be will be, Shifa Podikunju-Husain, an associate professor of school counseling, points out (Podikunu-Hussain, 2006).

Muslims in the U.S. must deal with an ongoing tension between the pull toward assimilation into the larger culture and the pressure to maintain religious and cultural norms, Podikunju-Husain, emphasizes. Here a school psychologist may find a role in helping a young person become aware of these tensions and clarifying a path forward. Since 9/11 Muslims have also had to deal with increased responsibility to defend basic religious rights and to cope with real or perceived prejudice. Muslim children may have to deal with conflicting values from home as they acculturate, which can mean shedding some of their Muslim identity, and, at the same time, face bullying in school for being Muslim (Podikunu-Hussain, 2006).

The complexity and sensitivity of these religious and cultural issues can be intimidating to a school psychologist unfamiliar with Muslim life. The best approach may be to allow the student to be your teacher. Let them explain their beliefs and allow them to guide you to a specific understanding of their cultural and religious perspective. Awareness of your own attitudes and biases will aid you in this process, Podikunju-Husain asserts. What counts in the end is that they know you are there to stand beside them (Podikunu-Hussain, 2006).

School Psychology Resources

The National Association of School Psychologists (NASP) has been ready to assist ever since the tragedy of 9/11. Charles Deupree, the president of NASP at the time of the terrorist attack, reported that within hours of the event, the organization posted handouts and help sheets online for parents and teachers. Over the traumatic ensuing days, NASP added several more handouts and shared site links, which were available at NASP National Emergency Assistance Team (N.E.A.T.) Resources. Also, NASP collaborated with the International School Psychology Association to make translations of them into several languages other than English. Thanks to trainings made available through NASP, school psychologists around the country have been trained in crisis response (Delisio, 2002).

In the years since the immediate crisis, NASP has published articles aimed at helping school psychologists cope with the effects of xenophobia on children. As a profession, we are ethically bound to address harassment and support its victims. Cultivating a safe school climate includes learning about how to overcome Islamophobia within the school community. An effective approach is to develop a Multi-Tiered System of Support (M.T.S.S.) in school communities which can address incidents and over time serve to prevent discriminatory behavior (Houri & Sullivan, 2016). Such a problem-solving framework can ensure improved outcomes for all students while targeting support for those who struggle.

At this writing, a great many more Americans can find Pakistan on the map than could in 1980, when I returned home. The intervening decades have brought many sad reasons for us to note what is happening half the world away and to ponder the impact of it on us. Islamophobia has become a part of our current vernacular, and we read often in the press about attacks on Muslims prompted by hate and fear. School psychologists need to understand the geopolitical history of the recent past and must be well informed about the challenges American Muslims and immigrants face.

As time passes, school psychologists and other members of school communities are becoming better informed. Just as we have worked for decades to demand equal treatment for students with disabilities, so we can join the call for equal treatment for all students, regardless of ethnic or religious background. We can take heart in the knowledge that many fellow citizens are sympathetic to the needs of immigrants. Some are from what many might consider unlikely places. I think of an example from my home state.

A Hopeful Sign

In 2019 the President authorized local governments to restrict the admission of refugees. The Burleigh County commissioners in the state of North Dakota were the first to consider such action. A public meeting was held, and several residents spoke in favor of allowing refugees to come. They referred to their Christian duty to do so, the history of their own ancestors who came as refugees from Scandinavia, and their worry that a vote in favor would gain the county a reputation as home to bigots. In a vote of 3 to 2, the commissioners ruled to accept the 25 refugees allocated to them, rather than reject them (Omdahl, 2019). Perhaps some will be children who will attend local schools. I trust there will be a school psychologist ready to assist.

This outcome seems particularly fitting to me, since our state is the site of one of the oldest still-existing mosques constructed in the United States. In 1929, immigrants from Syria and Lebanon constructed the building. It fell into disrepair and was removed in 1979. A new mosque was built to replace it in 2005, financed by donations from the family of its founders and Christian friends (Jenkinson, 2021).

References

Al-Khatahtbet, A. (2016). *Muslim girl: A coming of age.* Simon & Schuster.

Delisio, E. (2002). School psychologists' changing roles, responsibilities. *Education World.* www.educationworld.com/a_issues/chat/chat058.shtml

Houri, A., & Sullivan, A. (2016). Meeting the needs of Muslim American students. *Communiqué, 45*(3), 8.

Iyer, D. (2018, March 22). Courts were unfair to boy who brought clock to school. *CNN*. www.cnn.com/2018/03/22/opinions/ahmed-mohamed-discrimination-school-court-opinion-iyer/index.html/

Jenkinson, C. (2021). *Essays on the future of North Dakota: The language of cotton-woods*. Koehler Books.

Mitchell, C. (2016). How one Minnesota school district handles a rising immigrant population. *PBS*. www.pbs.org/newshour/education/how-one-minnesota-school-district-handles-a-rising-immigrant-population

Mohamed, B. (2018). New estimates show U.S. Muslim population continues to grow. *Pew Research Center*. www.pewresearch.org/fact-tank/2018/01/03/new-estimates-show-u-s-muslim-population-continues-to-grow/

Omdahl, L. (2019, December 26). A courageous stand for refugees. *Grand Forks Herald*, A4.

Pew Research Center. (2011, August 30). *Muslim Americans: No signs of growth in alienation or support for extremism*. www.pewresearch.org/politics/2011/08/30/section-1-a-demographic-portrait-of-muslim-americans/

Pillars of Islam. (2016). *Encyclopedia of world religions: Encyclopedia of Islam* (Ed. J. E. Campo, 2nd ed.). Facts on File. Credo Reference.

Podikunu-Hussain, S. (2006). Working with Muslims: Perspectives and suggestions for counseling. *VISTAS Online*, (22), 103–106. www.counseling.org/docs/default-source/vistas/working-with-muslims-perspectives-and-suggestions-for-counseling.pdf?sfvrsn=48dd7e2c_10

Radford, J., & Connor, P. (2016, December 6). Just 10 states resettled more than half of recent refugees to U.S. *Pew Research Center*. www.pewresearch.org/fact-tank/2016/12/06/just-10-states-resettled-more-than-half-of-recent-refugees-to-u-s/

Safe Schools Improvement Act of 2021, H.R. 4402, 117 Cong. (2021–2022). www.congress.gov/bill/117th-congress/house-bill/4402

United States Department of Education. (2017). *Newcomer toolkit*. https://www2.ed.gov/about/offices/list/oela/newcomers-toolkit/ncomertoolkit.pdf

United States Department of Justice. (2016). *Combating religious discrimination today: Final report*. www.justice.gov/crt/file/877936/download

Chapter 8

They're Just Talking Gibberish

English Language Learners

Like many Americans, I grew up within "hearing distance" of languages other than English. Because all my grandparents were immigrants, my parents spoke English as their second language. Their common language was English, so our family spoke only English at home, except for special expressions, such as saying goodnight each night to my mother in Norwegian (*god natt*) and to my father in Icelandic (*gotha nott*), and addressing the family dog in Icelandic. I could, for example, order our pet to "Fara hame!" (Icelandic for "Go home!") if I came upon it performing some mischief, such as chasing chickens just for fun. Code-switching—moving from one language to another—was commonplace in my community, and so I grew up thinking there was nothing unusual about it. Something else I took for granted was my mother's insecurity about her English. What I came to realize was that not only was her language "broken", but her intellectual self-confidence, too.

In my life as a teacher and school psychologist I encountered many children and families much like mine, with a wide assortment of variations on the main theme. Thanks to my own family history, I have always been intrigued by the dynamics attached to bilingualism. As a teacher and as a school psychologist I welcomed working with children from backgrounds different from my own, I suppose, ironically, because they didn't seem all that different. I saw that my family and I had been, and to some degree, still were, on the same path as the newcomers I encountered, just at different points along the way.

Teaching Standard English

As you have read, my first position as a teacher was in an all-Black American elementary school in the American South, so I was immersed in the language of African-Americans. Teaching in this context prompted me to consider how I felt about the controversy of promoting standard English at a time of rising Black cultural pride. Was it insulting to them to encourage mastery of standard English? And who should decide what

DOI:10.4324/9781003348344-8

the linguistic standard should be? These are ongoing questions for any-one working with people who speak a language other than standard English, the dominant world language used in commerce, diplomacy, science, and many other fields.

I decided it would be a disservice not to encourage mastery of stand-ard English, because so many opportunities in life require English lan-guage proficiency as a prerequisite. At the same time, I was determined to show respect to everyone's language and to respect anyone's language development as they acquired a second language. I would never want to repeat the harm done to people like my mother, who were made to feel ashamed of the way they learned to speak at home.

In the mid-1970s I spent several weeks as the teacher in a rural migrant program one autumn during harvest before they returned to Texas or Mexico. There, too, I was confronted with the same questions. Like other programs around the country, it was designed to provide school-ing for the children of migrant farm workers. Such programs had been around since 1966 when Congress authorized the creation of the Office of Migrant Education (Branz-Spall & Wright, 2004).

In North Dakota workers came north to work in the sugar beet fields and in the potato harvest. I was hired because the school principal had heard through the small-town grapevine that I was an English teacher who spoke Spanish, and he was desperate for someone to fill the short-term position. I warned him I was nowhere near to being fluent in Span-ish, but I had studied the language in high school and then in college for a year, and if that was good enough, I was willing. I was quickly hired to teach about a dozen elementary-aged children in a full English immer-sion classroom.

I was standing in the main office my first day when a school employee asked who I was. I explained I was there to help the migrant kids learn English, and she retorted that they never seemed to have any trouble understanding English when it came to money. I wondered if this would be the tone of the rest of my encounters with adults at this school. To my relief, the teacher aide in my classroom was a refreshing contrast. She had worked in the migrant program for a long time, loved the children, and was sympathetic to their parents, aware of how hard their lives were. I told her I would do my best, but I was walking in cold, and I needed her advice. I may have been the one with the credentials, but she had the experience. I was grateful that she didn't hesitate to share it.

The First Day

So how to begin? The children would be arriving shortly, and I needed to find a suitable way to break the ice and welcome them. I thought of my parents' experience in school, and I remembered them talking about how intimidating it was to go to school and be forbidden to speak their own language, so I decided to treat my students the way I wished my parents would have been treated. To soften the impact of being completely immersed in English, I began the day by greeting my students in Spanish. I wanted them to feel at home with me so they could relax and enjoy learning, and I figured hearing their teacher speaking their first language might help. My classroom aide pointed me to the classroom's small library of children's books, and I found one in Spanish. I knew enough Spanish to read aloud, and I chose one that I thought students of all ages would like. The children entered the classroom quietly; I could sense their anxiety about meeting their new teacher. I greeted them and introduced myself, and then I read the story. Afterward we went to work learning English. Before I knew it, it was time for recess.

At lunch one of the classroom teachers asked what I had done that morning, because she noticed a girl in her home room smiled for the first time. Evidently Lucia had not ever looked happy before that day, and the teacher said she was amazed to see her smiling and playing at recess after her morning with me. I don't know if being welcomed in Spanish made the difference, but the research on teaching English language learners emphasizes starting where the students are and respecting their native language and culture. That is what I tried to do.

Lucia had a lot of responsibility. Her four-year-old little brother came with her each morning because there was no daycare available for him. Their parents worked in the fields all day, so there was nowhere for him to go except to school. We didn't have a preschool, so he just tagged along to the migrant program. The little guy was no trouble. He would nap in his desk during most of the morning's lesson. Lucia was a very attentive second mother who made sure he was tended to and didn't cause any disturbance when he was awake. It wasn't surprising to me that Lucia didn't often act light-hearted, since she was doing double-duty, first as a student and then as a second mother to her little brother. Her life reminded me of my mother's when she was a girl; the big sister who had to grow up fast because younger siblings needed care, and circumstance required that she become the caregiver.

But today Lucia smiled and laughed, and out on the playground she joined in with other children to play. Maybe for the first time she did feel at home at school and so could relax and enjoy herself.

A Linguistic Puzzle

When I was a teacher in Pakistan, I taught many students who spoke English as a second language. In stark contrast to my students in the migrant program, some of them were as proficient as I was, or nearly so, Because they were from affluent families with well-educated parents who could afford to provide their children with excellent educational opportunities. These children were adept in their first language, and so acquiring English came relatively easily. Some of these children were also fluent in other languages. I had students who spoke at least one language other than English, such as Urdu, Arabic, French, German, Croatian, or Russian, for example. It was not unusual for my students to be fully functional in three languages. Their high linguistic proficiency illustrated the truism that the more you know, the more you can know. I had plenty of evidence right in front of me that with the right foundation, it is perfectly natural to speak several languages.

There was one, however, who did not acquire English easily. He soon became an unsolved linguistic puzzle for me, and I indirectly owe my career in school psychology to him. This boy had a fascinating combination of strengths and weaknesses; I must say I had never encountered anyone quite like him before, nor have I since. He transferred to our school after the term started, having moved back to Pakistan from Saudi Arabia. His linguistic background was diverse: His first language was an Indian dialect from the region from where his family originated; in addition, he spoke Urdu and at least one middle Eastern language, probably Arabic. He seemed to understand English, and he was able to make himself understood orally. Writing was by far his greatest challenge.

He diligently attempted all our written assignments, but what he produced was nothing short of word salad. He would capitalize the first word of his intended sentence and then produce a series of words that had almost no meaning, ending with a period. Had I not assigned the topic myself, I doubt I could have guessed what he was trying to write about. He had a vocabulary, and he knew how a sentence was supposed to begin and end but was unable to arrange words meaningfully. He also had an exceptional ability to draw.

I wish I could say I had been astute enough to figure out exactly how best to teach him, other than just to give him practice. I often wondered out loud to my principal about him, especially if there might be some sort of oblique connection between his exceptional artistic ability and his unusual linguistic difficulties. Because of my continuing concern for him, my principal asked if I would like to attend a conference at the American Embassy School in New Delhi, India. She thought that there might be an expert there who could advise me about the best way to teach him. I leaped at the chance to attend, but I didn't encounter anyone with the expertise I had hoped to find. What I did find was a school psychologist.

My Introduction to School Psychology

A school psychologist gave a lecture describing his work at the embassy school, and I was captivated. What I gleaned from his talk is that he spent his time trying to assist students who couldn't cope with the regular curriculum, whether because of learning problems, emotional difficulties, or disabilities. I realized that he was describing the students I spent most of my time thinking about. Before I heard his lecture, I didn't know school psychology existed as a profession. I was intrigued and made a mental note to follow up when I returned to the United States. Once I became a school psychologist, I welcomed the opportunity to work with students with unusual language difficulties. I quickly learned in graduate school that there was no magic involved in understanding them. But having a keen interest was a good starting point.

Advocacy

I typically encountered English language learners as part of the special education assessment process. When I began, my generation of school psychologists was taking our first tentative steps toward achieving nonbiased evaluation. There were even fewer bilingual school psychologists then as now, and there weren't many instruments to aid in achieving an accurate estimate of ability or achievement in the face of a complex linguistic background. Much was left up to our own judgment. As the following example will illustrate, many within special education were afraid of even attempting to assess, for fear of making serious errors. To some, avoidance seemed like a reasonable approach, because all our instruments were suspect.

Several years after my experience teaching in a migrant school, I was a school psychologist serving a rural school with migrant students. A young family arrived with three children who were all showing learning deficits. What to do quickly became controversial. Because of lawsuits brought against schools which had placed students from diverse backgrounds in special education, administrators were sometimes leery of getting involved.

One of our co-op speech/language coordinators tried to forbid testing of Hispanics to avoid potential discrimination suits. At the time there was a lot of controversy over fairness in testing, and she feared our lack of experience with bilingual assessment could lead to trouble. Hers was not a frivolous concern. According to a report written in 2009, Assistant Secretary Monroe of the Office of Civil Rights stated that a National Academy of Sciences survey from 1982 (which would be around the time this controversy arose in our cooperative) expressed concern over over-representation of minorities in special education programs and that more recent surveys had shown similar findings (Minorities in Special Education, 2009).

Despite the risks, the school psychologists balked at setting a blanket standard and protested. We felt we needed to advocate for evaluation because we didn't want children with demonstrated needs to be neglected and receive no services at all when they might require special help. Not assessing seemed as bad or worse than risking imperfect testing results if it meant disregarding children with disabilities altogether.

It would have been easy for us to sidestep our responsibility to these children. As a rule, the migrant Hispanic parents usually went on faith that the school knew best, so they did not question policy. Complicating communication was their lack of literacy in both their native language and English. Given the vulnerability of these families, we objected. It was too likely that educational rights would be violated. The coordinator relented after we presented our arguments against a ban.

Teasing out what is language based and what indicates a disability can be challenging, but our clinical judgment was improving with each new situation. We were becoming more confident that we could draw reasonable conclusions with enough information from parents and direct observation to supplement testing results. In the situation that prompted the confrontation with the speech coordinator, we ended up completing assessments with all three children from the family. All qualified for special education services, and as the years passed, we could see in each child's development we had made the right decision.

However limited, we did the best we could with what we had because the alternative seemed worse. With 20/20 hindsight, I realize the limitations of both our instruments and our knowledge may have led to misidentifying children. Our hearts were in the right place, but good intentions are not enough to guarantee a valid assessment. Assessment practices have been developed since then which give a more accurate estimate of the intellectual functioning of Students with Limited Interrupted Formal Education (S.L.I.F.E.) than my generation could derive.

Since the beginning of my career, our expertise has grown in response to our recognizing that inadequate training in assessment and pre-referral intervention has led to disproportional special education placement for linguistically diverse children. Rhodes, Ochoa, and Ortiz indicate that "inadequately trained examiners, inappropriate assessment practices, and failure to comply with federal and/or state guidelines" are factors creating disproportional placement (Rhodes et al., 2005, p. 31). At the heart of the issue is how well the examiner understands the meaning of acculturation, because "it dictates the manner in which all data can and should be viewed" (Rhodes et al., 2005, p. 135). School psychologists must grasp what acculturation means, because it is the frame of reference within which assessment data can be understood.

Refugees

Near the end of my career, a new population of non-English speakers arrived in my school community. Thanks to the efforts of Lutheran

Social Services and other agencies sympathetic to refugees, we had an influx of Somali children. What do we do when we encounter children who have had little or no opportunity to learn English?

Eventually some Somali students were referred for special education assessment. There were interpreters available to us from the Somali community, so we could interview parents through them. Once again, we had to do the best we could within our limitations. We relied on nonverbal assessments, in-depth parent interviews, and observation. It was important for us to pay close attention to what the mothers said about how the child compared with other children in the family. If the mother was worried about developmental delays, for example, then we were, too. One of the most challenging areas to assess was emotional/behavioral status.

The most dramatic instance involved a middle school boy who suffered from hallucinations. The school invited his parents in for a consultation to let them know our concerns and what we had to offer. At first, they were very hesitant about intervention at school or having a psychiatric evaluation at a clinic. The parents took him to see a faith healer back in Minneapolis first, and when that did not achieve a cure, they decided they would try Western medicine and, eventually, placement to receive special education services.

Conducting assessments of children who speak a language we don't understand tests our awareness of our own cultural biases and challenges our imagination. It becomes easier as we learn about their culture directly from them and their parents, so we can begin to get a feel for what their experience with us means to them. Keen observation combined with deep empathy is essential. It is always important to know the story besides the numbers so we can understand what testing results really mean. We also must do our utmost to guarantee we do not violate their rights by placing children in special education programs on scant evidence. Nor do we shy away from evaluation because of cultural difference; a child certainly can be an English Language Learner and, for example, have a developmental disability.

It has become a mantra within school psychology that tests do not evaluate; people do. Our judgments must be based on best practice, so we increase the likelihood that our decisions are just and fair. We must respect and accept where children are in their linguistic development while analyzing how we can best assist them, while we scrutinize the limits of our testing materials and of our own understanding. What is vital to keep in mind is that evaluations must be based on what we learn of the child's own linguistic background and culture, rather than by viewing them only through the lens of our own.

The best case for optimal language learning is for a child to have a fully developed first language with literate adult role models. Such a child will master the second language quickly and efficiently, as did my students in Pakistan. It is much harder for children who are not literate in their native language. These children are not prepared to learn in school using our traditional methods.

Minnesota, the state where I practiced school psychology for nearly 30 years, enacted an important piece of legislation in 2014, the year I retired. The Learning English for Academic Proficiency and Success (L.E.A.P.S.) Act was designed to provide increased support For English language learners. A feature of the Act was a definition of and account-ability reporting for S.L.I.F.E. Under the Act, schools must differentiate instruction to accommodate their multilingual students. This requires that educators must acquire the skills to foster English language profi-ciency (Minnesota Department of Education, n.d.).

One step forward is that the Act treats bilingualism and multilingual-ism as an asset. A student's first language is no longer viewed as a deficit in the effort to teach them English. Rather, bilingualism and multicultur-alism are respected and valued. If Minnesota schools can rise to the occa-sion and act on the intention of the L.E.A.P.S. Act, the language skills of New Americans will improve and, I suspect, so will their self-esteem.

Broken English, Broken Hearts

The emotional associations we have with E.L.L. issues run deep. We are a nation of speakers of several languages, whether immigrants and descendants of immigrants, or Indigenous. Over time, English came to dominate the linguistic landscape in the United States and consequently, gained the highest status. Correspondingly, those who spoke it as their first language could enjoy a sense of superiority over those who didn't, a prejudice that still holds true today. Within my own family, language mastery, especially of English, played an important role. My grandpar-ents were all Scandinavian immigrants, a heritage common to many in my part of the country. My father's parents came from Iceland and my mother's were from Norway. The Icelanders in general were highly lit-erate in their birth language and aggressive about becoming excellent speakers of English. My father was no exception to this pattern.

My mother's family also strove to master English, and many of my moth-er's siblings did very well in this regard. Unfortunately for my mother, she was the eldest daughter and was called upon to spend so much of her time tending her younger siblings when she was a girl that schooling took a back seat. Typical of girls of her era and place, she didn't go very far in school, quitting at the end of eighth grade. Because of her spotty attend-ance, she probably did not leave school with even eighth-grade skills. My mother was sent off to work as a hired girl at 17. As time passed, some of her younger sisters were able to further their education, and my mother sometimes gave them some of her earnings in support. But there was never time nor opportunity for her; she once commented to me that she really had never been a child.

I grew up thinking she wasn't very smart because of her comparatively poor English skills. She often expressed insecurity about how she spoke. She never ever would lead a reading in church, for example, or volunteer to teach Sunday school. She would have died of embarrassment. She frequently described her language as "broken". That word described so much more than syntax or vocabulary; it also summed up a part of her self-evaluation.

An expert in bilingualism reminded me of what my mother had experienced all her life. During his lecture at one of our annual M.S.P.A. conferences, he described his mother in much the same way I thought about my own. His testimonial redoubled my resolve to do whatever I could to help students struggling to learn English and to show respect to their parents, who often were also struggling, and additionally had passed the developmental window so that no matter how hard they tried, they would never sound exactly like a native speaker of American English.

The emotional stress bound to the experience of entering another culture and leaving the old one behind must be acknowledged. The first generation suffers the loss of the homeland and the trials of establishing a new life in an unfamiliar setting that may present difficult challenges. The documentary *God Grew Tired of Us*, for example, graphically demonstrates the loneliness, disappointment, and grief immigrants from Sudan feel, while at the same time they appreciate the opportunity for a better life (Quinn & Walker, 2006). The next generation faces the conflict of separating from the old culture in favor of the dominant culture. This generation has a hyphenated identity; my mother was Norwegian-American, and my father was Icelandic-American, with the American part shaping their future.

I am a member of that second generation of Americans that longs wistfully for the culture denied them through circumstance. I felt it especially in my youth, after a trip to Europe. There it was commonplace to encounter young people who were fluent in more than one language. One young European, upon learning of my background, was critical of me because I had not learned the languages of my parents. I tried to explain that there really wasn't any opportunity, but she was not convinced.

When I returned from my travels, I asked my father why he didn't teach me Icelandic when I was a child. I lived on a farmstead with four native speakers: my grandmother, an aunt, an uncle, and my father. They were all articulate and literate in Icelandic. I grew up listening to them speak to one another and to hearing my father reading Icelandic literature aloud. But other than learning a few words and phrases, Icelandic did not become a part of my life, except to hear it.

In my travels I spent one day in Iceland, en route to Amsterdam. I took a bus tour of the countryside, and I was struck by how much the people reminded me of relatives and neighbors from home. The tour guide's sense of humor was just like my father's, and as I glanced around at the stops we made, I felt like I could match the noses of the Icelanders I saw with people back home. It was almost eerie how familiar everyone seemed. I was saddened that I could communicate with them only in English.

My father's sympathetic reply was that it happened out of "dumbness". He went on to explain that it just didn't seem important at the time. But once childhood ends, there is no longer any chance of speaking like a native; the door is sealed shut. I, and many like me, felt the loss of a tremendous opportunity. My parents, meanwhile, were just trying their best to help me to become a competent member of mainstream America. English was the language I needed to master. They spoke to me in English and provided books in English, knowing it was the language that would shape my future. Most of the families in my community did the same.

Language and identity are closely intertwined. To have a healthy self-image we need to feel competent in our linguistic expression. I wish my mother had had a mentor like Reyna Grande did, when she was a young woman. In her memoir, *A Dream Called Home*, Grande confesses to a teacher how inadequate she felt when she visited Mexico, her native country. "Over there, everyone treats me differently, as if I'm not Mexican enough". The teacher replied. "In fact, the opposite is true. . . . You are now bilingual, bicultural, and binational. You are not less, you are more" (Grande, 2018, p. 96).

Later, Reyna encounters the work of Frida Kahlo for the first time and recognizes herself in *Las Dos Fridas*, a double portrait Kahlo painted of herself. Reyna projected herself into the painting, seeing two versions of herself, one Mexican, the other, American, grasping on to one another, and seeing herself as twice what she was (Grande, 2018). What a pity a bilingual background can result in strong feelings of being less than, when perhaps it should make one feel more than.

The Ongoing Need

Now, even more than at the beginning of my career, it is particularly imperative to gain the knowledge necessary to conduct fair assessments because we have so many children who are not first language English speakers. In 2016, there were 4.9 million English Language Learner students attending public school in the United States, compared with 3.8 million at the turn of the century. About 21% of California's total enrollment is E.L.L., representing both the highest number in any state and the highest share of English language learners nationwide.

Spanish is by far the most common first language among the E.L.L. school population at 77%. But more than 400 languages are spoken at home by E.L.L. students; it is a very heterogeneous group. For example, 16% of E.L.L. students in Minnesota speak the Hmong language. In general, rural areas tend to have far fewer E.L.L. students than do cities (4% rural, 14% urban). A fact that many Americans may not know is that most E.L.L. students are U.S. citizens (Bialik et al., 2018).

We also encounter their parents, and it is part of our responsibility to assure that parents understand their children's rights. To make sure they do, it is a legal requirement to provide them with an interpreter in their native language. Parents are also asserting themselves, as illustrated by an example from one of Natasha's schools, when a New American rejected the offer of an interpreter that the school had hired in favor of bringing his own.

The U.S. Department of Education cites examples of legal precedents that are the basis for delivering educational services to English language learners. In the U.S. Department of Education's "Newcomer Toolkit", three lawsuits are emphasized: In *Lau v. Nichols* (1974), the Supreme Court ruled that school must be affirmative in their actions so English language learners can participate in their education. *Plyer v. Doe* (1962) forbade states to deny immigrant students a free public education. In *Castaneda v. Pickard* (1981) a three-part test was established to evaluate how well a district's E.L.L. program complies with civil rights laws (Newcomer Toolkit, 2017).

The toolkit also lists information schools should provide to families with an E.L.L. student. The list includes informing them about special education services and the role of guidance counselors and other non-teaching staff. The Department of Education encourages parent participation so they can influence policies and procedures that affect their child, and school psychologists have a role to play in supporting such parents.

Accommodating refugee and immigrant students requires insight and sensitivity to the circumstance from which they have come. Assumptions about how to navigate through a school day must be examined, because these students may have no experience with a structured school day, coed classes, riding a school bus, and so forth. One way recommended to help students feel more at home is through literature, which can provide stories of young people facing similar challenges to their own (Newcomer Toolkit, 2017).

Today's school psychologist must be sensitive on many levels when dealing with English Language Learners as English language learning involves so much more than language acquisition. For people making a new life in a new country, it also means creating a new identity. Because children naturally pick up language more quickly than adults and, until early adolescence, can replicate sounds with no trace of an accent from their first language, they are wonderfully equipped to slip on a new language, and simultaneously, immediately sound as though they are native-born. Their parents cannot.

This innate linguistic facility carries over to culture. Kids assimilate much faster than adults because school immerses them in their new culture. School psychologists need to be sensitive to this dynamic and understand the parents' anxieties. Youth are pulled forward toward their own future, and that can mean leaving behind much of what their parents treasure, such as their native language. This can be difficult for parents to accept. School psychologists can build bridges with them by taking an interest in their native culture, their language and traditions, and their story.

Near the end of his life, my father inadvertently gave me a lesson in the significance of one's first language. He was old and very sick, possibly dying. During my visit with him in the hospital, he started speaking in an almost inaudible voice, and he didn't seem to be addressing anyone in the room. I asked my mother if she could grasp what he was saying, but try as she may, she couldn't, either. But the next day he was better, and I asked him if he remembered speaking the day before. He did, and he smiled as he told me he was reciting a poem in Icelandic about two old men in adjoining hospital beds, talking with one another about death. He was consoling himself, I realized, by using the beauty of poetry in his first language to do so.

In her memoir *My Broken Language*, Quiara Alegria Hudes describes how much language matters. Raised in a barrio in North Philadelphia, she came to her own understanding of literacy by recovering for herself and to herself the rich linguistic, religious, and cultural background of her mother's family of immigrants from Puerto Rico. Puerto Rican language combines Spanish with a large contribution of words from the Taino people of the Caribbean. Taino is an extinct Arawakan language, the language spoken by the Indigenous people prior to Spanish colonization. West African languages brought by enslaved people to Puerto Rico also enriched the local language. Finally, English combined with the rest to create what we know as Spanglish. Unearthing all the influences that had combined over time to create her background and bring them to light for herself and others allowed her to claim her cultural and personal identity (Hudes, 2021).

My linguistic history is one small variation on the main theme of what millions of Americans who grew up in a heavily ethnic setting experience. While continuing to cherish many traditions from the places our forebears came from, the mainstream culture absorbs us, to one degree or another, because that is the environment in which we need to survive. But even when the assimilation process is voluntary, aspects of it can be challenging to the point of painful. School psychologists can lend support to students and their families as they make this transition.

What we now understand about language learning is that knowing more than one language broadens our knowledge of the world; it makes us smarter. Those of us who speak only one language are misguided if we feel superior to those who speak more than one, because each language gives entrance into another linguistic world. Rather than a burden, it can be a joy to work with children who have this gift if we can overcome our fear of taking on the challenge. School psychologists can help to soften the hard edges of adapting to a new culture as children learn to navigate their new environment at school.

References

Bialik, K., Scheller, A., & Walker, K. (2018, October 25). 6 facts about English language learners in U.S. public schools. *Pew Research Center.* www.pewresearch.org/fact-tank/2018/10/25/6-facts-about-english-language-learners-in-u-s-public-schools/

Branz-Spall, A., & Wright, A. (2004). *A history of advocacy for migrant children and their families: More than 30 years in the fields* (ED481635). ERIC. https://files.eric.ed.gov/fulltext/ED481635.pdf

Grande, R. (2018). *A dream called home: A memoir.* Atria Books.

Hudes, Q. (2021). *My broken language: A memoir.* One World.

Minnesota Department of Education. (n.d.). *LEAPS act.* https:///education.mn.gov/MDE/dse/el/leap/

Quinn, C., & Walker, T. (Directors). (2006). *God grew tired of us: The story of lost boys of Sudan* [Film]. National Geographic Films.

Rhodes, R., Ochoa, S., & Ortiz, S. (2005). *Assessing culturally and linguistically diverse students: A practical guide.* The Guilford Press.

United States Commission on Civil Rights. (2009). *Minorities in special education.* www.usccr.gov/pubs/docs/MinoritiesinSpecialEducation.pdf

United States Department of Education. (2017). *Newcomer toolkit.* https://www2.ed.gov/about/offices/list/oela/newcomers-toolkit/ncomertoolkit.pdf

Chapter 9

Issues in Diversity

'There's No Way He'd Tell a White Woman That'

Talking Back, Politely

When injustices occur at school, school personnel must be ready to address them. During my years first as a teacher and later as a school psychologist, occasions arose which required that I help kids cope. For example, in Pakistan I had to help students deal with what they perceived as discriminatory behavior from another of their teachers.

One day my eighth graders came in from physical education class with a complaint. There had been an incident with the physical education teacher that they were upset about. Normally they were a level-headed bunch, so I took them seriously. They were angry and excited about the blatant discrimination they felt they had just witnessed—and if they were Pakistani—experienced on the playing field. The children felt that the teacher, a British citizen, had chosen positions based solely on ethnic background, prejudicially excluding Pakistani students from having the best positions. Whether her action was deliberate or unintentional, the class was furious as well as hurt. Their outrage and sense of helplessness were palpable.

After I listened to their complaint, I asked them to take out a piece of paper. I told them to write down exactly how they felt, holding nothing back. I told them that they had permission to write in a language other than English if that would help them express their feelings better. (Because we were an English medium school, all classes, except for language classes, were conducted in English.) They looked at me in amazement. "Anything? We can write anything?" I assured them they could, and they would not get into any trouble for doing so. They wrote with a fury, and when they were finished, I carried the waste basket around the room. I told them that now I wanted them to crumple up their paper and throw it away. And once that was accomplished, together we would develop a plan to address their complaint.

The class defined exactly what they were angry about, making sure their statements were accurate and fair. I had them choose a spokesperson

DOI:10.4324/9781003348344-9

who would tell the teacher their complaints in a polite manner. The rest of them would stand with her for support. We would take further steps only if it were necessary. I didn't want them to go straight to the principal because I had faith the teacher would see the merit of their argument and would change her procedure, and I wanted the students to take responsibility and speak for themselves. And that is what happened. They were all beaming and laughing when they entered the room the following day. They had confronted their teacher, she listened to their statement, acknowledged that they had reason to be upset, and changed her approach.

After class the previous day I had gone to the principal and told her what I had done. She gave me her full support. She was pleased the students were handling the problem themselves and looked forward to seeing how the story unfolded. I was relieved and glad to inform her of my students' success.

The Basis Is Trust

It isn't always that easy. My first job as a school psychologist was at a large rural co-op in western North Dakota. Consequently, I was frequently assigned to do evaluations in tribal reservation schools. I remember one particularly well. I was asked to do a comprehensive evaluation with a ninth-grade boy who was doing very poorly academically. I gave the standard assessments of an I.Q. test, an academic skills test, and a self-concept questionnaire. On the Piers-Harris Self-Concept Questionnaire he obtained a percentile score in the high 90s. If the score were to be trusted, he was leading an exuberant life.

The mother came in to meet with me, and after I told her about the results of the evaluation, she asked if he had told me about the deaths of loved ones that he had recently experienced. He had not. We went over several of the items on the questionnaire together, and she told me what he had gone through in the past several months. My heart was heavy by the time she related all the tragedies this young man had endured. "Why do you suppose he did not reveal any of this in the evaluation?" I asked. "There's no way he'd tell a White woman that", she said. I thanked her for her honesty.

It was painful to be confronted with the hard truth that a kindly smile and quiet voice were nowhere near enough to gain the trust of this young man. Based on what his mother said, our nation's history stood in the way; he felt there was no reason to believe my concern for his welfare was genuine. The score on the questionnaire I administered accurately measured one thing: his mistrust of White people, reflecting the impact of our tragic collective history.

I related this incident in a graduate seminar that I was attending, and the professor told me she had been asked by tribal leaders at another reservation to give an estimate of how well their children were doing emotionally. She had administered the same instrument I had used, and unsurprisingly to me, everyone scored in the above-average range, at least. She took the results at face value and told the tribal leaders that their students were doing just fine. Considering my experience, she contacted them to say she had serious doubts about the results.

The Interrelated Web

At the time this incident occurred, I was aware that in the past the U.S. government had violated treaties, waged genocide, and stolen land, impoverishing the surviving Indigenous people as a result. I was not aware, however, of the treatment many children received at the hands of teachers and clergy who ran Indian boarding schools. Had I known of the cruelty and disrespect shown to the children and their culture at the hands of school personnel, I would have better understood why the communities I worked in faced the problems they did. The impact of generational trauma is easy to grasp once one learns about the history of beatings, sexual abuse, hunger, and other cruelties—some resulting in murder—inflicted on Indigenous children. No wonder I was sometimes met with suspicion (Lajimodiere, 2019).

The importance of cultural identity and the need to preserve it cannot be underestimated. Renee Linklater has written a book based on personal stories, beginning with her own. She addresses the need for understanding the impact of colonialism on Indigenous people, the resulting trauma associated with it, and the usefulness of Indigenous healing methods (Linklater, 2014). Besides the growing interest in cultural healing, a testament to the importance of culture is the existence now of more than 30 tribal colleges and universities (T.C.U.s) nationwide, in the United States. These institutions provide a culturally supportive environment as well as access to education, and graduates tend to work in fields connected to native communities or tribal lands. Commenting on her experience at a tribal college in Wisconsin, Jasmine Neosh, a recent graduate said, "it wasn't only acceptable that I show up as my whole self. It was expected" (Weingarten, 2021, p. 14).

A few years after my enlightening experience with the self-report scale, I would learn of an important historical connection my own family had with Indigenous people. The Icelanders who immigrated to Canada and settled near Lake Winnipeg were assisted their first winter by the neighboring tribe who helped them gather food and ice fish. This story impressed upon me that the survival of my ancestors—and possibly, the reason I am here to tell this tale—was because of the compassion of Indigenous people. A horrifying tragic irony of their relationship was that the Icelanders also experienced a smallpox epidemic, which spread to the native people with devastating results. Both communities suffered a tremendous loss of life, and the story of the epidemic includes a grim connection to my family.

My great-grandfather arrived from Iceland with an infection on one hand, "which worsened into an illness not unlike smallpox" (Gerrard, 1985, p. 526). Whether or not there is any scientific merit to the claim that my ancestor brought smallpox to the settlement, I do not know, but the story has been passed down through the generations. What is known is that his wife, my great-grandmother, and their youngest child were the first victims of the disease within the Icelandic community. For me, this stark story represents the intimate relationship between Indigenous people and immigrants and how their lives intersected, sometimes disastrously, even with no ill intention.

Bridging the Divide

It would have been wrong for me to conclude that the cultural divide can never be crossed, however. Some years later, in a different district, I was asked to counsel an Indigenous junior high student. A teacher who had heard I would be working with him caught me in the hall and warned me that I better be ready to sit in silence, because the boy had a reputation for not speaking to anyone. By then I routinely used art and play in my counseling sessions, so I had some hope that using nonverbal forms of expression might have a positive effect.

The boy's sensitive, gentle nature was immediately evident, so I could see I needed to proceed slowly. After I introduced myself and described how I conducted the sessions, I showed him the sorts of activities he could do, one of which was drawing. He immediately chose to draw, and within moments it was obvious he was a naturally talented artist.

We developed a routine of having him begin our sessions by drawing, and inevitably, he would start to talk while he drew. I just had to bide my time and let him lead. He came as often as he was allowed, to the point where I had to set some limits, or he would have lived in my office. I often wondered if I would have been more effective with the other young man had I had the time to make friends gradually on his terms. Maybe it wasn't altogether so much a question of ethnic/racial difference, as it was my expecting too much of a child who was barely coping with burdens that would have challenged the strongest adult.

In a later chapter I describe in depth the use of the sand tray that I kept in my office. I encouraged students to create scenes in it, using small plastic figurines. Students liked to depict the dramas of their lives, sometimes reenacting actual events using human figures, or sometimes representing events symbolically, with animals substituted for people, for example. They were free to express themselves as they wished, so long as sand was not flung from the tray in the heat of a creative moment.

One day when an Indigenous girl was hard at work creating her scene, she abruptly turned to me and announced that she knew something about me; she knew I was Indian. I was startled by her statement, and I didn't know what to say, so I just responded with a smile. I now regret I didn't say thank you. She turned back to creating her scene, making no further comment. I still cherish her remark; I think she was saying that she trusted me. I felt honored, given our collective history.

Family Expectations and Personal Growth

A teacher referred Martina, an adolescent Hispanic girl, to me because she seemed depressed. She kept lingering after class to talk to the teacher, who said she felt she wasn't equipped to deal with the magnitude of the girl's problems. It soon became clear that Martina's situation was highly illustrative of how culture intersects with a person's individual path.

Martina had an older brother who was a senior and an outstanding student as well as a fine athlete. It was a foregone conclusion he would go on to college, and he was in line to win a scholarship to pay for it. Seasonal field workers were not highly paid, and there were other children in the family besides her and her brother, so it was unlikely the parents would be able to afford to pay for any of their children to go on beyond high school.

As it turned out, Martina was deeply demoralized because she had her own dream of a college education but feared it would never come to pass. She was not the stellar student her brother was, nor was she a fine athlete. She worked hard in school so her grades were adequate to attend college someday, but she could not count on a scholarship, as her brother could. In addition, Martina's parents were pressuring her, their oldest daughter, to work with them to earn money for the family.

Martina wanted to become an English teacher, what to me seemed to be a reasonable and possible goal. Maybe she wouldn't be eligible for a full scholarship, but I suspected she would be able to find adequate loans and grants. She was such a hard worker that I believed she could make it through a teachers' college curriculum, and with her bilingual abilities and ethnic background, she might turn out to be an ideal English Language Learner teacher. Here was an eager young woman, full of desire to better herself and contribute to her community, who might not be able to pursue her goal. She was afraid to go against her parents' wishes, but at the same time, she valued her own future.

I served as her sounding board so she could sort out her conflicted feelings. We talked through the likely outcome of not going to college and going to college; obeying her parents' wishes and going her own way. In the end she concluded that she probably would be able to help the family more if she became a teacher because she would earn more and could be an example to her younger siblings. It would just take time to get to that point. Martina grew more confident and seemed happier as she clarified for herself what she was willing and able to do.

As I witnessed this young woman plan her future, I reflected on the courage it would take. By pursuing a career, she risked disaffection from her parents whom she loved. She and her brother would be the first in their family to go to college, and he would do so ahead of her. While his achievement would be looked on as cause for celebration, her decision to further her education might be fraught with conflict since she would be stepping outside the traditional bounds of her role as a daughter. In the end, Martina was willing to take it on.

The Importance of Relationship

My career came full circle one day at an evaluation summary meeting that involved racial/cultural relations. A Black American high school girl was tested upon her mother's insistence to see if she would qualify for the specific learning disabilities program. She was already receiving support for her A.D.H.D. symptoms under a 504 plan, but her parents felt that was not enough. Her teachers, on the other hand, felt she was performing to her ability and was doing what could be expected. The mother kept insisting on testing, and so the school relented and proceeded with an evaluation.

I was struck by the irony of the situation of a Black parent insisting on a psycho-educational evaluation for her child. When I entered the field of school psychology, the state of California had forbidden I.Q. testing with Black Americans about a decade earlier, because a court case brought in 1979 had ruled that they were overrepresented in special education programs. The instruments were discriminatory (Larry P. v. Riles, 1979).

Some other states also followed the ban, but many did not, so standardized tests continued to be used in most states to determine placement. Move forward over 40 years, and I found myself sitting across from a Black American parent who not only didn't object to standardized testing for her daughter but demanded it.

Even with my many years of experience giving and interpreting I.Q. tests, I must admit I was uncomfortable when it came time for me to explain my results. I would not have been surprised if the parents had questioned their validity, given the legal history of testing Black Americans. I had some qualms myself. As it turned out, the parents felt our conclusions reflected a fair and accurate description of their daughter's achievement and abilities. Altogether, we could find no indication of a specific learning disability. Given the history of I.Q. testing and minorities, I wouldn't have been surprised had the parents not trusted our results.

In retrospect, I think I know why our meeting went so smoothly, and it had nothing to do with numbers. What I witnessed was a circle of teachers who all knew their student very well, and they were adept at describing her academic abilities and her behavior in their classes. Their respect and concern for her was obvious in the thoughtful manner they spoke to and about her. They knew her weaknesses and had suggestions for how she could overcome them, and they showed what had already been accomplished in that direction. It was clear that they were invested in her academic success. I admired them for their professionalism and their kindly relationship with their student, and I felt proud to be a part of their team. My portion was made easy because everything I had to say corroborated what the parents were hearing from the teachers; we were describing a consistent picture.

When I began as a school psychologist, however, a consistent picture might not have been sufficient to create trust. The way school personnel listened to the parents' concerns demonstrated respect for the family and brought assurance that we were on their side. They were reassured because our numbers matched what they considered their daughter's abilities to be, but I think the atmosphere of genuine caring in our meeting mattered most of all. I left feeling that maybe schools had made progress over the course of my career in meeting the challenge of fairness in evaluating Black Americans. It happened to be my final evaluation summary meeting before I retired, and I was grateful my circle had closed with an event that affirmed my best impression of what schools can be.

How We View One Another

It isn't always easy to bridge cultures. One Indigenous high school boy told me that at his school, kids wanted to beat him up "because he was an Indian". When he went to visit relatives on the reservation, kids there wanted to beat him up because he talked "too White". Exasperated, one day he exclaimed, "Why can't we all just get along? Why can't we all just be American? That's who we are, aren't we?" How that question is answered has been evolving over time, and the answer affects how we see and treat one another.

References

Gerrard, N. (1985). *The Icelandic River saga.* Self-published.

Lajimodiere, D. (2019). *Stringing rosaries: The history, the unforgivable, and the healing of Northern Plains American Indian boarding school survivors.* North Dakota State University Press.

Larry P. v. Riles, 495 F. Supp. 926 (N.D. Cal. 1979). https://law.justia.com/cases/federal/district-courts/FSupp/495/926/2007878/

Linklater, R. (2014). *Decolonizing trauma work: Indigenous stories and strategies.* Fernwood Publishing.

Weingarten, D. (2021, August 23). Tribal colleges honor students' past, prepare them for future. *The Christian Science Monitor.* www.csmonitor.com/USA/Education/2021/0823/Tribal-colleges-honor-students-past-prepare-them-for-future#

Chapter 10

Better Ally Than Savior

The narratives from the previous chapter revolve around trust and respect. My students in Pakistan had to trust that I and their physical education teacher would handle their complaint fairly. The Indigenous student who was asked to reveal personal information in a formal evaluation did not trust in the process he had no choice but to undergo. The Black American family had to trust the teachers and special education staff that our instruments and our interpretation of results were fair. So how do we gain the trust of those who view us as different from them in ways that they perceive as threatening? Where are we now on our path to equitable treatment for everyone? One way forward may be to improve our level of cultural understanding.

Raising Our Own Cultural Awareness

In *The Psychology of Multiculturalism*, Jones et al. advise how one can become more aware of culture, and consequently, more effective in working within a multicultural context. Wisely, the authors recommend starting with oneself. The first recommendation is to understand one's own culture (Green et al., 2009).

Even before that, it seems to me, the initial step is knowing you have a culture. It's easier for those of us who had parents and grandparents who were knowledgeable about family origins. I identify with Scandinavian culture because I was raised by people speaking Icelandic and Norwegian and grew up eating foods typical of nineteenth-century Scandinavian cuisine. (*Lutefisk* and l*efse*, anyone? Would you like another *pannekakur*?) Hearing stories of immigration and settlement, from those within a generation's reach of the actual events helped me build a sense of identity. These stories might imbue pride or shame, depending on circumstance. Regardless, learning the history is a necessary step toward understanding.

I traveled to Europe in my youth, and there I encountered a fellow who worked for the British foreign service. Unsurprisingly, he spoke a

DOI:10.4324/9781003348344-10

high-class British English, so I assumed he had been reared in an upper-class environment. He asked me where in the United States I grew up, so I told him I was raised on a farm in North Dakota. He said he was surprised I would admit that. Affronted, I told him I wasn't ashamed of my background, and I went on to describe the little Icelandic community I was reared in.

"Ah", he said. "That's different. You have a culture".

Doesn't everyone? I thought. Then the Englishman went on to confess he grew up in Boston, and after he fought in WWII in Europe, he decided to emigrate to England and adopt English ways, including learning the perfect accent. He had a prestigious career, achieved in part by obliterating connections to his place of origin. He had projected his own insecurities onto me when he expressed surprise at my willingness to admit my background. I was touched that he had the grace to tell me his whole story, since he was the one who was ashamed of his background, not I.

But what of those who are a mix of many backgrounds and don't identify as anything other than generic American? Irina Nevzlin, a Jewish immigrant from Russia, enriched her life by learning about her ethnic background—a history which had been suppressed. She offers insights into how to strengthen one's sense of identity, beginning by interviewing relatives, if possible, to gain information about one's family origin. Charting one's genetic path offers another means to uncover a hidden personal history, also. Our sense of identity can then be enriched by analyzing which aspects of our background we find most meaningful and help us connect to cultural traditions. Nevzlin encourages us to use this information to enjoy the richness of what each culture brings, not to feel superior to anyone but to appreciate the diversity around us. That we come from different backgrounds can create a common bond, a happy irony (Nevzlin, 2019).

Even without any new discoveries about our personal past, we can all deepen understanding of our identity as Americans by studying our collective history. Many writers, especially historians, are rising to the occasion with works explaining our American history in ways that are relevant to understanding who we are today, beginning with the first colonists, the first indentured servants and enslaved people, and the original people who inhabited this land before any immigrants arrived.

It is an unsettling and rich history, well worth reading, however painful, because it gives us a context from which we can evaluate current events. We need to study to understand why things are the way they are, not to accuse or condemn. For example, the history of immigration is highly informative to grasp the underpinnings of the attitudes of our own time, since xenophobia always has been an aspect of American life throughout our history. We can celebrate that Indigenous people are reclaiming and embracing their spiritual, linguistic, and cultural heritage and defining themselves on their own terms. To fully understand our nation, we need insight into their history and the impact of colonization on it. Likewise, we need to understand how our nation's economy depended on slavery, and the long, ongoing struggle for Blacks and other marginalized groups to achieve constitutional rights.

Recognizing Our Culture's Impact on Others

Once we have a grasp on our own culture, Jones et al. recommend learning what effect one's culture has on others (Green et al., 2009). As you saw earlier, I had a crash course in cultural awareness as I observed and interacted with the African-American students, teachers, and parents in our school community. How ideas of White supremacy had been accepted unconsciously by even the youngsters in my classes confronted me with the racial realities in our country. The acceptance of corporal punishment made me wonder if I was just culturally conditioned to abhor it. Was there a legitimate cultural justification I did not understand?

Only now, 50 years hence, I am coming to fully understand the impact of slavery on child rearing within African-American culture. Nor am I puzzled by how much some of the girls in my classes admired my hair, wanted me to buy them pretty clothes, perhaps wanted to be more like me. It was a sign of something much deeper than the normal admiration kids feel toward their teacher, and it had a tragic cause. They yearned for the privileges I could take for granted, among them—to be admired for the color of my skin and the texture of my hair. My experience in Pakistan educated me about racism internationally. There, too, I enjoyed special status because of my Whiteness, and I observed evidence all around me of the impact of British colonialism. My time in western North Dakota introduced me to the needs of Indigenous people in my own state. Learning their history is part of my ongoing education.

Five decades ago, I consoled myself with the fact that my ancestors settled in the United States decades after slavery was abolished. Consequently, I believed at the time that my predecessors were not complicit in this shameful aspect of our country's history. But I now know that the economy of our country was based on free labor for centuries, and even after slavery was no longer legal, its equivalent persisted, and prejudicial laws were devised which disadvantaged people of color and continue to do so to this day. Because I was in the lucky demographic, I was able to raise my economic and social standing, like others in my cultural group. Many people of color, like my African-American students, were not so fortunate. Now that I am much more aware of the implications of our shared history, I feel responsible for doing what I can to acknowledge that reality.

Respecting Other Cultures

The third recommendation the authors give is to respect and value other cultures and world views (Green et al., 2009). That means we must grow beyond our prejudices and recognize that other peoples can have knowledge and insight equal and even superior to our own. In my part of the world, that especially means reevaluating attitudes toward Indigenous cultures.

One source I find helpful is a history of the homesteading of reservation land in North Dakota. Karen Hansen, a great-granddaughter of a Norwegian woman homesteader, spent 15 years interviewing the elderly, reading firsthand reports, and studying historical governmental policies and regulations, treaties, and maps. She paid several visits to the Spirit Lake Reservation to learn about Dakota history. She also visited nearby towns that had been established by Norwegian immigrants to gain insight into how the U.S. government took Indigenous land and distributed it to Whites (Hansen, 2013).

This was of particular interest to me, because my ancestors also benefited from forced governmental acquisition elsewhere in North Dakota. To her credit, Hansen doesn't shy away from the fact that her own ancestor, and so, she too, benefited from such theft. In considering this history, Hansen gracefully tells the truth as she knows it, never seeking to justify; rather, to understand. Such histories help us face the truth that in the past had been concealed.

Her attitude reminds me of the conversation on guilt and responsibility between Margaret Mead, the famous anthropologist, and James Baldwin, world-renowned African-American poet. They agree that taking on the guilt for past wrongs is useless. As they point out, complicity at some level is inevitable, because we can never know enough to be fully responsible. What one must do, instead, is take responsibility to act fairly considering current knowledge and awareness and cultivate humility in the face of our collective history. In this spirit, I take heart from news of a $59M class-action settlement to the Ojibwe, who were forced to cede much of their land to the U.S. government in the nineteenth century.

Recipients included North Dakota's Turtle Mountain Band of Chippewa, Minnesota's White Earth Band of Ojibwe, the Chippewa Cree Tribe of Rocky Boy Montana, and lineal descendants who aren't enrolled members of any of the tribes. The settlement was finalized by the U.S. District Court in the District of Columbia on June 10, 2021, affecting 38,000 to 40,000 people. The treaty that took their land was signed in 1863, more than a century and a half ago. A few hundred soldiers and a Gatling gun accompanied the delegation from the U.S. government, so the treaty was signed under duress (Springer, 2021). The farm where I was raised is part of the land in question. I admire the determination of all the advocates who, over generations, refused to give up. Justice has been a long time coming, but it would not have arrived at all without the dedication of those who persisted, most of whom are now long dead.

Paul Dauphinais describes how he proceeds with Native American students in a formal assessment, showing how he, as an Indigenous school psychologist, uses a cultural framework to guide him. The framework, devised by the Indigenous American Subgroup (I.A.S.) of the NASP Multicultural Affairs Committee, includes a graphic addressing culture and identity through the four points of a red star, which incorporate four aspects of being human and are expressed as physical, social/behavioral, spirituality, and cognitive/academic; and four points of a black star, which show how relationships are constructed, including intentionality, reciprocity, sovereignty, and language.

In his illustrative case study, Dr. Dauphinais shows with great delicacy and sensitivity how he approaches the mother and the boy he is working with, avoiding any hint of shaming or belittling. His comment that generational trauma may be an element in the boy's learning difficulties places academic challenges in a grim historical context that we are now, at last, admitting, and so have some hope of coming to grips with (Charley et al., 2018).

Recognizing Differences Within Cultural Groups

Besides valuing other cultures generally, we also need to come to understand differences that can exist within cultural groups (Green et al., 2009). I was exposed daily to two, often three, cultural perspectives (Norwegian, Icelandic, American). Norwegians and Icelanders are both Scandinavian and so share much in common, but that does not make them identical. As I aged, I wondered more and more what it was like for my mother to go to live among the Icelanders after she married my father. One day I asked her.

"Well, she said. There was a lot to get used to!"

"Like what?" I asked.

She lowered her voice. "Even the men hug!"

Because the Norwegians I knew tended to be more reserved than were the Icelanders, I grew up realizing affection could be just as sincerely expressed with a hand squeeze and a warm smile as with a full embrace. My Norwegian relatives were physically affectionate with children, but at a certain point, touching beyond a handshake or pat on the arm was taboo. The Icelanders were much more physically expressive toward one another. I learned that I should judge a relationship by whether I felt cherished and respected in the presence of the person, rather than any outward physical expression. Through my mother, I had plenty of evidence that intense feelings can be fully expressed with great restraint.

My mother was right. The men did hug. When I returned for an annual community celebration some weeks after my father died, an elderly man approached my husband and me, asking who we were. I replied I was Rognvaldur's daughter. He responded by wrapping an arm around each of us in an embrace. We stood that way with him for several moments, while tears rolled down his face. Not only do Icelandic men hug, they cry, too.

One advantage of the school experiences I had among people with cultural backgrounds different from mine was that I was exposed to how different people could be within the same group. Unsurprisingly, there was great variation among personalities and behavior, and the daily exposure to these differences was a good education. We tend to stereotype people when we don't know much about them. The cure is to get to know them.

I have come to the conclusion that while we should not exaggerate our differences, we also must not underestimate or be dismissive of what makes each of us culturally distinct. We take so much for granted when we are immersed in our own culture, behaving automatically in social interactions, assuming our behavior is comprehensible, not worrying whether our words, dress, or gestures are acceptable. Now we have arrived at a time when we simply must expand our awareness and become more thoughtful of others. It requires effort and humility. Fortunately, our profession is dedicated to helping us move forward.

Gender Matters, Too

As I've mentioned, I fit the majority demographic of school psychologists, by being a White woman. Elizabeth McKenney examines how school psychology has been influenced by the acculturation of White women, which has been shaped by ideas of not only White supremacy but male supremacy. She posits that because White women have been taught to view themselves as powerless, our ability to champion school reform has been undermined (McKenney, 2021).

The people in power positions in my schools were almost invariably male. Especially during my early years as a school psychologist, having a female administrator was a novelty. Besides the power imbalance, female school psychologists on occasion also had to navigate the sexual politics of having male administrators who overstepped their bounds.

I agree with McKenney that women in school psychology need to quit censoring themselves for fear of offending those in power and use their voices to work for change. A great deal of progress has been made in this direction since my career in schools began, not only in our country but worldwide. When we speak up to ensure the rights of children are respected, dynamics can change.

The Pull of Affiliation

Sulkowski and Picciolini address a grim topic relevant to multiculturalism that needs to be addressed. They write about the rise of violent extremism among our youth, pointing out that extremist groups may vary in their ideologies, but their recruitment strategies are remarkably similar, exploiting the adolescent's unmet social and emotional needs, giving the young person a stronger sense of personal identity and group affiliation (Sulkowski & Picciolini, 2018).

I saw the need for affiliation cannot be underestimated, as the following example illustrates. In one of my high schools an African-American boy new to the school started hanging out with a White boy who was a kind of wannabe White supremacist. He doodled the symbols on his notebooks and liked to wear clothing suggestive of such affiliation. He didn't have many friends, and when the African-American boy moved to town, he befriended him. Soon the new boy was imitating his White friend, drawing symbols on his notebooks. White supremacy symbols were not allowed at school, and so the assistant principal called the boy in for a talk.

It soon became clear that he had no idea what any of the symbolism meant. He went along with it because he needed a friend. And my guess is, the White boy befriended him for the same reason. They were both left-outs, and they had found each other. The assistant principal gently explained what the symbolism represented, and of course the African-American boy was very surprised. His unquestioning faith in his new friend illustrates how deep our need for belonging is. I suspect flirting with White supremacy was a way the White student gained a sense of affiliation, perhaps without understanding fully what it meant.

Moving Forward

It is heartening but not surprising that NASP created its own Social Justice Task Force in 2016. In April of 2017, social justice was officially designated as one of NSAP's five strategic goals. A large task ahead is to define how school psychologists can be most effective in the cause of promoting educational justice. Our profession is just beginning to formalize the study of this effort, through both qualitative and quantitative approaches. Shriberg and Kim note that school psychologists need to be personally committed in addition to having professional knowledge at the level of best practice (Shriberg & Kim, 2018).

What is best practice for being an ally? The short answer is to deepen our understanding of the cultural and linguistic backgrounds of the children we serve so we can respond in a sensitive and appropriate manner. We must read and study to enrich our knowledge of history and culture, and when we are in the presence of people from backgrounds other than our own, we must listen and observe with respect. Having a keen interest in people from other cultures and ethnic groups is an excellent start. If we show genuine interest in others, particularly through a willingness to listen, most likely they will share insights with us when we seek to understand.

We must proceed with humility, knowing that we may give offense, however unintentionally. What collective noun to use in referring to tribal people serves as an example. I remain at a loss, because all the terms I have used in this chapter, save the specific names of tribes, are labels our English language dominant culture has bestowed.

Our best attempt so far at nondiscriminatory language is the use of "Indigenous" to label tribal people, but by necessity, it is an English word. It is a way to label people as other than "White", with White also a nonspecific, race-based term. As Dan, the revered grandfather in Kent Nerburn's book *Neither Wolf nor Dog*, explains, he doesn't care what term White people use for his people, because they invariably get it wrong. For example, "Indian" names them after a place across the sea, and "Native American" names them after an Italian (Nerburn, 1996). We can be blissfully unaware, but our language betrays our ignorance. The least we can do and the most we can do is to continuously strive to correct our misconceptions.

Our mistakes can serve as lessons. Helpful guidance for practitioners about what concrete steps to take is available from NASP on their website. Their "Self-Assessment Checklist for Personnel Providing Services and Supports to Children and their Families" is a tool to raise one's awareness of what one can do to increase sensitivity to the needs of those from a different cultural background than one's own. The checklist offers advice about communication styles, with, for example, ways to adapt to someone's limited English proficiency; how to equip your physical environment to suit those from other cultural and ethnic backgrounds, and how to view your own attitudes and values in relation to those from other groups (Chen & Kang, 2010). In my experience, the day-to-day activities and encounters of school psychology practitioners invariably offer ample opportunity to fold in a social justice perspective.

References

Charley, E., Robinson-Zañartu, C., Melroe, M., Dauphinais, P., & Baas, S. (2018). Multicultural affairs using the NASP framework for effective practice with indigenous youth, families, and communities. *Communiqué, 47*(1), 24–25.

Chen, E. C., & Kang, A. E. (2010). Self-assessment checklist for personnel providing services and supports to children and their families. In C. S. Clauss-Ehlers (Ed.), *Encyclopedia of cross-cultural school psychology* (pp. 872–873). Springer. https://doi.org/10.1007/978-0-387-71799-9_380

Green, T., Cook-Morales, V., Robinson-Zanartu, C., & Ingraham, C. (2009). Pathways on a journey of getting it: Multicultural competence training and continuing professional development. In J. Jones (Ed.), *The psychology of multiculturalism in the schools* (pp. 83–113). National Association of School Psychologists.

Hansen, K. (2013). *Encounter on the Great Plains: Scandinavian settlers and the dispossession of Dakota Indians, 1890–1930.* Oxford University Press.

McKenney, E. (2021). Reckoning with ourselves: A critical analysis of white women's socialization and school psychology [special series]. *School Psychology Review.* https://doi.org/10.1080/2372966X.2021.1956856

Nerburn, K. (1996). *Neither wolf nor dog: On forgotten roads with an Indian elder.* New World Library.

Nevzlin, I. (2019). *The impact of identity: The power of knowing who you are.* Self-published.

Shriberg, D., & Kim, D. (2018). Quantitatively measuring one's capacity as an agent of social justice. *Communiqué, 47*(1), 16–17.

Springer, P. (2021, April 7). $59M settlement addresses 1800s Ojibwe land grabs. *Grand Forks Herald.* www.grandforksherald.com/community/59m-settlement-addresses-1800s-ojibwe-land-grabs-in-minnesota-and-north-dakota

Sulkowski, M., & Picciolini, C. (2018). The path into and out of violent extremism, part 2: Deradicalizing and leaving violent extremism. *Communiqué, 47*(2), 18, 20–22.

Chapter 11

Rites of Passage

Becoming a School Psychologist

My varied teaching experiences provided a good background for me to become a school psychologist, but circumstances also conspired in that direction. After returning home from Pakistan, I found there were few teaching positions open where I wanted to live. To pay the bills, I substitute taught while I reflected on what I should do next. Remembering the fascinating lecture from the school psychologist at the U.S. embassy school in New Delhi, I decided to see if there was a program available anywhere nearby, and luckily, there was. I talked with the head of the school psychology program at the Moorhead branch of the University of Minnesota (M.S.U.M.), and we agreed that my interests and background fit well with school psychology. Also, there was a shortage of school psychologists, so I would be practically guaranteed a position after I completed the program. My next adventure was about to begin; this time, close to home.

I graduated a year later with an M.S. in School Psychology and accepted a position with a large rural cooperative in western North Dakota. They were happy to hire interns, because it wasn't easy to attract people to such a remote area. I grew up in a rural setting, so I was not discouraged by the location. I was just grateful to have employment and begin my life as a school psychologist.

In my part of the world, school psychology was—and still is—underpublicized. Understandably, my older relatives hadn't ever heard of this career. I left teaching to do—what exactly? Because school psychology is a composite of other, better known, fields, it wasn't surprising my relatives didn't know what to make of it. It didn't fit with what they knew of school or psychology, so they overrode their confusion by just enquiring if I still liked teaching, whenever we had a visit. After many unsuccessful attempts at explaining school psychology, I finally gave up and I would just answer that yes, I did.

A Brief History of School Psychology

School psychology was a recent discovery in my life, but the profession had existed since the end of the nineteenth and beginning of the

DOI:10.4324/9781003348344-11

twentieth century, when at last children were the focus of social reform. Child labor laws were passed, and juvenile courts were created. Compulsory schooling became mandatory in 1918, and with that requirement, children with disabilities appeared in school. Attitudes toward children and childhood had changed, so that schools became to be seen as a location for intervention to eradicate societal problems. If children could grow up to be healthy, productive adults, the country would benefit. To accommodate their learning needs, smaller classes with alternate teaching methods were created, some as early as 1910 (Fagan & Wise, 1994).

School psychology as a separate field of study grew out of clinical psychology and educational psychology. Early on, exceptionality was defined in terms of "mental, physical, and moral" impairments. As the nation's public health improved, there became fewer children identified as physically handicapped, and "mental" and "moral" impairments were redefined (Fagan & Wise, 1994, p. 26). School psychologists became the "gatekeepers for special education", there to determine who qualifies and who doesn't. This definition of our profession has persisted, despite the field expanding to address other purposes. At present, the role has expanded from strictly individual intervention to influencing systemic change within school districts (Fagan & Wise, 1994).

The American Psychological Association's Thayer Conference in 1954 defined what roles and functions school psychologists should perform and what their training should entail. The 1975 Education for All Handicapped Children Act (Public Law 94–142) sanctioned school psychologists. The profession came to serve all children experiencing learning difficulties, not just those who qualified for special education services (Fagan & Wise, 1994).

Psychologists considered to have had the greatest early influence on the development of school psychology were Lightner Witmer (1867–1956) and G. Stanley Hall (1846–1924). Witmer opened the first psychological and child guidance clinic in 1896 at the University of Philadelphia. He focused on a child's progress, rather than emphasizing deficits, and used his clinic to help individual children overcome their limitations, an idiographic approach. In contrast, G. Stanley Hall emphasized studying group norms to understand special needs. Over time, these two perspectives combined to form the basis of school psychology (Fagan & Wise, 1994).

The American Psychological Association had determined in 1945, about 40 years before I joined the ranks, that school psychologists should have their own division, which is called Division 16. Membership was limited to only Ph.D.-level psychologists. Had they had the final word deciding my status, I would not have been allowed the title school psychologist. Fortunately for those like me, the National Association of School Psychologists was formed in 1969 to strengthen the identity of the profession (Fagan & Wise, 1994). Under the auspices of NASP,

I eventually gained the title of Nationally Certified School Psychologist (N.C.S.P.). Certification was distinct from licensure. I could not become a licensed school psychologist without a Ph.D., but I was designated a school psychologist because of my national certification.

Right now, entry level for practitioners in all U.S. states and territories is the specialist-level degree. In some states, the degree is considered sufficient qualification to go into private practice. A comparatively small number of practitioners have a doctoral degree, while the majority hold the specialist degree. On a practical level, the question about what constitutes a real school psychologist has been settled, with the specialist degree winning out. To ensure that our skills stay current, continuing education credit must be earned throughout one's career to maintain licensure, because our profession is continually changing, and it is essential that practitioners keep pace (National Association of School Psychologists, n.d.-a.).

Who We Are and Who We Aren't

To explain school psychology, I often defined my occupation by what it wasn't and what I didn't do. Other mental health-related occupations overlap with school psychology in important ways, and we share some common responsibilities, but each requires different qualifications and has unique job expectations. Like school counselors, I offered counseling, but I had to have signed parent permission to speak with each child, unless it was an emergency, such as suspected suicidal intent. Typically, I served kids enrolled in special education programs, but I also counseled regular education students considered at risk. I performed formal psycho-educational assessments using tools like I.Q. tests, which school counselors and school social workers did not. Unlike a school counselor, I did not help students choose their course of study in high school or assist them with college admission.

Nor was I a school social worker. Because of their specialized training, school social workers serve as the main liaison with county social service agencies. Although I did make child protection reports from time to time, it was not a primary function of my position to report child abuse and neglect. Like school psychologists, school social workers do individual counseling and group work, but do not perform comprehensive individual assessments required for special education placement. However, like school counselors and school psychologists, they are a member of child study teams, which identify children suspected to need special education services.

My perspective was also different from that of a clinical psychologist. Like clinical psychologists, I had a strong background in psychology and child development, but I was trained more intensively in aspects of special education and school organization. Clinical psychologists have more training in psychopathology and are more likely to engage in long-term therapy. Most states require clinical psychologists to have a doctoral degree, while school psychologists are granted credentials by the state at the specialist level (National Association of School Psychologists, About School Psychology, n.d.-b).

School psychologists are vulnerable to the accusation of not being a "real" psychologist when compared with clinical psychologists. In retrospect, I wish I had done more not only to emphasize but indeed to celebrate the "school" in school psychology when I was asked to distinguish between the two professions. School psychologists have an advantage in that they work within a natural environment that children inhabit. Consequently, we are well informed about what their educational setting is like. Because we also spend our day at school, we are acquainted with the teachers, administrators, janitors, paras, and other adults they encounter day to day. We can observe children directly as they perform in class and interact with teachers and other adults at school, and we have immediate access to samples of their schoolwork.

We also directly observe the social world the child inhabits, because we are in and out of classrooms, lunchrooms, playgrounds, and other settings where we see how children are interacting with one another. We have opportunity, for example, to witness the isolation of a child sitting alone at lunch, shunned by peers. If a child has conflicts with other children, it is entirely possible we are acquainted with his/her adversaries, or, on the other hand, we may know his/her friends. We can also catch children enjoying activities, rounding out our impression of what their life at school is like. We usually have firsthand information, so we do not have to depend on a secondhand report. Also, we are accessible. Because we are right in their school, it is easy for them to keep appointments. Children do not have to be transported to an office somewhere else to meet with us.

Stereotypes and Us

Because the term "psychologist" is laden with associations, I sometimes longed for a different title, but I didn't know what it should be. As school psychologists became more common in schools, confusion, and suspicion about who I was and what I did were lessened. But, for example, when a parent refused testing for their child by saying they didn't want any "atheists, humanists, or psychologists" working with their children, I must admit I rather wished the nomenclature identifying my occupation was something other than what it was. Truth be told, the title of psychologist caused me dismay on more than one occasion.

The beginning school psychologist soon realizes the impact of the word "psychologist". It can be loaded with all sorts of associations, not all of which are positive. Once while attending a child study team meeting for a child with many behavioral issues, I felt the brunt of the negative stereotype. It was my turn to speak, and I began by saying I had some suggestions for modifying the child's behavior. Before I even concluded my beginning statement, the principal announced emphatically that he "did not believe" in behavior modification. In response I shifted my posture away from him and toward the teachers who were as shocked by his statement as I was. Ignoring the principal's remark, I said my piece and we carried on through the meeting.

Afterward I was visited by a teacher who was mortified by how the principal had spoken to me and assured me that the others in attendance did not feel as he did. She also said she was going to talk to the principal about his, in her words, very rude behavior. I said that wasn't necessary, but she was adamant.

The principal soon summoned me to his office to apologize to me, saying I did not deserve such treatment. Then he went on to explain that he had a family member who was a psychologist, who he described as an "insufferable know-it-all". "But", he said, "you never acted like she did, and it was unfair of me to treat you the way I did". I accepted his apology. We worked well together after that, as we had before, and I never again heard any negative comments about behavior modification or anything else I proposed. I would have been grateful to anyone for such a gracious apology, but it was especially meaningful coming from an administrator because of the power intrinsic in his position.

A Composite With Its Own Identity

School psychology is a hybrid profession. To address the school part of school psychology, we must understand how school systems work. Beyond that, we must know how to work within them, so consultation and collaboration are very necessary skills. We need to be familiar with the roles other school personnel play, such as speech clinicians, occupational therapists, school counselors, school social workers, and of course, teachers and administrators. We must know how teachers teach and how children learn; thus, educational and developmental psychology form the backdrop to our stage. We also need to understand why children don't or can't learn, and we need to know how to figure out what to do when they don't or can't. Because learning problems stem from a wide range of possible causes, we need to understand the principles of clinical psychology and applied behavior analysis as well as child and adolescent development and psychopathology. Family dynamics must also be well understood, as well as the role of societal effects, such as racism and poverty.

Besides being trained in the nuts and bolts of psycho-educational assessment, school psychologists must be able to provide counseling services with students and crisis intervention should a tragedy or natural disaster occur. School psychologists must be well versed in how to conduct fair assessments with children with disabilities, bilingual children, and others from protected groups. Our profession is governed by a code of ethics, and we must adhere to state and federal laws, to avoid violating children's rights. Most recently, school psychologists are also expected to be adept at data analysis to help guide teachers in planning academic and behavioral interventions.

What to call us? For my own part, I became quite fond of the title, "that lady".

A poignant incident involving a little boy perhaps illustrates who I was and what my role meant, at least to him. He had recently come to one of my schools and got referred to me almost immediately because he was such a handful in the first-grade classroom. We learned that his biological father had recently died. The little guy just had way too much to deal with, and his coping took the form of some acting out. I met with him each week when I came to his school, and he seemed to be gradually settling in. Then his mother died. Her partner, to his credit, treated the boy as his own. He soon found a better job in another community, and they moved away to start their new life.

All this happened suddenly, between visits. The next time I came to the school, the secretary told me about the move. The previous day had been the little boy's last day. Near the end of the day, he was brought down to the office because he was upset. The secretary told me he sobbed and sobbed, saying he "wanted to say goodbye to that lady". Our visits had been few and relatively brief, but, evidently, important to him. At the end of the day, what title we carry is irrelevant. What counts is what our efforts mean in the lives of children.

My Course in Human Relations

We need to know quite a lot about many areas, and our training programs usually do a good job of preparing us. When my generation of school psychologists entered the profession, school personnel often didn't know what we did. Part of our task was to inform them about what we were qualified to do in their school. Our wealth of knowledge could come to naught if we couldn't find our place in a school system and learn how to communicate and work well with the whole range of folks who were a part of it.

Conducting special education assessments with two brothers almost immediately after I began my internship proved to provide a quick course in human relations at school. I was assigned to assess two brothers, newly enrolled in elementary school: one a kindergartener, the other a second grader, whose Air Force father had just been transferred from England to a base in western North Dakota. Their classroom teachers sought special education evaluations for them immediately. Usually, children were given some time to adjust before formal assessment was considered, but these teachers were in a panic. Their classrooms were in an uproar because the children were so physically active, and besides that, the teachers were having a terrible time communicating with them. The language the brothers spoke was almost incomprehensible, so their teachers didn't know what to do.

In both instances, their teachers suspected the children to be developmentally delayed. I performed the typical school psychology tasks of observing them in their classrooms and administering I.Q. tests and had teachers and parents complete Vineland questionnaires. The younger of the two scored high enough on the academic and I.Q. tests that developmental delay was ruled out. He was quite hyperactive, and his language was difficult to understand, but he clearly was able to learn within average limits. His older brother, however, scored within the qualifying range on the assessments, and his teacher, as well as the learning disabilities teacher, who even stated that she "knew in her heart" the boy was developmentally delayed, were both convinced he should be labeled Mildly Mentally Impaired (M.M.I.). If one only looked at the numbers, that was a possibility. But there was so much more to consider.

These two children had arrived quite recently from England, where their father had been stationed for two years. Before that, they had lived in Okinawa. Their mother was Jamaican and their father was from Alabama. Because of my experience teaching in the all-Black school, I could understand them fairly well, so I was able to understand a lot, even if not all, of what they said. Also, I paid several home visits where I saw the brothers conversing together, proof they clearly could communicate very effectively with one another. I asked the mother if she understood what they were saying. "Most of the time, but not always", was her reply.

All was revealed when the speech clinician did a language evaluation, and she concluded that these two boys spoke a kind of twin language consisting of elements of Jamaican creole, Alabama Black dialect, Japanese, and cockney English. Her results confirmed all my impressions. Through a parent interview we learned that the two boys had watched a great deal of Japanese cartoons on TV while living in Okinawa, and they picked up some of the language. Living in England, they were exposed to a cockney English, a dialect quite different from the one spoken in western North Dakota. I will be forever grateful for the expertise shown by the speech clinician. She was already a highly respected member of the school staff and having her results and mine match saved me from having to try to convince the child study team all by myself.

The Meaning of a Number

But the I.Q. test with the older brother fell within the M.M.I. range, and the principal and teachers were adamant that I place the boy, based on that number. At our in-house meeting to share testing results I told the child study team that I could not in good conscience say that the second grader met M.M.I. criteria, given the unusual language history and the fact that he had just undergone a tremendous change, moving from England to North Dakota. It was true that he was hyperactive, but that could be a symptom of the stress of making this transition to a new location. At least for the time being, I didn't feel he fit any special education criteria. There just wasn't enough information to justify such action.

The principal was very displeased with me. He had asked me earlier what the boy's I.Q. score was, and I had told him. Unbeknownst to me, he had called the special education cooperative and asked someone what such a score meant. Without getting any information about the child, the person told him that the child met M.M.I. criteria. I was just a rooky, so my judgment was discounted. We had another meeting, at which the principal pounded his fist on the table, exclaiming, "Numbers don't tell the whole story!" I repeated that my score was compromised by several confounding factors, such as the boy's unique language experience and likely emotional stress from the move. I fully agreed with him that numbers don't tell the whole story, which I stated at a much lower volume than he had, and that was why I was going to use this case in my internship seminar, so my graduate program professor could give her opinion. Neither he nor the teachers were satisfied with my answer.

In North Dakota at that time, it was legal to place a child in a special education program on a trial basis if the assessment process was inconclusive, so the team asked if I would be willing to agree to do that. Because I knew and trusted the special education teacher who ran the M.M.I. program, I said I would agree. She had many years of experience and seemed to be very savvy, so I put my faith in her judgment. The next time I came to the school the principal immediately called me into his office. I wondered if I would again be put on the hot seat. Instead, he told me that the M.M.I. teacher had called him one day after the second grader had been placed in her room. She demanded to know what kind of idiot school psychologist they had hired, that she would place this child in her classroom. With wonderful grace, the principal replied that the school psychologist was not the idiot.

Learning From Mistakes

I got the placement question right, but on another front, I indeed was in the wrong, so I could identify with the well-intentioned principal. Because these children and their parents were Black, and because where we lived hardly anyone else was, I thought it would be a good idea to invite an African-American air base chaplain to be on the team. I was told he had attended other school meetings in the past. I asked permission of the family and they agreed. But after our final meeting, the father took me aside and commented that he couldn't see any good reason why the chaplain was there and very pointedly asked why he was invited in the first place, and (with tension rising in his voice) who exactly had had the stupid idea to invite him. I confessed, "You're looking at her". He stared at me in disbelief, then shook his head and laughed.

As I stood there, absorbing this blinding glimpse of the obvious, I realized the error of my thoughtless reasoning. Having another Black person on the team would not automatically help to balance the playing field for them. I had not taken the time to find out if the parents trusted this chaplain or if they considered him an ally. Skin color was not enough of a reason to invite him, a lesson I was glad I learned early in my career. In today's language, I committed a microaggression.

Once on the job, it doesn't take long to learn that a school psychologist must be someone who thrives when solving problems in a group setting and enjoys facing real-world challenges—this is not an ivory-tower occupation. Day in and day out, we need to please many people who may not really understand what we do. What they are very clear about is whether they like how we treat them. Survival as a school psychologist requires a high level of diplomacy as we navigate among the whole range of people whom we encounter day to day. We need to know how to communicate technical information in a manner that lay people can easily grasp without distorting the meaning of the information or talking down to them. We also must be able to stand our ground, but in a way that doesn't alienate those with whom we work. With so many personalities in the mix, this can be quite challenging.

Because of the need to protect confidentiality, we must be happy working in the background, not necessarily having anyone know our successes or even understand all that much about what we are doing. This aspect was problematic at the start of my career; administrators didn't always realize the value of a school psychologist because we performed our duties quietly, and, because of our code of ethics, we kept secret much of what we knew about kids in their schools. I had many adventures along the way as I honed my skills, especially in working with the people who held the most power—the administrators. The process was often an education for us both.

Shifting Ground

Because of the financial problems in school districts exacerbated by the pandemic, comments from my friends who were practitioners finishing out their 2020–2021 school year unfortunately did not reflect much optimism. Two disturbing realities in their school communities had them worried. First, practitioners voiced how overworked they were, and as a result, what a great need there was for more of them. Their second concern was that there weren't enough school psychologists to fill the need, even if funding were available.

Not only practitioners themselves have raised this cry but national organizations, such as the American Psychological Association, have been expressing this concern for years (Weir, 2012). The importance of a lower student-to-school-psychologist ratio has been emphasized for decades. It was alarming that at a time of grave need, school district budgets were tightening even further, placing school psychology positions in jeopardy. So not only was there a need for more school psychology practitioners but existing positions were being considered for elimination. Some of my younger friends were fretting that their current position might not even exist the following year. Ironically, at the same time, school psychology ranked 19th in the category of social service jobs and 27th in best S.T.E.M. jobs (National Association of School Psychologists, n.d.-c).

Bear in mind that these estimates were made before the coronavirus appeared. At the beginning of the twenty-first century, the need to have mental health services available at school, combined with increased awareness of the role of mental health in learning, has meant school psychologists were in greater and greater demand, even before the pandemic. School psychology training is designed to meet what schools need at any given time, but state and local funding all too often is not always adequate to cover the cost.

During my final year before retirement, I experienced firsthand that positions sometimes go unfilled in rural areas for lack of applicants. Because of a resignation, some of my school psychology colleagues and I were assigned an extra school district to pick up the slack. We just had to do more with less, with no extra compensation except a heartfelt thank you from our director. This example is replicated in many locations across the country. There needs to be support for increasing the number of positions and once people are on the job, support for them as they deal with problems unique to our country's less populated regions.

When school psychologists are stretched too far, there is not enough time to do much more than complete mandatory special education assessments. For many, this can be a formula for burnout. One reason I left my first position was to have more variety in my work, so I could use the wide range of skills I was trained to perform. Decades later, I had thankfully already planned to retire at the end of the year I was assigned the extra district. I must admit that I was so exhausted by the end of May that I was grateful and relieved I wasn't under contract to go back.

In addition, while individual positions were in jeopardy, school psychology training programs were also on shifting ground. For example, the school psychology program at Minnesota State University at Moorhead (M.S.U.M.), my alma mater, was placed on a list of programs under consideration for discontinuation in the summer of 2020. The underlying reason was strictly financial; the program and its faculty were highly respected. The only criticism levied against them was that they were not bringing in enough revenue. In an era of inadequate funding for public education at all levels, they were expected to provide for their own financial needs, regardless of their educational contribution to the region.

I joined in protest with many alumni and others who recognized that shutting it down would be a grave disservice to schools and children in our region. One reason was that graduates from this program are well schooled in the needs of Indigenous children, and regional tribal reservation schools benefit from being able to hire them. Furthermore, our region has depended on this program to supply school psychologists for several decades. There is no easy replacement available should the M.S.U.M. program close. Fortunately, the hardworking faculty overcame the objections by adapting their program and gaining support from several quarters, not least of whom were special education directors.

Not only are school positions going unfilled but also trainer positions at the university level (National Association of School Psychologists, n.d.-d). NASP reports there is also a shortage of school psychologists with doctoral-level training. In an ideal world, education at the Ph.D. or Psy.D. levels would be available to anyone in the field with the ability and interest to attain it. Right now, such training is unfortunately out of reach for the majority of those who work in rural areas, unless they are willing to relocate.

Perhaps graduate school psychology programs can be reimagined so the next generation of school psychologists can continue beyond the specialist degree in a way that wouldn't disrupt their lives and the continuity of service in the schools where they work. We know it isn't good for schools to have high turnover of their school psychology practitioners. Might there not be ways to shape doctoral programs to consider the practical realities that have prevented participation? This would be one way to lend support to rural schools.

That rural school psychologists need more support is not to suggest practitioners in urban settings do not. Both rural and urban areas across the country need school psychologists representing diverse populations to join their ranks, because all the children we serve need to have someone they can identify with. Research studies are showing that children do better in school when the demographics of the faculty match that of the student body. There is evidence that this is particularly beneficial for economically disadvantaged Black male students

(Gershenson et al., 2018). To address this challenge, NASP combines addressing our workforce shortage with our educational justice responsibility through the NASP Exposure Project (Barrett et al., 2019). In the hope of being better able to serve all of our nation's children, NASP is working to attract a much broader cross-section of our population to school psychology.

The Long View

Fagan and Wise end their history of school psychology published in 1994, over a quarter of a century ago, with a section on the future of the profession. They include a 1933 quotation from Leta Stetter Hollingworth, early pioneer in psychology, who predicts that 25 years hence school psychology will offer sound scientific practices which will assure that schools will be designed to suit children's needs. "True idealism demands impersonal truth as a basis for action", she said. Fagan and Wise conclude that Hollingworth would be pleased with the state of knowledge within our profession but disappointed in how well schools can apply what we have to offer (Fagan & Wise, 1994).

The authors take a cautious approach to predicting how well our ideals will match reality in years to come. For example, they do not foresee the NASP-recommended service ratio of one school psychologist for every thousand students to be uniformly realized in all districts (Fagan & Wise, 1994). Now the recommended ratio is 1: 500. Presently, the national ratio is 1:1211 (National Association of School Psychologists, n.d.-e).

Nor do they expect school psychology to move away from individual assessment; rather they expect us to retain aspects of traditional assessment for identifying the need for special education services. Fagan and Wise foresee the likelihood of school psychology embracing mental health issues to a greater degree than in the past, and they expect NASP to maintain its central role in determining standards for the profession. They accurately predict the increasing feminization of the profession, and they acknowledge there is a dire need to attract people of color to join our ranks. They warn against aligning too closely with political movements to avoid being left behind when the political atmosphere changes, and they express concern that we can become polarized over issues such as doctoral versus nondoctoral training and credentialing, inclusion versus traditional special education, and a focus on academic learning versus mental health (Fagan & Wise, 1994).

I particularly appreciate their distinction between "roles and functions". They defend the traditional assessment role of the school psychologist, suggesting that rather than abandoning assessment, we need to "adjust the functions of the assessment role to include more instructionally relevant forms of testing or appraisal . . ." (Fagan & Wise, 1994,

p. 287). This insight is particularly relevant, with the assessment of English language learners under scrutiny.

Professional burnout, serving the entire school population and a broader age range, concern for society at large, continuing professional development, and roles clarification are topics Fagan and Wise hope will be given close attention (Fagan & Wise, 1994). Since the publication of their text, these topics have been and are being addressed on an ongoing basis. In many ways the past predicted the future. But the twenty-first century had a big surprise in store for our profession and the world. One topic Fagan and Wise could not have predicted as a central concern was how to cope with a pandemic at school.

The effects of the pandemic also heightened awareness of the need to address educational inequity, because of the disruption in learning caused by Covid-19. Inequities existed before the pandemic, but the unequal impact of the pandemic on students' lives, both at home and in school, made them more apparent. There have always been students struggling because of insecure housing, nutrition, and adequate medical care, services the affluent take for granted. The question now is whether this increased awareness will prompt long-overdue remedies.

As the cliché goes, history doesn't repeat itself, but it rhymes. Our profession has always complemented the public health movement that became a force in schools over a hundred years ago. We found a place among those concerned for the welfare of society and the future of the entire school population, regardless of ability or disability. Now the need presented by the pandemic of the twenty-first century prompts our profession to emphasize systemic interventions, in addition to intervening one child at a time. The next two chapters are devoted to the connections among public health policy, action taken by schools, and political influences on school funding, all of which combine to affect the daily life of a school psychologist.

References

Barrett, C., Heidelburg, K., & Malone, C. (2019). The NASP exposure project: Addressing workforce shortages and social justice. *Communiqué*, 47(5), 8–10.

Fagan, T., & Wise, P. (1994). *School psychology: Past, present, and future*. Longman.

Gershenson, S., Hart, C. M., Hyman, J., Lindsay, C., & Papageorge, N. W. (2018). The long-run impacts of same-race teachers (NBER Working Paper No. 25254). *National Bureau of Economic Research*. https://doi.org/10.3386/w25254

National Association of School Psychologists. (n.d.-a). *School psychology: A career that makes a difference*. www.nasponline.org/about-school-psychology/a-career-that-makes-a-difference

National Association of School Psychologists. (n.d.-b). *About school psychology*. www.nasponline.org/aboutschoolpsychology/selecting-a-graduate-program/a-career-in-school-psychology-frequently-asked-questions#

National Association of School Psychologists. (n.d.-c). *About school psychology.* www.nasponline.org/about school psychology/selecting-a-graduate-program/a-career-in-school-psychology-frequently-asked-questions#

National Association of School Psychologists. (n.d.-d). *Shortage of school psychologists.* www.nasponline.org/research-and-policy/policy-priorities/critical-policy-issues/shortage-of-school-psychologists

National Association of School Psychologists. (n.d.-e). *Shortages in school psychology challenges to meeting the growing needs of U.S. students and schools.* www.nasponline.org/research-and-policy/policy-priorities/critical-policy-issues/shortage-of-school-psychologists

Weir, K. (2012). School psychologists feel the squeeze. *Monitor on Psychology, 43*(8). www.apa.org/monitor/2012/09/squeeze

Chapter 12

Health in School

The small North Dakota rural community where I graduated from high school was featured in a video on the BBC in December of 2020 because of the desperate situation at the local hospital resulting from the Covid-19 pandemic (Ostasiewich, 2020). I have my own vivid memories of health care in this small town, particularly because it was where I spent a week in the hospital receiving intravenous antibiotics after a bout with measles. This occurred in 1964, before there was a measles vaccine, and every so often, an epidemic of measles would break out. Schools provided an ideal environment for transmission.

I got sick near the end of a six-week grading period, and my teachers wanted everyone to do their make-up work quickly so the six weeks could end with no loose-ends. I liked to please my teachers, so I kept going to school once the measles passed, even though I wasn't well. I was running a fever, and it would rise throughout the day in school. I'd go right to bed when I got home and stay there until the next morning, when I got ready to leave for school again. I toughed it out until Thursday, which was when our school week ended, because Friday was the start of our Easter vacation. We would have an entire week off.

The next morning, I vomited what my dad thought was liver bile, and he immediately drove me to a doctor in the town that decades later, the BBC featured. The doctor hospitalized me immediately, because my whole body was infected. I would need to be on intravenous antibiotics for several days. I was unaware at the time that one reason people died from epidemics wasn't just because of the virus that spread but because the disease would weaken one's immune system, laying one vulnerable to bacterial infections that could be fatal. Fortunately, the antibiotics worked, and I was returned to full health. I was able to return to school without missing a single day, but I had spent almost my whole spring break in the hospital. That Monday, our English teacher went around the room, asking everyone how they spent their vacation. Her jaw dropped when I told her what my experience was.

DOI:10.4324/9781003348344-12

Disease and School

Public schools have had to consider the spread of dangerous diseases throughout their history and so have needed to take several steps to protect the health of students. Consequently, public health policy has greatly influenced the behavior of American public schools, not only during the health crises caused by epidemics and pandemics but day to day. Concern for health gained momentum at the end of the nineteenth and the beginning of the twentieth century, when school population increased dramatically, as did the nation's population in general. For example, making sure drinking water was safe and classrooms were well ventilated became priorities, as well as regular inspections to determine whether children carried head lice. Tuberculosis was an ongoing concern. Lina Rogers, the first school nurse hired in the United States, served four schools in New York City, and her impact was soon evident. Within six months of her hiring, student absences fell by 90% (Pruitt, 2020).

Because they were deemed to be comparatively safe, schools in many of our nation's large cities stayed open during the second wave of the "Spanish flu" pandemic of 1918. This was done because authorities such as Dr. S. Josephine Baker, director of the New York City Department of Health Bureau of Child Hygiene, believed children would be safer in school than at home because sanitation was better and sick children could be identified and treated more quickly because of regular inspections. This proved to be true (Pruitt, 2020).

In 1957, a virus known as the Asian flu (H2N2) moved through the world, beginning in China. By late summer, the U.S. Surgeon General issued a warning that it would create a dangerous outbreak in the United States by fall. Fortunately, a vaccine became available in time to stem the tide. In the end, the death toll in the United States was estimated to be 116,000; certainly, a high number, but not nearly as many as it would have been without the vaccine. Over a million died worldwide (Kelly, 2020). Schoolchildren in the United States were significantly affected, when much of the transmission occurred among children (Cauchemez et al., 2014).

The next two pandemics had scant effect on schools. The H3N2 virus was next to arrive, first noted in the United States in September 1968. No school closings occurred. The estimated number of deaths was 1 million worldwide and about 100,000 in the United States and affecting mainly people 65 years and older. This virus continues to circulate worldwide as a seasonal influenza (Centers for Disease Control and Prevention, n.d.-a).

In 2003, the Severe Acute Respiratory Syndrome (S.A.R.S.) came to the United States and also did not have an impact on schools. By

March 24th of that year, there were 39 suspected cases here. By April 4th, a total of 115 cases from across 29 states had been reported. Fortunately, there were no deaths, and by May 6th, the virus had been contained (Centers for Disease Control and Prevention, n.d.-b).

Then in 2009 the H1NI pandemic arrived, known as the swine flu, which was first detected in the United States in the state of California. Its spread was rapid, across both our country and the world. By June of 2009, all 50 states, the District of Columbia, Puerto Rico, and the U.S. Virgin Islands had reported cases of the infection. On April 28th, the CDC issued the first "CDC Interim Guidance on Closing Schools and Childcare Facilities", recommending a seven-day dismissal in schools and childcare facilities. Unlike the Covid-19 pandemic, 80% of related deaths occurred in people under age 60 (Allen & Jernigan, 2020). This recommendation was modified on May 1st, recommending dismissing school for 14 days, but the recommendation in the United States was reversed on May 5th and school closure was no longer recommended (Cauchemez et al., 2014).

An *Education Week* article from May 4, 2009, reported that more than 500 U.S. schools in over 24 states were closed that day, due to the flu (The Associated Press, 2009, May 5).

In Minnesota, where I was working at the time, all schools closed in Orono, one in Minneapolis, and one in Cold Spring. Altogether, a total of more than 700 schools in the United States closed in response to the pandemic (Klaiman et al., 2011). I remember the anxiety I felt during the weeks the virus was gaining a foothold in the United States, including among some communities in Minnesota. I couldn't help but fret about children in my districts with medical conditions that made them particularly vulnerable. What excellent vectors I and other itinerants would be, moving from one school to another over the course of our day, and sometimes from one community to another, as well. Fortunately, my schools remained unaffected. On August 10, 2010, the World Health Organization declared the global pandemic had ended. The virus continues, however, as a seasonal flu virus, but we have a vaccine to protect us (Centers for Disease Control and Prevention, n.d.-c).

Vaccination and Anti-vaccination

Because vaccines have been so effective in preventing outbreaks of life-threatening diseases, we have come to consider it a matter of social responsibility to have them, and so children attending public school have been required to be vaccinated before admission, with few exceptions. The first time vaccination was required in the United States was in response to an outbreak of smallpox in Massachusetts near the end of the nineteenth century. This action was upheld in court at both the state and federal levels. Most recently, in the 1970s, schools advocated for required vaccination against measles, because it was clear disease rates were drastically lower in states which enforced vaccination requirements compared with those that didn't. Currently, schools have the authority to require vaccination when a disease arises (Flanagan-Klygis, 2003).

Over time, the number of unvaccinated children has fallen to a very small percent (1.3% of those born in 2015 were not vaccinated, the 2017 National Immunization Survey-Child reported). Reasons included inadequate access to health care and cost (Hill et al., 2018). Had there been a measles vaccination available when I was a freshman in high school, I very likely would have been spared my stay in the hospital.

At this time, the anti-vaccination movement that has gained momentum in recent years threatens public health. A study done in Colorado indicated that unvaccinated children ages 3–18 were at 60 times a greater risk for acquiring measles and 16 times for pertussis. Risks for vaccinated individuals also increased, indicating the public at large was paying a price for the refusal of some parents to have their children vaccinated. Convincing parents to have their children vaccinated requires overcoming the misinformation and disinformation that has been spread about the dangers of vaccination. This is one of the challenges schools face in partnership with public health entities, so school psychologists should be well informed about the issue (Flanagan-Klygis, 2003).

The Debunking Handbook, an online publication written by experts drawn from the fields of psychology, political science, journalism, education, and others, offers guidance about how to counter misinformation and disinformation, such as arguments used to promote anti-vaccination (Lewandowsky et al., 2020). In the *Handbook,* they explain the psychology behind our susceptibility to falsity and how to counter it. Whether simple misinformation or disinformation—that is, misinformation intended to mislead—there are methods to employ to counter them. Fact-checking helps, but once misinformation has been introduced, it can remain an influence. Scholars call this the "continued influence effect" (Lewandowsky et al., 2020).

We need to inoculate ourselves, metaphorically speaking, by learning the strategies used to mislead us. Then we can be on guard against them. It can be particularly helpful if we have information about manipulative strategies prior to being exposed to false information. We can't always get ahead of the game, however; we also must know how to debunk false claims. To be effective, we need to explain clearly why this information is incorrect and state what the correct information is. The authors emphasize it is important to give detailed explanations, because without them, our objection may not take hold. We also must be aware that the more familiar the misinformation becomes, the easier it is to believe it. Repeating misinformation makes it more believable. Furthermore, it is often delivered using highly emotionally charged language intended to persuade. Even presenting an idea by asking a question about it, such as, "Are vaccinations safe?" can introduce doubt (Lewandowsky et al., 2020).

If possible, people should be warned ahead of time that they may be exposed to misinformation. "Prebunking" forewarns the receiver that the information may not be accurate. Such forewarnings have been shown to be quite effective. If one must debunk, the authors recommend leading with a factual statement explaining why the misinformation is untrue. Warn the listener that you are going to mention the myth and state it only once. Then give your explanation about why this belief is incorrect and why its alternative is true. End by repeating the facts of the matter that explain why the myth is inaccurate. If possible, point out how the misinformation relies on selective use of data, designed to mislead (Lewandowsky et al., 2020, p. 7).

Across the Atlantic, the European Commission published a press release in September 2020, concerning the disinformation being circulated about the coronavirus. It contained guidelines for Facebook, Instagram, and Twitter to provide information from public health resources, such as the World Health Organization, and to restrict disinformation spread by advertisers. Ongoing efforts to counter manipulation of the public and promote trustworthy information were emphasized (European Commission, 2020).

Concern for the ill effects of misinformation and disinformation in the United States was also growing, in part because of the divisiveness created by politically motivated propaganda related to the pandemic. Facebook and Twitter, for example, became stricter about what sorts of information could be posted, but such efforts were insufficient. Since the time Covid-19 entered the United States, a great deal of misinformation and disinformation has been circulated.

Public Health as a Priority

Meanwhile, public health in public school became a topic of critical importance around the world after Covid-19 appeared. The contrast between the priority Germany and the United States, for example, gave to providing public education is an interesting study. Germany favored keeping kids in school over keeping businesses such as bars and restaurants open. Their philosophy was that education had to be their top concern because the problems resulting from absence from school cannot be solved with money. Lost learning and psychological problems caused by school absence would have long-lasting effects in the lives of individual children, but also on the whole economy. Germany decided that providing equal educational opportunity to its children was its highest priority. Bars and restaurants, for example, could receive funding from the government to keep afloat during the crisis. Germany also wanted to ensure its public schools retained students, knowing that their closure would result in affluent parents choosing private options, weakening the public education sector (Llana & Chu, 2020). In comparison, the United States was not as protective of its public schools.

In 2020, the Organisation for Economic Cooperation and Development (O.E.C.D.) produced a study that estimated school closings will reduce the average lifetime earnings for affected students by 3%. That the most disadvantaged children will be hit the hardest is deeply concerning. The World Bank's educational global practice experts also warned that the effect of the coronavirus would have a serious long-term impact. The United States would not be exempt, they said. Although the United States spends more money on average on education than many other developed countries, our weak cultural valuing of teachers and schools in general would undermine our ability to collaborate to preserve education during the pandemic, said Andreas Schleicher, director for education and skills at the O.E.C.D. (Llana & Chu, 2020).

Was Schleicher's criticism fair? We know that at its inception and for much of its history, the United States fostered public education. Each state has a provision for it in its constitution, requiring that the state provide funding. But Derek Black, a law professor at the University of South Carolina, sees us shirking our responsibility toward public education to a greater degree than ever before. Writing during the pandemic, he insisted education should be the last place states should cut funding if the coronavirus crisis required cutbacks to services. Black quotes language from the Supreme Court decision *Brown v. Board of Education*, which states public education "is the most important function of state and local governments" and the "foundation of good citizenship" and "democratic society". According to Black, it is at our peril that we shortchange the institution through which we transmit our democratic and constitutional norms to our youth (Black, 2020, p. 257).

Because of our long history of racial and socioeconomic inequality, equal educational opportunity for all has remained beyond our grasp in the United States. Part of the reason we have failed, according to Douglas Downey, author of *How Schools Really Matter*, is that we don't measure progress accurately, which creates the impression that schools, rather than circumstances outside of school, are the problem. According to Downey, if we measured student progress seasonally, at the end of the school year and at the end of summer, we would get a more accurate picture. He and several others have done this, and their data points to schools being far more effective at helping children keep pace than what the general public believes (Downey, 2020).

Addressing Children's Needs Beyond School

School performance is affected by the quality of the environment beyond school. An environment with inadequate food, shelter, emotional support, and health care stymies a child's chances of overcoming learning deficits and achieving the kind of academic progress they deserve.

The harsh reality of the lives of disadvantaged children during the pandemic revealed the weaknesses in our social support system. For example, food insecurity tripled in the United States between March and May of 2020, and by October, over 40% of children were undernourished. Loss of jobs and inadequate federal benefits played a role. In addition, school closures meant millions of children were denied breakfasts and lunches, because they could not access their free or reduced-price meals when the school doors were closed. It is ironic that children were kept home to protect them from the pandemic, only for those in greatest need to suffer from hunger (Piser, 2021).

Prompted by the crisis of the coronavirus, millions of hungry children were aided when food assistance to families in need came to be increased through public funding. According to James P. Ziliak, expert on nutrition programs, the increase to SNAP benefits, formerly known as food stamps, represented a significant change. Not since the food stamp program was established in 1977 had we seen such a dramatic increase in food support (DeParle, 2021).

Besides the need for more support for children's physical health, kids in school also need robust mental health services to help them thrive. School psychologists can play a critical role in providing services which will lead to better academic performance as well as improved social-emotional outcomes. For them to become better recognized within their school communities as a mental health provider, school psychologists need to publicize the range of services they can offer and assume leadership in this effort (Splett et al., 2013). Recognizing this reality was one of the reasons I wrote this book.

Children also need a safe and healthful educational environment. That means their physical environment also must be well maintained. Many school buildings are substandard, with physical plants that haven't been updated in years. For example, modern ventilation systems must be provided to protect against the damage of pollutants, as well as a safeguard against viruses (Persico, 2021).

The basic responsibility of public schools, according to our tradition, is to teach all the nation's children to be literate so that in adulthood they will be equipped to vote and participate in civic government. For public schools to adequately prepare students for this responsibility, children must be physically and emotionally fit to take full advantage of what the school offers. Many of our children cannot, because of the disadvantaged circumstances under which they live.

Schools cannot fulfill their mission unless children come to them in reasonably good health and are able to concentrate, so they are ready to learn. We need commitment at the state and federal levels to provide a strong enough safety net so that all children are provided the basic needs of secure shelter, adequate nutrition, and timely medical care. Many organizations around the country are continually lobbying Congress to address these matters, believing good nutrition, health care, and housing should be considered basic rights for all Americans, particularly children. Whether or not we are amid a crisis like a pandemic, every child should feel protected and secure in the knowledge that not only their family, but their nation wants to take good care of them.

References

Allen, J. U., & Jernigan, D. B. (2020). The Asian flu: The H2N2 influenza outbreak (1957). In M. L. Issit (Ed.), *Opinions throughout history: Diseases & epidemics*. Grey House Publishing. Credo Reference.

Black, D. (2020). *School house burning: Public education and the assault on American democracy*. Public Affairs.

Cauchemez, S., Kerkhove, M., Archer, B., Cetron, M., Cowling, B., Grove, P., Hunt, D., Kojouharova, M., Kon, P., Ungchusak, K., Oshitani, H., Pugliese, A., Rizzo, C., Saour, G., Sunagawa, T., Uzicanin, A., Wachtel, C., Weisfuse, I., Yu, H., & Nicoll, A. (2014). School closures during the 2009 influenza pandemic: National and local experiences. *BMC Infectious Diseases, 14*, 207. https://doi.org/10.1186/1471-2334-14-207

Centers for Disease Control and Prevention. (n.d.-a). *1968 pandemic (H3N2 virus)*. www.cdc.gov/flu/pandemic-resources/1968-pandemic.html

Centers for Disease Control and Prevention. (n.d.-b). *2009 H1N1 pandemic timeline*. www.cdc.gov/flu/pandemic-resources/2009-pandemic-timeline.html

Centers for Disease Control and Prevention. (n.d.-c). https://www.cdc.gov/flu/pandemic-resources/2009-pandemic-timeline.html

DeParle, J. (2021, April 4). Biden effort to combat hunger marks a profound change. *The New York Times*. www.nytimes.com/2021/04/04/us/politics/biden-hunger-programs.html

Downey, D. (2020). *How schools really matter: Why our assumption about schools and inequality is mostly wrong*. University of Chicago Press.

European Commission. (2020, September 9). *Disinformation: EU assesses the Code of Practice and published platform reports on coronavirus related disinformation* [Press release]. https://ec.europa.eu/commission/presscorner/detail/en/mex_20_1601

Flanagan-Klygis, E. (2003). School vaccination laws. *Virtual Mentor, 5*(11), 386–388. https://doi.org/10.1001/virtualmentor.2003.5.11.pfor1-0311

Hill, H., Elam-Evans, L. D., Yankey, D., Singleton, J. A., & Kang, Y. (2018, October 12). Vaccination coverage among children aged 19–35 months—United States, 2017. *Centers for Disease Control and Prevention*. www.cdc.gov/mmwr/volumes/67/wr/mm6740a4.htm?s_cid=mm6740a4_e; www.cdc.gov/flu/pandemic-resources/1968-pandemic.html; www.cdc.gov/flu/pandemic-resources/2009-pandemic-timeline.html

Kelly, J. (2020, March 17). In 1957, a new flu appeared in Asia. The world watched and waited for it to spread. *The Washington Post.* www.washingtonpost.com/local/in-1957-a-new-flu-appeared-in-asia-the-world-watched-and-waited-for-it-to-spread/2020/03/17/9f5205b4–685f-11ea-b313-df458622c2cc_story.html

Klaiman, T., Draemer, J., & Stoto, M. (2011). Variability in school closure decisions in response to 2009 H1N1: A qualitative systems improvement analysis. *BMC Public Health, 11*, 73. https://doi.org/10.1186%2F1471-2458-11-73

Lewandowsky, S., Cook, J., Ecker, U. K. H., Albarracín, D., Amazeen, M. A., Kendeou, P., Lombardi, D., Newman, E. J., Pennycook, G., Porter, E., Rand, D. G., Rapp, D. N., Reifler, J., Roozenbeek, J., Schmid, P., Seifert, C. M., Sinatra, G. M., Swire-Thompson, B., van der Linden, S., Vraga, E. K., Wood, T. J., & Zaragoza, M. S. (2020). *The debunking handbook 2020. Databrary.* https://doi.org/10.17910/b7.1182

Llana, S., & Chu, L. (2020, December 3). Bars or schools? How nations rank education in pandemic priorities. *Christian Science Monitor.* www.csmonitor.com/USA/Education/2020/1203/Bars-or-schools-How-nations-rank-education-in-pandemic-priorities

Ostasiewich, A. (2020, November 23). Covid in North Dakota: One day inside a rural US hospital's fight. *BBC.* www.bbc.com/news/av/world-us-canada-55024447

Persico, C. (2021, May 19). Now is the time to invest in school infrastructure. *Brown Center Chalkboard.* www.brookings.edu/blog/brown-center-chalkboard/2021/05/19/now-is-the-time-to-invest-in-school-infrastructure/

Piser, K. (2021, February 19). How public schools became America's social safety net. *TheNation.* www.thenation.com/article/society/community-schools-coronavirus/

Pruitt, S. (2020). At height of the 1918 pandemic, NYC and Chicago schools stayed open. Here's why. *History.* www.history.com/news/spanish-flu-schools-new-york-chicago

Splett, J., Fowler, J., Weist, M., McDaniel, H., & Dvorsky, M. (2013). The critical role of school psychology in the school mental health movement. *Psychology in the Schools, 50*(3), 245–258. https://doi.org/10.1002/pits.21677

The Associated Press. (2009, May 5). Flu-related school closings spread to 24 states. *Education Week.* www.edweek.org/policy-politics/flu-related-school-closings-spread-to-24-states/2009/05

Chapter 13

The Health of Schools

Overview of Public Policy

In *The Vanishing Middle Class*, author Peter Temin observes that the current demise of public schools around the country coincides with an era of unprecedented wealth (Temin, 2017). How has this come to pass? A quick history of public policy toward schools in the United States reveals what has happened to schools over the past 40 years. At its inception as an independent nation, the United States deemed education to be a fundamental right. Our founding fathers, most notably Thomas Jefferson, John Adams, and James Madison, supported the notion that a democratic republic necessitated an educated populace. Otherwise, demagogues could manipulate the ignorant and subjugate them, destroying our republic. It was of paramount importance, therefore, that Americans be literate. Education had to be a fundamental right for all, and that required adequate funding (Black, 2020).

This was the prevalent attitude toward schooling during my education. But in the decades since I became an adult, the trend has been toward an ever-widening gap between the rich and the poor, with people of color overrepresented among the impoverished. Contemporary writers such as Robert Putnam, author of *Our Kids: The American Dream in Crisis*, echo this sentiment and warn against the danger to our society that comes from being so economically segregated, as we are now (Putnam, 2015).

For much of the last century, the federal government supported the expansion of services to children in school through vaccination and providing school meals. The goal was to keep kids healthy and in school, and providing such services achieved that end. Under President Ronald Reagan, however, funding for services delivered through public schools was drastically reduced. Since then, schools have been scrambling to continue to provide a safety net, but without the federal money they depended on. They have been put in the untenable position of being expected to deal with children's needs but denied the dollars necessary to fulfill the responsibility (Piser, 2021).

DOI:10.4324/9781003348344-13

With schools relying heavily on local funding derived from property taxes, districts with the highest need are invariably those with the weakest tax base. As a result, schools with the greatest number of children in need of social supports have the least ability to provide them. The pandemic required unforeseen investments such as laptops for distance learning and other emergency expenditures. The school districts that were already hurting financially were unable to do more when the need was greatest (Piser, 2021).

Besides economic segregation, at the time of our country's founding a great many people were excluded based on the color of their skin. It is a measure of how highly education was valued, however, that after the Civil War, rebel states were readmitted to the Union *only if* their state constitution guaranteed equal education as a fundamental right. This standard was undermined in short order after Reconstruction, because of racist attitudes. The case of *Plessy v. Ferguson* in 1896 established the "separate but equal" principle that legalized racial discrimination for decades to come (Black, 2020).

This was not the final word on educational rights. In 1954, half a century later, the U.S. Supreme Court ruled in *Brown v. Board of Education of Topeka* that separate was not equal. Then came the era of school desegregation in which I played a tiny role (Black, 2020). But now, in the third decade of the twenty-first century, our schools are as racially segregated as they were in 1968, despite hard-won legal precedents against it (Contreras, 2021).

Impact of Reduced Investment

These trends match the reduction in spending on public schools. In late 2017, The Center on Budget and Policy Priorities issued a report summarizing the shrinking public investment in public schools throughout the United States over a ten-year span. The authors caution that not restoring funds that have been cut not only risks reducing the quality of education we can offer our children but also means a loss of jobs and a negative impact on the economy (Leachman et al., 2017). And this advice was written before the pandemic appeared on the scene.

Concerned public policy makers have recognized the challenges public schools face and for decades have tried to improve the quality of public education but without increasing revenues. The charter school movement is an example. The idea originated in 1974 with Ray Budde, a professor of education from Massachusetts. He wanted states to grant charters for experimental programs in existing public schools. These programs would try to find the best ways to address the educational needs of children who were falling through the cracks in traditional public schools. The idea lay fallow until a decade later, after *A Nation at Risk: The Imperative for Education Reform* reported in 1983 that our public schools were not competitive on the world stage. This warning motivated leadership to find ways to dramatically raise academic achievement. In 1991, Minnesota was the first state in the nation to pass a charter law. In 2017, only seven states, all rural, did not allow charter schools. Over time, enough charters were granted so that we now have a parallel system of education financed with school dollars (Jason, 2017).

And therein lies the rub. Traditional school districts have come to resent the loss of revenue from declining enrollment that charter schools have imposed on them, to the point that the controversy has risen to the level of a polarized battle. The titles of books and articles addressing the situation are very telling; for example, *Charter Schools and Their Enemies*, by Thomas Sowell, defends charter schools because of their success with children of color who were failing in traditional public schools (Sowell, 2020). On the other side of the argument, *A Wolf at the Schoolhouse Door* by Jack Schneider and Jennifer Berkshire warns of charter schools being used by profit seekers to make money at the public expense, with little oversight. They reported that there were over 7,400 charter schools nationwide: some very successful and deserving respect—others not (Schneider & Berkshire, 2020).

An overview of school spending provided by the U.S. Census Bureau for the 2020 fiscal year indicated the amount the United States spent per pupil for public elementary and secondary education increased by 3.4% to $12,612 per pupil in 2018, compared to $12,201 per pupil in 2017. In 2018, public elementary and secondary education revenue, from all sources, amounted to $720.9 billion, up 3.8% from $694.2 billion in 2017 (United States Census Bureau, 2020). At first glance, one might conclude all public schools have more resources than ever. But this is not the case, because schools are not funded equitably. Why aren't they?

How much money is available through local property taxes determines to a great extent what resources are available for local schools. The rich can afford to pay higher taxes than the poor, so wealthy communities can provide fully adequate facilities and learning opportunities, and impoverished communities cannot. The situation has become so extreme in the state of Delaware, for example, that a retired chief justice of the state Supreme Court accused leaders of ignoring their "moral duty". "Kids who have less need more", he said (Dobo, 2019).

Effects on Rural Schools

In my part of rural America, schools have always been affected by public policy affecting farms. The beginning of my school psychology career coincided with the farm crisis of the 1980s, and school psychology itinerants watched school populations dwindle in what seemed like an inexorable process. Schools closed as districts consolidate to survive. Now we see the effects of climate change, with drought drastically affecting the ability to raise cattle and grow crops. We have reached a point where many small towns need an economic boost so people will be able to remain in them, or they must attract people from larger areas to move there so the economic base can expand and schools can be supported.

With larger towns and cities providing better schools and healthier communities, the future of the small rural community school looks bleak. Because property taxes provide a significant portion for local school funding, the current farm situation bodes ill for rural schools. Since farmers own most of the land in rural districts, a lot of funding that is used to pay for school expenses depends on taxes that they pay. But farmers fearing the loss of their land cannot afford to vote in favor of a new school bond. This means referendums to raise money can stand a good chance of failing. But there are efforts to balance this tax responsibility. The state of Minnesota, for example, created a tax credit from the state government to farm owners who pay taxes for school bonds. The result has been an increase in the passing of local bonds, a welcome change (Gunderson, 2019).

Mark Joseph, in his article about the education crisis in rural areas, points out that most of the people lacking a high school diploma live in rural areas. At the same time, the number of rural students is more than the combined number of students attending the 20 largest urban school districts. As the economic vitality of rural communities shrinks, they cannot provide career opportunities for their young people. Youth leave for economic opportunity in cities, creating a "brain drain" in rural parts of the country (Joseph, 2017).

A Distributive Justice Failure

This is a failure of distributive justice. For educational opportunity to be equitable, funding must be. Cutbacks since the recession of 2008 have cost many schools highly qualified teachers, safe buildings, strong pre-schools and kindergartens and other necessary resources that combine to make a good school.

In recent years, funding for education has become a topic of hot debate. Those who support school choice would like to see the per pupil funding that goes to public school districts be available to go to parents who want to choose a different educational setting, whether it be a private school or their own home. Parents in neighborhoods with deficient schools understandably welcome the freedom to send their children to a better educational setting. For-profit schools like the idea, and in several states, funds have been diverted from public schools to private institutions. This is an international trend, not unique to the United States. Several countries worldwide have embraced the neoliberal idea that free market principles can be effectively applied to schools to increase learning. The results overall appear to be benefiting the affluent while increasing the opportunity gap (Sahlberg, 2021).

Researchers report that in many instances what we've got as a result is a loss in learning, demoralized teachers—to the point that many are leaving the profession—and opportunities for self-interested entities to gain profit. In the opinion of some experts on education in the United States, public schools have been blamed and punished for society's ills, and we are not adequately facing up to the actual causes (Black, 2020). Because of the added economic pressure of the pandemic, school budgets were under threat of being reduced even further (Turner, 2021).

Pandemic Support to Schools

Beginning in 2020 and continuing into 2021, Congress passed pandemic assistance legislation that gave K–12 schools funds to address the cost of the pandemic. This came in the form of $13 billion from the C.A.R.E.S. Act passed in the spring of 2020, $54 billion more passed that December in follow-up legislation, and $122 billion as part of the American Rescue Plan, in March of 2021. These funds were distributed according to a formula that gave preference to high-need districts, with qualifying schools getting approximately $2,400 per student (Turner, 2021).

The School Superintendents Association surveyed 400 school administrators to find out what schools invested in besides necessary Covid-19-related needs. The survey found that money was being directed toward financing summer school, high-intensity tutoring, adding specialized staff, such as counselors, social workers, and reading specialists; technology; particularly to purchase devices and provide connectivity to students, social-emotional learning, and/or trauma-informed instruction for educators, and renovating old or building new buildings. One possible shortcoming is that Congress mandated a shorter timeline for spending than school leaders like. The funds are supposed to be used by late 2024, a deadline that school leaders would like to see extended to ensure building projects can be completed (Turner, 2021).

Georgetown University scholar Marguerite Roza commented that the American Rescue Plan is "the largest one-time federal investment in public education in this country" (Turner, 2021).

This infusion of support can have positive consequences that can go far beyond coping with the pandemic. The crisis has shown us how much families rely on schools to provide education for their children and structure in their lives, and political leadership has acted in response. It is heartening that the needs of public schools are beginning to be recognized and addressed, but much more needs to be done to restore public education to where it deserves to be.

With the right resources, schools can provide the services needed to help mitigate the destructive impact of traumatic events on kids. Because of the pandemic, our youngest generation experienced a crisis with a deep and long-lasting impact. Suicides rose; for example, Clark County School District in Nevada which serves over 300,000 students, reported 19 student suicides in 2021, more than double that of the previous year. Officials viewed school reopening as a way to lessen caustic stress on young people (Stuart & Asmelash, 2021).

On an encouraging note, early in the pandemic the Centers for Disease Control and Prevention reported that schools didn't appear to be responsible for the widespread of the virus, and so lent hope for the possibility of a safe return to school (Centers for Disease Control and Prevention, 2021). An article in the *Christian Science Monitor* noted that to do so would require communities to act to limit the spread in other ways, such as foregoing eating meals in restaurants. The authors questioned whether the United States would be willing to sacrifice for its schools (Llana & Chu, 2020).

With enough political will on a broad scale, we can address the weaknesses in our social safety net that the coronavirus revealed, with particular attention to those affecting children and the schools they depend on for their future. The U.S.D.A. extension through the 2021–2022 school year of universal free meals in school was an important step in the right direction (U.S. Department of Agriculture, 2021). This action and many more are necessary to meet the needs of our nation's children. I wonder what lessons they will have learned from their pandemic experience. I hope they will have good reason to report that schools helped them face their losses and rebuild their hope for the future. We cannot leave their future to luck, however. Concerned citizens must insist that elected officials provide the resources the next generation needs to thrive.

References

Black, D. (2020). *School house burning: Public education and the assault on American democracy.* PublicAffairs.

Centers for Disease Control and Prevention. (2021, February 12). *Science brief: Transmission of SARS-CoV-2 in K-12 schools.* www.cdc.gov/coronavirus/2019-ncov/science/science-briefs/transmission_k_12_schools.html

Contreras, R. (2021, January 13). The resegregating (and diversifying) of U.S. schools. *Axios.* www.axios.com/2021/01/13/schools-segregation-increasing

Dobo, N. (2019, December 19). "Kids who have less, need more": The fight over school funding. *The Hechinger Report.* https://hechingerreport.org/kids-who-have-less-need-more-the-fight-over-school-funding/

Gunderson, D. (2019, November 3). New tax credit for ag land might help rural Minn schools. *The Grand Forks Herald*, B5.

Jason, Z. (2017). The battle over charter schools. *Harvard Ed. Magazine.* www.gse. harvard.edu/news/ed/17/05/battle-over-charter-schools

Joseph, M. (2017, June 1). Crisis in rural American education. *HuffPost.* www.huffpost. com/entry/crisis-in-rural-american-education_b_59305c2ce4b09e93d7964875

Leachman, M., Masterson, K., & Figueroa, E. (2017, November 29). A punishing decade for school funding. *Center on Budget and Policy Priorities.* www.cbpp.org/ research/state-budget-and-tax/a-punishing-decade-for-school-funding

Llana, S., & Chu, L. (2020, December 3). Bars or schools? How nations rank education in pandemic priorities. *Christian Science Monitor.* www.csmonitor.com/ USA/Education/2020/1203/Bars-or-schools-How-nations-rank-education-in-pandemic-priorities

Piser, K. (2021, February 19). How public schools became America's social safety net. *TheNation.*www.thenation.com/article/society/community-schools-coronavirus/

Putnam, R. (2015). *Our kids: The American dream in crisis.* Simon & Schuster.

Sahlberg, P. (2021). *Finnish lessons 3.0: What can the world learn from educational change in Finland?* Teachers College Press.

Schneider, J., & Berkshire, J. (2020). *A wolf at the schoolhouse door: The dismantling of public education and the future of school.* The New Press.

Sowell, T. (2020). *Charter schools and their enemies.* Basic Books.

Stuart, E., & Asmelash, L. (2021, January 26). A rise in student suicides has pushed the 5th largest US school district to speed up a return to in-person learning. *CNN.* www.cnn.com/2021/01/26/us/clark-county-school-district-covid-suicide-trnd/index.html

Temin, P. (2017). *The vanishing middle class: Prejudice and power in a dual economy.* The MIT Press.

Turner, C. (2021, September 1). Schools are getting billions in COVID relief money. Here's how they plan to spend it. *NPR.* www.npr.org/2021/09/01/1033213936/ survey-school-superintendents-federal-covid-relief-money-spendingapproved

United States Census Bureau. (2020, May 11). *Spending per pupil increased for sixth consecutive year* [Press release]. www.census.gov/newsroom/press-releases/2020/school-system-finances.html

U.S. Department of Agriculture. (2021, April 20). *USDA issues pandemic flexibilities for schools and day care facilities through June 2022 to support safe reopening and healthy, nutritious meals* [Press release]. www.usda.gov/media/press-releases/2021/04/20/ usda-issues-pandemic-flexibilities-schools-and-day-care-facilities

Chapter 14

Speaking Up
Civic Action Through Lobbying Elected Officials

Over the course of my career as a school psychologist, I engaged in only two civic advocacy actions intended to influence policy governing schools: I wrote a letter to the editor supporting the elimination of corporal punishment, and I wrote a letter to my state legislator on the same topic. A law forbidding corporal punishment in Minnesota schools was passed shortly thereafter. My state school psychology association had a lobbyist at the state legislature, and I knew my director of special education cultivated relationships with elected officials and would on occasion make the 630-mile round trip to St. Paul and back in support of special education legislation. NASP tended to business at the federal level. So far as I could see, they had politics covered.

At least for a while, my career spanned what seemed like an optimistic era for special education. Programs were being put into place and expanded. The fact that school psychologists were coming to be considered a necessary part of a school community felt like a victory; federal and state laws sanctioned my presence, and more and more young school psychologists were joining our ranks.

As highlighted in the previous chapter, the past few decades have become increasingly less hopeful for public education. Then Covid-19 entered the picture, and the need to respond to the crisis created by the coronavirus meant a new phase in national politics. The weaknesses the pandemic exposed in our public-school systems showed the necessity to create positive change. It was time for political leaders to rise to the challenge.

It was also time for concerned citizens to step forward. By then I had already been retired for a few years, and I had aligned myself with an advocacy organization through which I lobbied Congress. Once I no longer had day-to-day experience in schools, I felt it would make sense for me to focus on public policy. On the recommendation of a retired teacher/attorney, I joined RESULTS, a nonpartisan organization which works to eradicate poverty, both domestically and globally. I liked that the broad issues RESULTS addresses often affect how well children can perform in school, and so support educational aims, whether directly or indirectly.

DOI:10.4324/9781003348344-14

What Is RESULTS?

The list of accomplishments RESULTS can claim is impressive. In the recent past, RESULTS was a strong influence in the fight to keep the Affordable Care Act (A.C.A.). RESULTS has worked very hard to protect SNAP, otherwise known as food stamps. RESULTS also went to bat for C.H.I.P., the Children's Health Insurance Program, when its funding was in jeopardy. On the Fourth of July in 2017, a *New York Times* article about civic action referred to RESULTS as "one of America's best kept secrets" (Bornstein, 2017).

Beginning in someone's living room in 1980, the organization now conducts two campaigns, one global and one domestic. There are volunteers in all 50 states in the United States, as well as chapters in 20 other countries. For 2019, 2020, and 2021, for example, the main domestic campaign addressed the issue of affordable housing, and the global campaign focused on the coronavirus and treating tuberculosis worldwide, as well as public education, particularly for girls.

As I learned early on, schools are shaped by politics. What does or does not happen depends on the strength of the political will exercised by governing bodies. Civic action is one avenue available to us to influence those making critical decisions. After spending a few years developing my advocacy skills through RESULTS, I realized I wanted to also apply them on behalf of school psychology. I began by informing the Minnesota School Psychology Association's (M.S.P.A.) legislative committee that RESULTS was willing to provide educational webinars about advocacy that might be useful to them. I was delighted when they accepted the offer.

As time passes, I am becoming more and more convinced that it is essential for school psychologists en masse to insist on a chair at the political table. I fear our profession may cease to exist if we don't, thanks to funding shortages. I wonder if recruiting new retirees at both the state and national levels wouldn't be an effective way to advance the cause. They have a lifetime of stories to tell, and finally have the time to tell them. With the proper training, these experienced people could form a veritable advocacy army. Furthermore, becoming an advocate to support school psychology could bring deep meaning to the next phase of their life.

NASP's Public Policy Institute

As Hahrie Han, political scientist, explains, it is useful to join an organization that teaches you how to be an advocate. She calls it "transformational organizing" when an organization invests in developing the activist's capacity to act, which then creates a heightened sense of personal agency, and clarifies a sense of purpose (Han, 2014). To be effective, organizations must thoroughly educate their members. This will enhance the members' knowledge and personal confidence, which can then be aimed toward a particular goal.

The National Association of School Psychologists responded to this need in 2010 when it created the Public Policy Institute (P.P.I.) in conjunction with George Washington University. The P.P.I. is a function of NASP.'s Government and Professional Relations Committee, which from its inception has covered public policy and advocacy. Through the Public Policy Institute, school psychologists and other people in education-related fields, as well as graduate students, can go to Washington, D.C., to learn about public policy and how it affects the lives of students in school. In the years since it began, the institute has increased its emphasis on advocacy, including the very important skill of conducting conversations with legislators (National Association of School Psychologists, n.d.).

NASP created a framework for action that defines what legislative aims need to be addressed for each legislative session. For example, their *Federal Policy and Legislative Platform* for the 117th Congress includes seven broad goals, along with specific recommendations for each of them. The goals address personnel shortages, ways to ensure that outcomes for all students will be equitable, that the environments they live and learn in are supportive for everyone, that students with disabilities will have improved outcomes, school safety and crisis response will be comprehensive and evidence-based, mental and behavioral health services in school will become more accessible, and M.T.S.S. will be accessible for all students (National Association of School Psychologists, 2020).

Through the Virtual Advocacy Academy attendees learn the components of advocacy. I find it interesting that the process sounds remarkably like what school psychologists do on a small scale in their day-to-day practice at school. Advocates have to build strategic relationships, communicate using evidence to support one's position, which may include providing data, and share stories. They have to speak with those in power and approach them in a timely manner. All of these aspects of advocacy are not new to a practicing school psychologist.

The NASP website provides a treasure trove of pertinent governmental and policy information and guidance for advocates on the local, state, and national levels. The Government and Professional Relations (G.P.R.) Committee members provide guidance for local and state advocacy, and NASP G.P.R. staff cover Congressional action. We are fortunate to have highly qualified people serving as the NASP director of Policy and Advocacy, the director of Professional Policy and Practice, and the NASP manager of Policy and Advocacy as well as the members of the Government and Public Relations Committee to guide us. For example, Becca Murdoch, NASP manager, Policy and Advocacy, noted that almost 3,000 letters were sent to members of Congress from school psychologists across the nation during the 2022 NASP convention. They were in addition to the 700 that were sent in January and February before the convention (Murdoch, 2022).

Such an avalanche of advocacy does not go unnoticed. On March 11, 2022, President Laurie Klose sent a message to NASP membership announcing that $111 million in federal support for the current fiscal year for state and local educational agencies (S.E.A.s and L.E.A.s) efforts has been accomplished, which will increase the number of school psychologists and other school-employed mental health professionals that can be hired. She goes on to say that we will continue to press for funding such that every L.E.A. is able to have one school psychologist for every 500 students (L. Klose, personal communication, March 11, 2022). The lesson I take from this is, never dream small, even though progress may be incremental.

Thanks to NASP's online Public Policy Institute held in the summer of 2021, I was able to benefit from formal instruction on how to conduct conversations with my elected officials in Washington, D.C., about school psychology concerns. When I took NASP's online class on grassroots advocacy I saw that the guidelines NASP taught matched what I had been learning from RESULTS. RESULTS aligns well with NASP, because both organizations teach the nuts and bolts of advocacy while addressing issues that affect children and promoting racial and social equity.

More About RESULTS

RESULTS' name is an acronym. It stands for "Responsibility for Ending Starvation Using Legislation Trimtabbing and Support". (No wonder that RESULTS dropped the full name in favor of the acronym. But it was a useful beginning.) The organization was formed in 1980 by Sam Daley-Harris, a former music teacher and percussionist for the Miami Philharmonic. At its outset, RESULTS focused on building political will to eradicate hunger globally. Over time the emphasis has broadened to eradicating poverty, viewing hunger as one symptom of it, and has expanded to addressing poverty domestically, here in the United States (Daley-Harris, 2013).

The key letter in RESULTS is the letter *T*, which stands for trim tabbing, in reference to a miniature rudder that is used to help turn a big rudder on a large ship. It's small but has a huge influence. Likewise, a RESULTS volunteers can nudge the ship of state, creating change through individual action. As Natasha astutely observed, "Much like special education services" (N. Olson, personal communication, October 17, 2021).

So how does RESULTS shape its volunteers into trimtabs? By ongoing mentoring of each volunteer in advocacy skills such as letter writing, laser speeches, community outreach, and building relationships with elected officials, combined with monthly informational webinars and conference calls about current issues. Progress is incremental much of the time. But like a trimtab turning the direction of a ship, the efforts of a civic action volunteer can help to shift the direction of our ship of state. When adequately trained and following a systematic plan, one person can have more influence than one might think, and a whole lot of people joining together can achieve a great deal.

I began my association with RESULTS by taking a few tentative steps. I looked over their website (results.org) and listened in on a RESULTS conference call at the invitation of a friend, a retired teacher and former attorney, who was already a member. From there I started attending their informational online webinars once a month. After getting a close-up view of how the organization worked, what it offered its volunteers, and what was expected of them, I decided to join.

Due to my membership in RESULTS, I have been able to focus my attention on a few pieces of legislation and support them under the guidance of experienced advocates. Like NSAP, RESULTS focuses on outcomes and works through established channels to achieve specified goals.

Planning One's Advocacy

We know that wishing as well as hoping is insufficient to accomplish a goal. That's why RESULTS helps its members construct a personal yearly plan of action so volunteers can easily monitor themselves. This plan is not hard and fast; it is a guide to follow that can be changed as circumstances dictate. For example, my plan usually includes writing a letter to my local newspaper at a rate of about once every two months. I may write more, and I may write fewer, depending on my specific circumstances. Each year I try to learn something new. For example, this year I have been studying how to partner with allied organizations in my state. Knowing I have a plan helps to keep me on track, so I can measure progress.

The Importance of Relationship

RESULTS teaches its volunteers a range of skills which can be applied to influencing Congress to pass legislation. Key to their success, however, is that RESULTS recognizes that having specific skills for individual tasks is not enough to achieve lasting results. Relationships, combined with effective advocacy skills, are what count. We learn how to build productive relationships with elected officials, the media, members of other nonprofits sharing similar concerns, the people whose cause we are representing, and other volunteers. This emphasis on relationship is key to RESULTS' success.

Current research on building a constituency affirms the RESULTS approach. Hahrie Han, along with Elizabeth McKenna and Michelle Oyakawa, analyzed the essential components of effective grassroots organizations. Their research indicates that leadership has to be strategic; that is, it has to be "simultaneously top down and bottom up, with power distributed so that constituents develop strategic independence, yet centralized enough that the constituents' decentralized leadership can be brought into a negotiation for power" (Han et al., 2021). And they emphasize that this kind of leadership occurs through respectful relationships.

I find these ideas compatible with my training and experience as a school psychologist, and with the advocacy guidance NASP provides its members. Like school psychologists, RESULTS volunteers work with others to achieve mutually agreed-on ends. RESULTS members come from a wide variety of diverse backgrounds, so we not only bond with those of a similar demographic but learn to bridge with those who are not, just like members of a school community need to do.

Both RESULTS and NASP have offered training in motivational interviewing (M.I.) to its members, to enhance our ability to engage effectively with those with whom we need to find common ground and perhaps influence. M.I. is used in therapeutic relationships to help a counselee overcome their ambivalence toward change, such as in addiction counseling. When applied to political policy, it can be a tool to encourage one's political representative to shift position to one closer to what you favor. At the very least, it encourages empathic listening.

Both NASP and RESULTS coach volunteers on how to conduct a conversation with elected officials and their staff. We learn the practical skills of how to set up meetings and how to make our points in the presence of our elected leaders. Ideally, over time one establishes a cordial relationship with officials that transcends a particular issue. In that way, a volunteer can become a trusted resource. Rather than viewing Congress people as potential adversaries, they are viewed as decision-makers who need the best information available to decide wisely. A good advocate shows respect to everyone, regardless of whether they are an ally on every point. Through persistence, a volunteer can gain influence.

RESULTS also concerns itself with the relationship its volunteers have with the people they are trying to represent. For example, RESULTS educates people like me (a retired White person) on how to be true allies of people living in poverty, rather than would-be saviors. We also examine political forces underlying the causes of poverty. This includes, for example, the construct of race and its implications for public policy. Here again, NASP and RESULTS align well.

RESULTS provides guidance on many topics related to citizen action, often with step-by-step advice, such as how to write an effective letter to the editor or how to approach an elected official about an issue. If you are planning a meeting with a member of Congress, RESULTS will coach you as to how to proceed. And on that note, RESULTS, like NASP, hosts a conference every summer that culminates with attendees visiting their Congressional delegation on Capitol Hill, or, as the case was in 2020, a virtual conference with meetings on ZOOM calls.

Useful Skills

Having more tools in one's advocacy toolbox can't hurt, whether they are used in day-to-day work at school or on Capitol Hill. For example, a letter to the editor can influence people in leadership positions because it serves a dual role: It is both a public statement to the readership and a message to one's Congressional delegation.

The approach RESULTS teaches is to begin the letter with a hook, an attention-grabbing statement. For example, it might be a reference to a piece of news recently reported in the paper or a startling statistic. This serves as a segue to the middle part of the letter, which provides the main content. The final paragraph is a call to action, where one asks one's Congressional delegation to support specific legislation.

To write efficiently, RESULTS recommends composing the letter backward, by writing the final paragraph first. That way you have clearly in mind what the goal of the letter is. Then write the midsection, which builds your case in support of the request being made in the final paragraph. Finally, compose a hook that will draw your readers in and capture their attention.

After I have a letter published, I then email a copy of it or send a link to each of my members of Congress, reiterating that I hope they will support the legislation I advocated for in the letter. Elected officials want to know what their constituents are thinking, and they know that if one person has written a letter stating a particular point of view, there may be others who are thinking the same thing. Just because your local paper may not be widely read by the general public doesn't mean your Congressional delegation isn't paying close attention.

Besides writing letters, I also call or write my Congressional delegation to give my opinion about a particular bill that is to be voted on. I am as respectful as I would be in a meeting at school because my intention is to build relationships, besides asking for support for a particular policy. Before long, I will return to lobby for another issue. I draw my strength from my fellow civic advocates, knowing that together we can achieve what I believe are good ends. I have seen that our persistence can, and often will, pay off.

When the Senate was deciding how or whether it would respond with further funding during the coronavirus pandemic in the summer of

2020, I emailed the chief deputy officer to my senators with whom I had spoken several times in the past. I recommended support for funding of school psychology positions in the schools as part of a relief package. I received an instant reply, saying he would be sure the senator saw my letter. His quick, supportive answer encouraged me, reinforcing the value of building relationships with Congressional personnel.

Giving a Laser Talk

Besides letters to the editor, another way to influence a decision-maker is through a laser talk. A laser talk is a brief—no longer than two minutes—but compelling statement on a specific topic, akin to an elevator speech. RESULTS uses the acronym, **EPIC**, to shape a laser talk. The letters stand for: **E**NGAGE by stating the **P**ROBLEM, **I**NFORM or **I**LLUSTRATE what the solution might be, and ending with a **C**ALL to action. This is one of the most important tools an advocate can use.

The laser talk is useful in a phone conversation and in person with a legislator in a town hall meeting or other brief encounter. An example follows.

ENGAGE YOUR AUDIENCE

Make a one-sentence statement to engage your listener.

In Grand Forks, we have over 2,000 students in our public schools who qualify for free and reduced lunch, and 122 children in our city meet the criteria for homelessness. These children are expected to perform in school amid relentless stress.

STATE THE PROBLEM

Identify the cause(s) of the problem. How serious is it?

Besides providing adequate food and housing, we also need to provide mental health support services in school to help children cope. At present, however, our schools are understaffed. For example, our local special education director reported that she only has funds to cover 7 school psychology positions, when there should be 16.

INFORM ABOUT SOLUTIONS

The Grand Forks School District requires better funding to fill mental health positions. Fortunately, there is legislation being developed to address this need. The Increasing Access to Mental Health in Schools Act would address the lack of staff.

CALL TO ACTION

Present a question that can be answered in yes or no, so you can come back later and follow up to see if your listener has taken the action you desire. "Will you vote in favor the Increasing Access to Mental Health in Schools Act?"

The laser talk format is the backbone of RESULTS' advocacy work because it provides an efficient and effective means to communicate essential information. If you are one of their volunteers, they will provide live practice by phone, so you can rehearse your talk before you attend a meeting.

Building Partnerships

Another aspect of building political strength through relationship is creating partnerships with like-minded groups. School psychologists have a host of fellow travelers to collaborate and cooperate with. The list is long: school social workers, school counselors, clinical psychologists, physical therapists, occupational therapists, speech/language clinicians, special education and regular education teachers, directors of special education, school administrators, pediatricians, parents, and more. Over the winter of 2021–2022, the Minnesota School Psychology Association legislative committee, for example, reached out to several other organizations representing other support staff in the schools such as school social workers, school counselors, and school nurses. They now collaborate to address forthcoming bills in the state legislature that would affect the well-being of children, families, school communities, and the future of our professions.

RESULTS teaches its members to partner with others, because joining together can make us more effective than going it alone. RESULTS even provides direct assistance to potential partners by teaching them advocacy skills. For example, in the summer and fall of 2020 and spring of 2021, Jos Linn, grassroots coordinator, created four instructional webinars upon my request, to share with the M.S.P.A. legislative committee.

The first webinar presented an introduction to advocacy that was shared with school psychologists across Minnesota, Wisconsin, and North Dakota, and the second addressed collaboration with like-minded organizations and was shared with the legislative committee. Then Jos followed up in the fall with a third webinar addressing advocacy during an election season. The fourth combined elements of advocacy skills with emphasis on telling your own story and understanding why an issue matters to you. Such instruction boosts the likelihood that advocacy will have a greater impact.

Where We Are

The good news for school psychologists is that we have a solid knowledge base to address the problems that beset our schools. We know that a nurturing environment achieves far and away better results than punishment does. We are rapidly coming to better understand child neuropsychology and the effects of generational and other forms of trauma. How kids best can learn and what schools can do to support physical and emotional health are fundamental to our training. We know how to prevent avoidable crises and how to organize and prepare ourselves for the unavoidable. We understand what standards we need to follow to achieve equitable treatment of all children in our schools. At this point, however, our know-how and understanding far exceed our means to remedy.

Political leadership over the past several decades has not adequately addressed the fate of impoverished children growing up without the educational advantages necessary to lead healthy, productive lives and participate fully in the democratic process. Public schools in the United States were created to educate the population so we could maintain a representational democracy. How fitting if school districts became models of participatory democracy, creating opportunities for the public to engage in identifying community needs and approaches to meeting them. All levels of our government need to address the underlying factors which undermine education. Achieving this end will require the deliberate and concerted effort of determined citizens.

As the Public Policy Institute instructors emphasize, school psychology practitioners get advocacy experience all the time, whether they realize it or not. For example, consider that school psychologists continually meet with all kinds of people and find common ground through respectful listening and careful questioning. They get constant practice translating technical language into lay language while presenting their perspective to parents or school personnel. They regularly collaborate with other school personnel to achieve mutual goals. Further, they gain deep insight from observing what is happening in and to our schools and its impact on children and families, which can be applied to evaluating public policy. Add on their knowledge of child development and how children are affected by inadequate housing, poor nutrition, and other environmental deficits common to many. Round it off with the dedication to kids and educational rights a school psychologist brings to their work, and potentially, what we have before us is a passionate, knowledgeable advocate.

As a currently practicing school psychologist, Natasha is acutely aware that at times it is necessary to advocate for one's role at one's workplace.

For example, she counsels some students who are not on an individualized education plan (I.E.P.) to help prevent their having to be on one. From a Response to Intervention perspective, prevention is best practice. But there can also be pressure to serve only kids already on I.E.P.s, because school psychologists fall under special education funding. It's worthwhile having more tools in one's advocacy toolbox, whether they are used day to day at school or on Capitol Hill. Pleading on behalf of children in need is basic to the work of school psychologists. Shouldn't it be easy to go from pleading on behalf of one child to asking on behalf of all children?

Building Courage

The reality is that the challenge of taking that short step can be more difficult than it might appear. Besides having to learn civic advocacy skills, one must also develop the courage to speak up in public to address leadership on Capitol Hill. School psychologists get a lot of practice speaking up in meetings, but it's usually on their own turf. Consequently, this seemingly small step can feel like it spans a deep chasm.

Despite my years of experience in schools developing the diplomacy needed to handle encounters with all kinds of people, lobbying was unnerving in the beginning. I kept asking myself why this should be. I have concluded it's because school psychology advocacy is usually performed amid colleagues who respect our training and who usually share our perspective. There can be occasions when one must face opposition, but typically that happens infrequently, and one often has a law to cite to settle a conflict.

The political realm is a far different environment. When we are talking with legislators, we are engaging with those who make the laws. The reason we are speaking with them is because a law governing our concern has not yet been enacted. Our senator or representative's vote can be the deciding factor in determining whether the conditions people live under are improved or made worse. By casting a vote, they can, for example, determine whether children receive the food, shelter, education, and medical care they need. Consequently, the stakes are very high. We can cast our vote at election time, but they hold the purse strings to governmental spending. As officeholders, they wield far more power than we do.

Furthermore, the mystique of Capitol Hill in Washington, D.C., or even a state capitol is intimidating, all by itself. The friend who invited me to join RESULTS admitted she also felt like I did at first, even with her years as an attorney, arguing in front of judges in courtrooms. I think it's because we are acutely aware that legislatures are where the course of our nation's history is often determined. The consequence of our potential failure is sobering, and we do not want to face the discouragement that would come from a disappointing outcome.

My antidote to this anxiety is to remind myself that a constituent has every right to be a part of the conversation; voters can and should insist on being heard. Like becoming a school psychologist, growing as an advocate requires getting one's impostor syndrome under control. We must shift our focus from the power of those in authority to what insight and expertise we can bring to influence the decisions authorities must make. We also must convince ourselves that trying and failing is better than not trying at all, because progress is cumulative, through increments. Understandably, it can take a while to become comfortable performing in this new role.

Most legislators, whether state or federal, want to please their constituents and do not cast a voter aside lightly. Legislative staff are expected to be cordial and polite to voters, whether they favor the legislator's position on a particular issue. It is the exception, rather than the rule, that advocates are ignored or treated rudely. In the best of circumstances, a school psychologist may become a useful resource to their legislators by providing evidence-based recommendations to help them make wise decisions.

Nevertheless, as with any new skill, becoming comfortable with civic advocacy requires practice to build endurance. It gradually gets easier as one develops friendly relationships with Congressional or state legislative offices. Anxiety is only overcome by building experience.

The process can even become enjoyable, as experienced advocates claim. Like other school personnel, school psychologists advocating for kids have a particular advantage, which should not be underestimated. We have firsthand stories about children and schools to share with elected officials, and there is nothing that impresses politicians more than a story that effectively illustrates your point. As Jos Linn, grassroots coordinator at RESULTS, is quick to point out, facts make us credible, but stories make us memorable. Also, people in Washington appreciate conversations with advocates who are pleading on behalf of a worthy cause. More than one staff person has thanked me for my efforts.

Strength in Numbers

Joining with others makes advocating easier. The Public Policy Institute concludes with meetings with Congressional offices to present our requests (or "asks" in advocacy jargon) concerning upcoming legislation. Attendees from each state approach their senators and representatives as a group, so there is strength in numbers. When I participated, our North Dakota school psychologists were given a warm reception by staff people who expressed deep interest and concern from the beginning of the conversation.

School psychologists can develop a habit of contacting our elected officials to share what school psychologists have to offer and our expertise about what children need. Fortitude comes with having the experience firsthand on a regular basis. For my own part, I have found that joining the ranks of fellow citizens who feel strongly enough to do the work of advocacy can be deeply rewarding. With the expert guidance that NASP and other organizations such as RESULTS generously provide, public advocacy is becoming more possible than ever before.

However small or large your commitment to civic advocacy may be, it is never too early or too late to start. Taking advantage of ongoing instruction and proceeding in manageable, incremental steps will build the confidence to speak up in support of legislation that you favor. Also remember that any action, however inconsequential it may seem, can have an impact beyond what you expect, and just may contribute toward creating important public policy.

When positive change seems out of reach, let's remember Judy Heumann's observation based on the perspective she gained while being the head of the Office of Special Education and Rehabilitation Services. Like the rest of us, Heumann didn't like that change doesn't occur as rapidly as we would like. It often happens painfully slowly at first, gains some momentum, and then, perhaps surprising us, the tide turns, and what we wish for happens (Heumann, 2020).

References

Bornstein, D. (2017, July 4). Putting citizenship back in Congress. *The New York Times*. www.nytimes.com/2017/07/04/opinion/putting-citizenship-back-in-congress. html

Daley-Harris, S. (2013). *Reclaiming our democracy: Healing the break between people and government*. Camino Books.

Han, H. (2014). *How organizations develop activists: Civic associations & leadership in the 21st century*. Oxford University Press.

Han, H., McKenna, E., & Oyakawa, M. (2021), *Prisms of the people, power and organizing in twenty-first century America*. The University of Chicago Press.

Heumann, J. (2020). *Being Heumann: An unrepentant memoir of a disability rights activist*. Beacon Press.

Murdoch, B. (2022, March 2). Advocacy during the NASP 2022 annual convention. *National Association of School Psychologists*. www.nasponline.org/ research-and-policy/policy-matters-blog/advocacy-during-the-nasp-2022-annual-convention

National Association of School Psychologists. (2020). *Federal public policy and legislative platform*. www.nasponline.org/research-and-policy/policy-priorities/ nasp-policy-platform

National Association of School Psychologists. (n.d.). *Research and policy*. www. nasponline.org/research-and-policy

Chapter 15

Adversary or Ally
Working With Administrators

To be effective as a school psychologist, one must have the backing of those who wield power in our school communities. Consequently, how well we work with our school principals and superintendents directly affects our ability to perform. I was fortunate to encounter many who supported me in my role, and I will always appreciate their good will. During my more than three decades as a practitioner, I met only a very few along the way who seemed ambivalent about having a school psychologist in their building. Coming to grips with their anxieties provided valuable lessons in patience and diplomacy that I might not have learned otherwise. Through these encounters, I was forced to consider the whole range of perspectives administrators might have of a school psychologist.

Becoming a School Psychologist

My first position was with one of the geographically largest rural special education cooperatives in North Dakota. Some of the schools we visited were over 70 miles away from our main office, where co-op employees had their office space. I was grateful most of our referrals were much closer, so far distances were an occasional, not a daily, challenge. But unless the weather was truly awful, I never minded making the long treks, because I felt deeply appreciated by the school staff.

People were as hospitable as rural folks have a reputation for being. Because the co-op was understaffed, they were accustomed to waiting a long time for a visit from a school psychologist, so when I arrived, it was an event, not something to take for granted. Once I entered the building, I was often greeted warmly by a teacher or administrator eager for my arrival. I felt more like an honored visitor than a worker there to perform required tasks. School administrators, whether superintendents or principals, regularly gave up their office space for me to use when I was present, and they did so graciously. Sometimes I was even treated to a free school lunch.

I realized that my warm welcome sprang from the scarcity of school psychologists in this part of the country. Schools were eager to stay in

DOI:10.4324/9781003348344-15

compliance with special education regulations, a goal that sometimes couldn't be achieved in a timely manner because previously school psychologists were stretched too thin for evaluations to be completed on time. My appearance meant they could serve their students better, and I felt well appreciated.

Unaccustomed to having someone like me at school, one of the special education teachers I introduced myself to took for granted I was not from there, and not even from the same state as she. "You're not from North Dakota", she said, assuming such an origin would be impossible. "Oh, yes", I replied. "I grew up in North Dakota". "Where?" she asked. "On a farm about eighty miles northwest of Grand Forks", I said. "Well", she scoffed, "that's Minnesota". Factually she was in error, but culturally, she was right.

After two years in North Dakota, I accepted a position at another rural cooperative, this time in Minnesota, our neighbor state to the east, a move the special education teacher probably would have predicted. It was the early 1980s, and the region was in the middle of a farm crisis. People burdened with debt were losing their farms because of a crash in market prices, and school districts, dependent on local financing, were vulnerable, too. As a matter of fact, one of the school psychologists within our rural cooperative had a side practice doing therapy with farmers suffering from depression. Small rural school districts were negotiating mergers with one another, in tight competition for whose town would get to keep their school, which everyone knew would have a huge impact on the town's survival. School administrators had a lot to deal with, and the future looked uncertain.

I had the good fortune of working for special education directors who communicated well with superintendents and principals, so the school administrators usually knew about new requirements before special education people came to them with requests for more staff to serve kids that hadn't been served before. Still, when special education teachers and school psychologists quoted the law about providing services for kids with disabilities, we sometimes caused distress. Even with forewarning from our special education director, we could make administrators wince.

Expanding Special Education Services

The requirement to provide services to kids with behavioral, social, and emotional deficits caused the most tension because this was a new area for all of us to address. More than once, I think an administrator would have liked to escort me to the door after stating a child qualified for services under the Emotionally/Behaviorally Disordered category because that meant money—which invariably was in short supply—had to be spent to provide these services. I had one principal insist that there were no children in his school with mental illness, even when I was standing with a report in my hand from a nearby mental health center indicating the contrary.

But in the face of state and federal law, denial was not an option. It was important for me to realize the source of resistance usually wasn't because they didn't care about kids; it was because they didn't always know where the money would come from to provide services. I had to keep in mind that they were from the era when children with severe disabilities had been sent off to residential placements and the local school did not have to deal with them. Also, more and more children were surviving premature birth and other conditions that used to result in early death. Now an increasing number were showing up who required intensive special education services. And if they needed residential care, the school district was responsible. The life of a school administrator was becoming more complex, and the stakes were getting higher.

Special education kept pressing for more and better services, and it was hard for us to accept when changes did not occur as quickly as we liked. There was a period of adjustment and depending on the personalities involved, that process could provoke some discord as we moved toward our new normal. To their credit, most of the administrators I worked with did their very best to accommodate the new rules. Part of it was out of self-preservation; the realization that they might be placing their school in legal jeopardy if they were out of compliance was a strong motivation to act in a timely manner. To some, I suppose the presence of a school psychologist in their building represented a threat to their authority. Most, however, came to see us as protecting them from a potential lawsuit. Furthermore, they wanted to do right by kids as much as their school psychologist did.

There was one, however, who would hide the child's special education file when a new student moved into his district. We wouldn't know about the child's needs until the parents realized the child was not being given services. The special education teacher would receive an irate phone call and would then realize it was time to ask for the file from her superintendent.

Although I disapproved of his methods, I must admit I even developed some sympathy for him. His objection to special education was that he didn't like to see kids singled out, fearing they would suffer socially. He had a point; special education carried with it a stigma, but he was blind to the benefits time in the resource room provided the children. He happened to have one of the most competent special education teachers I ever encountered, and she did her utmost to shield her students from harm. So far as I could see, they usually wanted to be in her classroom, but I suppose he felt he was, at least temporarily, rescuing them.

How We Are Perceived

A potential pitfall for school psychologists is the perception that psychologists tend to be arrogant. Unfortunately, an even greater pitfall is that sometimes we are. Occasionally I heard anecdotal evidence from administrators I worked with that this unflattering characterization is sometimes true. (Perhaps the examples were intended as a kindly hint to me—I will never know.) When we behave this way, I suspect it often stems from insecurity. To prove our competence, it can be tempting to try to demonstrate it by using a lot of jargon and talking too much.

We need to recognize that our credentials alone are enough to be intimidating. Entry level to the profession requires graduate-level training, with some school psychologists beginning their practice with even a Psy.D. or Ph.D. in hand. We work right next to classroom teachers who enter with a B.S. or B.A. The professional jargon that is familiar to us can sound like a foreign language to them. If we don't take them into account, recognizing they have not received the same training and so may need a translation, the less we are able to communicate. This dynamic is especially destructive when it prevents us from engaging effectively with those at school who hold the most power, the administrators.

School psychologists must expect their reception will be colored by people's prior impressions of psychologists in general and should not be surprised when stereotypes are applied to us, at least at the beginning of the relationship. I think the most effective way to challenge stereotypes is to get to know the administrators in one's buildings so they can come to understand and appreciate the unique skills a school psychologist brings to the school community. If communication channels are open, difficult moments can be handled in the context of a strong working relationship.

Change Is Always Possible

From time to time the co-op would hear a member district was questioning the value of continuing with us. Districts were understandably very cost-conscious, so if leaving the co-op was a financially sound choice, of course, they considered it. There was one district where this issue seemed to arise more often than in others. I happened to be assigned to a school headed by a principal who held stronger reservations than most. He seemed unaware of what co-op employees brought in the way of expertise, so he didn't know what he would lose by our absence. His interest in getting rid of us would wax and wane, but it was always present, an elephant in the room. Because I was assigned to his building, I encountered his skeptical attitude fairly often. Fortunately for me, his staff never seemed to share his opinion. The special education teachers were supportive of me, so for the most part, I enjoyed my time working in his school. However, I realized he probably wouldn't have minded seeing me—and the rest of my co-op colleagues—gone.

Then one day one of his most trusted special education teachers needed extended sick leave. Her classroom served some of the most challenging students in his school, and she handled them so well that they were rarely a problem for him. But without her, things unraveled. In desperation he resorted to calling her at home, and every time he did, she would suggest he talk to me to get ideas about how to deal with the situations as they came up. I imagine this was not what he wanted to do, but he really didn't have any other good options. He took her recommendation and started coming to me for advice. After a few incidents, our working relationship was transformed. He became thoughtful and respectful toward me and followed through on my suggestions. In time I came to be a trusted advisor. The thing is, I hadn't changed one iota. All that had changed was his perception of me. Fortunately, thanks to my school psych training, my suggestions were good enough that he came to trust me as he had his special education teacher. He never reverted to his former attitude.

When I reflect on this situation, I remind myself that what feels on the surface like a personal slight can be a symptom of a much larger issue. For a time, this principal was convinced that the district was wasting precious funds by belonging to the co-op, so he resented my presence. He underestimated what a school psychologist had to offer and, consequently, didn't realize what I accomplished in his school. But to his credit, once he was forced into a position to learn, he based his impressions on his actual experience, rather than his former opinion. I had to respect that his desire to handle delicate situations with students brought him to seek my help. In retrospect, I count him as one of my best motivators for the years I worked next to him, because I didn't want to provide any reason to confirm his worst opinion of us. I always wanted to do right by students and meet the standards of my profession, but the additional pressure of his skepticism motivated me to observe best practice to the utmost.

On the other hand, in some schools I was immediately viewed as a very close ally by the administration. Principals would want me to check-in with them first thing upon arrival. They would have a list of questions for me about how they were handling various situations with special education students and their parents, eager to see if I agreed with their decisions. Usually, the steps they had taken were equal to or beyond what I would have done, but if not, they accepted my advice gladly. Their respect for my opinion of course made me feel highly valued, which helped me deal with the less than enthusiastic response described in my previous example. I was also aware that they appreciated a meeting with me because they didn't have many people to talk with who weren't directly subordinate to them. They welcomed an itinerant showing up once a week who could spend some moments discussing their concerns at school.

Going Toe-to-Toe

We can find ourselves balancing on a tightrope, though, if we stand in opposition to an action taken by an administrator. It can be particularly problematic in situations where our ethics contradict a legal administrative decision.

Until 1989, it was legal in Minnesota for school personnel to use corporal punishment in disciplining students. Before this law was passed, children could be spanked and paddled without any legal repercussions. By the time I entered school psychology, the practice had been almost completely abandoned in North Dakota and Minnesota. But it arose in one of my schools one day, and the story I am about to tell shows what a special education teacher and I did to prevent it from happening again.

The elementary school had recently admitted a child who happened to be in special education who had moved in from another district. The parents were divorced, and the mother was remarried. The father had visitation rights, and after a weekend with him, the child would invariably misbehave in class Monday morning. At her wit's end, one day the teacher sent the child to the principal's office to deal with the misbehavior. He responded with a spanking. The school secretary overheard the child's cries and told me that she had never heard a child sound so terrified. The principal had parental approval and the sanction of state law, so it looked like there was no recourse to challenge his approach. At first it looked like there was nothing we could do. But the special education teacher and I decided we had to try.

We put our heads together and came up with a plan. It was pointless to call social services since no wrongdoing had occurred, under law. But there was one thing we could do. I went to the principal and told him that I wanted to call a team meeting for this child. He realized instantly that I had heard about the spanking and replied that we didn't need a meeting. I said that I thought it would be useful to write a behavior plan and perhaps come up with some alternative interventions. He paused, then said, "And you know the law, and the law says that any member of the team has a right to call a meeting. All right. We will have a meeting".

The meeting was arranged, and the principal presided. He began by saying that he had called us together because he thought it would be wise to come up with some interventions to deal with the child's behavior since Monday mornings were so difficult. He glanced my way, and I smiled and nodded. Then we proceeded to write the plan. To my knowledge, the child was never struck again in school.

I was rewarded with what I considered to be a high compliment from this principal a long time later, whether he intended it to be. I had driven to another school, only to find it closed for the day, and so I shifted my plan for the day to his school where I also had things to do, even though it wasn't my regularly scheduled time to be there. I stopped at the main office to check in and said to the secretary, "Might there be room at the inn for a poor, helpless school psychologist who needs office space?" Before she could reply, the principal popped his head out of his door and replied, "You? Helpless? You are as helpless as a rattlesnake!" Both the secretary and I paused in stunned amazement for a moment and then dissolved into silent laughter after his door closed.

The next week there was a large, pink metal button waiting for me in my mailbox. It had a picture of a coiled rattlesnake with long, curly eyelashes, and glued to the perimeter was a delicate edging of lace trim. Inscribed around the rattlesnake was the phrase "Helpless as a Rattlesnake". The secretary caught my eye and grinned; it was clear who had created it. Tempted though I was, I didn't wear it in front of the principal; instead, I carried it in my bag as a reminder of one small triumph on behalf of a child. I will always remember the courage of the school secretary and the special education teacher who joined me in the effort. They both had a lot more to lose than I did, had they received any fallout from my action. The principal was their boss, and they worked in his building every day.

What Exactly Do They Do?

In the early years of my time as a school psychologist many administrators had very little idea about what exactly we did. This was both unfortunate and inevitable, because of the confidential nature of much of our work. They could see us testing kids and attending I.E.P. meetings, but they typically wouldn't know about the counseling and consultation we did, nor did they know how much time we spent writing reports. While we could be frantically busy in a school district, the administrators could be unaware of all that we were accomplishing.

At one point the committee of superintendents who governed our cooperative decided we needed to be held more accountable. Some even suspected that our mileage checks were so large because we just went out and drove around to boost the reimbursement. For a few weeks, we were required to document specifically what we did every half hour throughout our day. It didn't take long to show the superintendents we were not padding our reimbursement checks, nor were we underscheduled. From their perspective I suspect we seemed too independent, because our schedules were so flexible that there could be opportunity for abuse, should one want to take advantage of the situation. As administrators became more familiar with the nature of our position, they came to trust our judgment and our intentions.

We Have Grown to Be a Part

By the time Natasha entered the field, school administrators had become accustomed to having a school psychologist on staff. My generation of administrators was not accustomed to having us around; a few even believed special education was just a fad that would fade away, and so they didn't have to take it (or us) seriously, and others, at the opposite extreme, were intimidated by our presence because identifying behavioral and emotional needs meant having to hire staff to deal with them and raised the possibility of lawsuits. By the time I retired I felt school psychologists were considered a welcome member of the school team particularly when special education issues came up and when crises, especially those related to mental health concerns, needed to be addressed. We have become much more an ally and much less a threat.

Over time, schools figured out how to address the new challenges. Most administrators came to realize that our cooperative provided cost-effective services, and since the alternative would be to find the same services on their own—probably at a higher cost—they saw we were a bit of a bargain. If they weren't already converts, having a crisis such as the death of a student in their school usually convinced them there was a need for us.

Chapter 16

The Changing Role of School Principalship

New Perspectives

In 2018, Stephanie J. Hull, executive vice president and chief operating officer for the Institute for Citizens & Scholars (formerly known as the Woodrow Wilson National Fellowship Foundation) summarized four skills that principals need to master if they are to be effective in their role. On her list were: (1) grasping the use of new learning technologies, so principals can choose well what best fulfills their school's need; (2) knowing how to connect students to social supports and services their students can benefit from; (3) understanding the impact on education of systems on the local, state, and federal level; and (4) identifying professional development needs and making the best use of funds to meet them. She emphasized that principals will be expected to show through data what the likely best path forward should be, and commented that in the near future a master's degree in business administration might be the best education for a prospective principal to attain (Hull, 2018).

The same year that Hull's article appeared, so did an article addressing principalship written by a renowned expert on educational reform, Michael Fullan, a Canadian and Global Leadership Director, New Pedagogies for Deep Learning. Fullan cites three interrelated ways principalship has changed since 2013. They are: first, moving beyond a focus on literacy, numeracy and high school graduation to what Fullan calls "Living in the real, real world" (Fullan, 2018). To do so, students must become competent in the 6Cs: "character, citizenship, collaboration, communication, creativity and critical thinking", which Fullan terms "Global Competencies" (Fullan, 2018, pp. 18–19). Ultimately, these skills will be linked to literacy and numeracy.

Second, school leaders must, in Fullan's words, "Mobilize the masses" with the goal in mind of changing the world for the better. He expects principals to learn alongside teachers and students as they work to make a difference. Third, principals will need to lead "outward and upward", which is to say, they will need to participate in the school hierarchy, but

DOI:10.4324/9781003348344-16

at the same time, engage with other school leaders as well as the larger community. A principal should be a skilled collaborator who will inspire students and staff to work for change (Fullan, 2018, p. 19).

These two perspectives, one attuned to the business perspective of the global economy and the other to twenty-first-century world justice issues, would have seemed foreign to the principals I worked alongside, 40 years ago. Now school principals are having to redefine themselves and their relationship with staff and students in ways that would have seemed well beyond their scope when I began working in schools.

When I entered the school world several decades ago, principals were at the top of the hierarchy in their building, from which position they led staff meetings, attended to the school budget and state and federal requirements, oversaw the physical plant and busing, and represented the school within the community. As the head manager, they dealt with concerned parents and disciplined students with the most severe behavior problems. A school psychologist might have been invited in for consultation in such instances, especially if the student was enrolled in a special education program.

I usually engaged with principals only at I.E.P. meetings or in their office when they wanted to discuss the path forward for a particular student or when parents came in to talk about a special education issue. Otherwise, in my daily routine they were usually in the background. They were not seated at a computer analyzing data as the school C.E.O., as Hull described; nor were they assisting their staff and students in addressing current issues on a global scale, such as Fullan articulated.

Corporal Punishment and Congress

Over the course of my career, how a principal handled school discipline was often one of the most important aspects of the position that had the greatest impact on me. Fortunately, current practice is shifting from dealing out consequences for misbehavior one student at a time to adopting school-wide approaches that are proving themselves to be far more effective than the "get tough" actions that they have replaced. That is just one among many changes affecting the role of a school principal, and I am grateful for it.

For the first few years of my career, it was still legal in the states where I worked for principals to engage in corporal punishment with children. As the example given in the previous chapter illustrates, this was of particularly vital concern to me when the child being punished was someone with a disability. Thankfully over time, many states have abolished the practice. In 1867, New Jersey was the first to do so. Several states followed suit in the 1970s and 1980s, including the ones where I worked (Chen, 2020).

Currently, however, corporal punishment is still legal in 19 states: Except for the two western states of Texas and Wyoming, all are in the South. Interestingly, these states have higher rates of child mortality and children living in poverty as well as lower per pupil spending on education than the states that have banned the practice. In a nutshell, these are high-needs schools serving high-needs children. On the national level, there are now a great many professional organizations which publicly oppose the use of corporal punishment, including, among many others, the National Association of School Psychologists, the American Medical Association, the American Psychological Association, the Council for Exceptional Children, the National Parent Teachers Association, and the American Bar Association (Chen, 2020).

In response to the growing awareness of its negative effects, there has been an attempt in Congress to ban corporal punishment in all schools throughout the country. The late Representative Alcee Hastings of Florida introduced House Resolution 727 on 1/23/2019 to "end the use of corporal punishment in schools, and for other purposes". No action was taken, and so he reintroduced the bill on February 23, 2021, some weeks before his death. It was not expected to be enacted into law, but Representative Hastings persisted in proposing the abolition of corporal punishment in schools, nonetheless (Ending Corporal Punishment in Schools Act of 2019, H.R. 727, 116 Cong., 2019–2020). I hope the cause will find another champion in Congress who will carry it forward.

Eight findings by Congress are given in the proposed Ending Corporal Punishment in Schools Act of 2019, H.R. 727, 116 Cong., 2019–2020). The first is the need for all behavioral interventions to preserve the dignity of children. The second states that there are "safe, effective, evidence-based" alternatives to use instead of the traditional ones relying on physical punishment. The third finding indicates "school personnel have the right to work in a safe environment and should be provided training and support to prevent injury and trauma to themselves and others" (Ending Corporal Punishment in Schools Act of 2019, H.R. 727, 116 Cong., 2019–2020).

The fourth finding lists School-Wide Positive Behavior Interventions and Support as a worthy alternative. The fifth emphasizes the frequency with which such punishment occurs, noting that it happens "every thirty seconds during the school year" (Ending Corporal Punishment in Schools Act of 2019, H.R. 727, 116 Cong., 2019–2020).

Sixth, the fact that 19 states continue to allow their public school to use corporal punishment with children is cited. The seventh finding emphasizes that the main method used is paddling, and lists possible injuries that can result, including some which are life-threatening (Ending Corporal Punishment in Schools Act of 2019, H.R. 727, 116 Cong., 2019–2020).

The eighth and final finding for abolishment addresses the disproportionate rate that Blacks are administered physical punishment, compared with Whites. Although Blacks make up only 18% of the student population, they comprise 40% of all students subjected to this form of punishment. They are eight times more likely to receive such punishment as Hispanic children, and nearly two and a half times more likely than Whites (Ending Corporal Punishment in Schools Act of 2019, H.R. 727, 116 Cong., 2019–2020).

As Natasha pointed out to me, the findings in this legislation could have been written by a school psychologist, given the points of emphasis. From what they encounter every day at school, practitioners can affirm the wisdom of this House Resolution. I am hoping that not very many more years have to pass before corporal punishment is banned from all schools in our land. Several other countries throughout the world have forbidden it. As of 2020, 60 nation-states had bans against it and 28 others were committed to reform (Global Partnership to End Violence Against Children, 2021).

Student Resource Officers

How best to manage disruptive and dangerous behavior at school is an ongoing challenge for principals. The government has responded by funding Student Resource Officers, whose performance has been met with varied reviews. The first S.R.O.s were first hired in the 1950s, but their presence became much more commonplace in the 1980s during the "War on Drugs" era, and then their numbers increased again in the late 1990s, after horrific school shootings (Ryan et al., 2018).

Under the best circumstances, they collaborate well with administrators and school staff and have positive relationships with students. Unfortunately, there have also been instances where S.R.O.s have exacerbated challenging situations, and have overstepped reasonable bounds, intruding where principals need to assume authority. Their presence raises concerns about unnecessarily harsh and ultimately, counterproductive, intervention. Their intent is to reduce crime and protect students, but depending on their level of training and skills, this may or may not be the case (Ryan et al., 2018).

Ryan et al. recommend school resource officers serve as team members on school-wide positive behavioral support teams, and that they not be used to address student misbehavior except when the behavior is criminal. They recommend training for S.R.O.s in child development, behavior management, and disability issues, contending that it is crucial that S.R.O.s need to learn to communicate with young people effectively. Equitable treatment among groups is also a concern, because children of color are more likely than Whites to attend schools with S.R.O.s (Ryan et al., 2018). Ideally, an S.R.O. in Natasha's schools would serve next to her on P.B.I.S. teams, where she plays an important role by identifying students needing services in and beyond high school in a nonbiased manner and collaborating with community agencies to find appropriate settings for them.

An S.R.O. should be a force to diminish, not increase, the likelihood that youth will be arrested. Over the past decade we have become more and more aware of an unfortunate path to incarceration, through what has come to be termed the "school to prison pipeline" (Stop the School-to-Prison Pipeline, 2011/2012).

Because suspension is an important predictor of whether someone drops out, it then raises the chances of their becoming unemployed, and eventually, ending up in prison. Suspensions rose dramatically as a result of zero-tolerance policies implemented across the country in an attempt to limit the illicit drug trade and reduce violence. But even after crime in schools declined in the early 1990s, zero-tolerance policies did not. Sadly, there were examples of unreasonable arrests of even young children.

About a decade later, in 2021, the National Association of Secondary School Principals published an article addressing the role of S.R.O.s in schools. They acknowledge "the legitimate concern about their impact on school climate, discipline, and the school-to-prison pipeline, especially with respect to disproportionate, and at times, unwarranted, enforcement toward students of color". They go on to say that S.R.O.s need to be properly vetted and trained and their role clearly defined. They emphasize that S.R.O.s should be educated to mentor students, and they should serve as a link for students to public services, such as legal aid, public health, and social services. That school administrators, not S.R.O.s, are responsible for handling school disciplinary situations is noted (National Association of Secondary School Principals, 2020).

In Minneapolis, with the scene of ongoing racial unrest following the deaths of Blacks at the hands of police, the public school system has hired safety specialists who have no police powers, so are unarmed and cannot arrest anyone, in the effort to move in the direction of providing increased mental health services and restorative justice practices. The need to add more school social workers, school counselors, and teachers of color to their staffs has gained a lot of traction (Sheasley, 2021).

A Role for School Psychologists

Finding alternatives to suspension, which in our era unfortunately has been practiced even at the preschool level, is one way school psychologists can assist. For example, they know how to apply the principles of Positive Behavioral Interventions and Support (P.B.I.S.), which can deliver the procedural social justice necessary for constructive intervention in school. P.B.I.S. teams strive to prevent a student's behavior from getting to the point where suspension from school is necessary. Counseling, restitution, and behavior monitoring are a few nonpunitive approaches that can be tailored to suit an individual student. By working to create a positive school climate, schools can shift from addressing problems after they arise to preventing them before they can occur.

Because of their position of responsibility, administrators must address the rising level of stress among all facets of the community. They must promote equity among groups, find staff to fill positions, try to satisfy state and federal mandates for performance, reduce violence and bullying in their building, foster good relations among employees, communicate with dissatisfied parents, and, in this litigious era, administrators be alert to the possibility of lawsuits. They must know how to handle crises, which in the twenty-first century, includes coping with a pandemic. The responsibilities are challenging enough in districts with ample resources, but in poorly funded schools, the role is even harder. Principals are often the first to arrive at school in the morning and the last to go home. The role requires tremendous stamina of body and spirit.

We have always been aware that teachers have a profound effect on their students' ability to achieve. In recent years, we have realized that principals have an even greater impact, because they affect all the students in their school. Now the literature on principalship addresses not only how to build a supportive and productive school community but also how to build a better world.

References

Chen, G. (2020, February 14). Teachers in 10 states allowed to physically punish students. *Public School Review.* https:///www.publicschoolreview.com/blog/teachers-in-19-states-allowed-to-physically-punish-students

Ending Corporal Punishment in Schools Act of 2019, H.R. 727, 116 Cong. (2019–2020). www.congress.gov/bill/116th-congress/house-bill/727

Fullan, M. (2018). The principalship has changed: 2020 here we come! *Principal Connections,* 22(1), 18–19. https://michaelfullan.ca/wp-content/uploads/2018/09/The-Principalship-Has-Channged-M.Fullan.pdf

Global Partnership to End Violence Against Children. (2021). *Prohibiting all corporal punishment of children: Laying the foundations for non-violent childhoods.* https://endcorporalpunishment.org/resources/global-report-2021/

Hull, S. J. (2018, January 9). The job of a school principal has changed a lot. Here's how we help them do it. *Ed Post.* https://educationpost.org/the-job-of-a-school-principal-has-changed-a-lot-heres-how-we-help-them-do-it/

National Association of Secondary School Principals. (2020, March). *Position statement: School resource officers and law enforcement in schools.* www.nassp.org/school-resource-officers-and-law-enforcement-in-schools/

Ryan, J. B., Katsiyannis, A., Counts, J. M., & Shelnut, J. C. (2018). The growing concerns regarding school resource officers. *Intervention in School and Clinic, 53*(3), 188–192. https://eric.ed.gov/?id=EJ1163923

Sheasley, C. (2021, April 20). In a roiled Minneapolis, schools are testing new model for safety. *Christian Science Monitor.* www.csmonitor.com/USA/Education/2021/0420/In-a-roiled-Minneapolis-schools-are-testing-new-model-for-safety

Stop the School-to-Prison Pipeline. (2011/2012). *Rethinking Schools, 26*(2). https://rethinkingschools.org/articles/editorial-stop-the-school-to-prison-pipeline/

Chapter 17

Remember to Breathe

Crisis Intervention

In my experience, nothing gained a school psychologist recognition faster than effectively responding to a crisis, particularly the death of a child. The first time I was called on to do so, one of my colleagues and I received a call around ten o'clock on a school night informing us of the death by suicide of a 15-year-old boy who shot himself at home with a hunting rifle. Neither of us had had any direct experience with crisis intervention, so we turned to our most experienced colleague, Dr. Steve Olson, to ask that he accompany us to the school the next morning. On the way there, my colleague and I shared our anxieties with one another, hoping out loud that Steve would know what to do, because we felt we did not. He usually did, but this was a new situation for him, too.

We would be meeting with school staff at 7:30, an hour before school started. There we would lay out our plan for the day. The situation was especially delicate because the boy was the child of a staff member. Also, he was from a large family, so there were several siblings attending school in the district. In small rural communities such as the one he lived in, it was likely that every teacher in the district would have worked with him or a sibling at one time or another. We knew that the effect on the school community would be profound.

Steve had an easy, warm manner; he was naturally gregarious, and he had worked for our co-op for many years so almost everyone knew him. He had been doing crisis intervention in his private practice with farmers who were suffering from depression, and the skills he brought to them saved us that day. After the staff were assembled, he walked to the front of the room and began by simply saying, "Good morning". His voice was strong and reassuring, and at the time I realized that Steve would find whatever good there was to be found in this day.

He reviewed the concrete plans to keep things as normal as possible while at the same time showing proper respect for the loss. We volunteered to accompany teachers to their classrooms, especially those who had had the boy in class. We advised staff to stick to the facts and to allow students to go to a quiet area that would be set aside for grieving. It was

DOI:10.4324/9781003348344-17

evident from Steve's presentation that we were reasonably equipped to help people handle their shock and to support the staff and the family. Staff expressed concern for students who were especially emotionally vulnerable, and we, with the help of county social workers, were planning to address their needs. By the time the meeting ended, a complete plan was in place and the staff was on board with us. Evidently the superintendent trusted our plan, because shortly after this meeting he left to go to the post office. He did not return until several hours later, leaving us co-op school psychologists to attend to the business of the day.

Steve and I visited the family, and again Steve's kindly manner put everyone at ease. He told the parents what the school was doing to address their son's death, and he spoke with them about any special wishes they had. They impressed upon us that they wanted their son's friends to feel free to stop by. We were happy to convey their message, and it was received with gratitude by the students.

Later we went to the elementary school in a nearby town. Two towns had consolidated their school districts, so the high school was in one town and the elementary in another. Steve and I sat in the teachers' lounge, waiting for anyone to ask us to relieve them of their class if they felt they needed a break. No one came, and after a while Steve left because he had his own schools to tend. Deeply moved by the dedication shown by the teachers, I contemplated what it might be like to be a teacher in a small town, to know every child from every family, and to share in everyone's sorrow when an event such as this occurred.

Community Involvement

A group of parents requested that I meet with them once a week on an ongoing basis to sort through what their community might do to prevent another suicide. At our first meeting a parent asked, "Can a whole community grieve?" I replied that I believed I was witnessing one.

Within the year schools in the region held a day of instruction on mental health for students in grades 7 through 12. I was asked to talk to groups about suicide and its prevention. Nearly all, if not all, of the participants had either known the boy who had died or knew a classmate or family member. I emphasized to them how important it was that they tell a trusted adult when a friend appeared to be contemplating suicide, because help was available. It wasn't tattling or betraying a friend if they revealed such a dangerous secret; rather, it could be lifesaving. At the end of my talk with each of the groups, I asked everyone to put their head down on their desk and close their eyes. Then I asked that they raise their pinky finger if they would go to an adult when they heard a friend contemplating suicide. Throughout the entire day, not one finger was raised. I left quite disheartened.

Years later, I was asked by one of my principals to administer a "violence test" to a student whose behavior had teachers worried about his mental health status. There was no such test, but I met with the boy for counseling. Meeting with him was unnerving. His face was mask-like, and his speech was uninflected. There wasn't anything wrong, he said, so he didn't need to talk to anyone. His girlfriend of several years (the only one he had ever had) was dating someone else, but he asserted he was certain they would get back together. According to him, they had their entire lives planned together. It was evident that there was room in his imagination for only one possible narrative. Each session he just repeated his faith that his ex-girlfriend would return to him, so all was well. I reported to the principal that I had made no progress and I remained deeply concerned about what he might do.

Months passed. Then one day some students tipped off an adult that the boy was contemplating violence. Thanks to that report, he was prevented from carrying out a destructive desperate act, and a tragedy was averted. Had this scenario played out some years earlier, I doubt classmates would have sounded a warning. By the time I retired years later, students were coming directly to adults such as school psychologists, teachers, counselors, parents, principals, and school social workers to intervene. Once I had a girl practically drag her friend to me and say to her, "Now tell her what you told me!"

Flying Solo

A few years after the first suicide, my fellow school psychologists and I were again called to duty after the accidental deaths of two elementary school children. By then Steve had moved on to a position at a nearby mental health center, so we led the response without him. Thanks to Steve's mentoring, we faced the next tragedy with much less anxiety, because now we had a procedure to follow.

The deaths occurred before our co-op schools had created crisis committees to deal with such situations. Fortunately, what we had was a wise superintendent as well as school personnel, local clergy, and social workers with knowledge of crisis intervention beside us. Not long after, our rural cooperative had standing crisis committees in its schools, which further defined precisely what roles everyone would play.

We arrived early and met with school employees, including cooks and janitors, first thing in the morning, as we had when Steve led us. A statement restricted to the facts surrounding the deaths was given to teachers to read to their students. We fielded questions about what to say to grieving students, emphasizing that students needed to know the truth, but it wasn't necessary to go into detail. Nothing speculative should be stated. We requested a "quiet" room be set aside for grieving students to gather, supervised by adults throughout the day.

When it was time for school to start, we began our classroom visits, starting with the classrooms of the deceased. Because we didn't have enough crisis team members for every classroom, we had to rotate among classes. In this way we did our best to lend support to the teacher as well as to the students. We volunteered to read the descriptive statement to the class if the teacher felt unable, and we answered questions about the incident. Crisis team members escorted students to the designated quiet room and were alert for behavioral indicators which might suggest a need for further intervention, such as referral to a mental health agency.

Midmorning, we were summoned to the superintendent's office to help him handle the press. In a stroke of diplomatic genius, he managed to handle them in a way that satisfied them and at the same time protected children and teachers from intrusive questioning and cameras. A journalist and photographer had come to gather material for what would become a front-page story. Rather than trying to discourage them, he welcomed them into the school, immediately escorting them to his office, which was at the far end of the building, away from any classrooms. He had already summoned my colleague and me, so we were waiting for them, ready to be interviewed about the procedure the school was following in response to the deaths. After we laid out the plan for the day, the journalist commented on what an up-to-date approach we were using, despite, she said, our rural location. The next day, the front page of her newspaper featured an article about our response. In accordance with the superintendent's plan, students had been shielded from cameras, so the only photo they had to show was of two school psychologists seated in the superintendent's office.

Being rural was no excuse not to develop this expertise. By this time crisis intervention was getting a lot of scholarly attention nationwide, and our state school psychologist organization and NASP were addressing the topic. Furthermore, we already had weathered our own crash course and so learned firsthand what needed to be done.

At the end of the day, we held an after-school meeting with all staff to share information and support. Before and after school meetings continued to be held for some days, until the staff decided they no longer felt a need. My colleague and I paid a visit to the bereaved family when they were ready to meet with us. We conveyed our concern and assured we would do what we could to carry out their wishes at school.

All parents received a letter at the end of the first day with an overview of what we did and a fact sheet describing the tragedy. They were invited to return comments. At the end of the week, we once again paid a visit to the classrooms to see how everyone was doing. By then students were talking calmly about the ones who had died. We composed a letter for the school staff, encouraging them to take care of themselves and acknowledging how well they had met this difficult challenge. We gave each person a copy in our final meeting.

Throughout the week my colleague and I urged one another to get as much rest as we possibly could so we could maintain our stamina. We tried to focus on what actions we needed to take and avoid worrying about anything else. Because we had gone through a similar crisis once before, we believed we could handle this one, too.

Later in the year another school in our co-op experienced the death of a high school student in a car accident. By then we felt equipped to respond, thanks to our recent experience. Shortly thereafter crisis plans were developed in most of our schools, involving school administrators, counselors, school psychologists, interested teachers, local clergy, social workers, and other community figures familiar with crisis intervention. We had come a long way in a few short years; of course, saddened by the reason, but glad that our crisis intervention raised awareness of the need to address mental health concerns in schools.

A Finger Pointed at Me

Several years after the first suicide, we faced another situation where, again, a boy had shot himself. By then our cooperative had its crisis plan in place, so each school knew who to call and what to expect. Several co-op school psychologists converged for a day of listening to students and staff and doing our best to help them cope. I was assigned a group of students from the boy's class, so many of his closest friends were present.

One student raised her hand and asked, "You're a psychologist; why didn't you stop him?" She said that I should have called the whole school together to address them in an assembly. I replied that I dearly wished I could have prevented his suicide, but the sad truth was that no one can predict with certainty who will commit suicide at any given point, and that holding group events and focusing on suicide seems not to be effective. I told her it was most helpful for those closest to someone contemplating suicide to intervene and get them individual help.

What interested me was that I was not their assigned school psychologist. I had never met the boy who had died. Yet this young woman was convinced that I would have had the power to prevent his death if only I had talked to the student body. I told her that every mental health worker would be glad to give talks and do whatever else if we knew it would have the intended positive effect. But lectures to groups had not been shown to be effective.

Years earlier in graduate school I heard one lecture on what to do about suicide and its aftermath in a school. The professor introduced his talk by acknowledging how traumatic a suicide would be, but that the likelihood of any of us having to deal with such a situation was so slight that he would just give us a quick overview. Seven years out into the field as a school psychologist, I wrote my specialist paper on the topic of dealing with death at school.

In my oral exam for the degree, one of my examiners asked a provocative question. He said small towns are usually close-knit communities that come together in a crisis. Of what use, then, was an outsider like me? When I walked into one of my schools in the early morning the day of my first experience doing crisis intervention, this question was paramount in my own mind. Would I be a helper—or an intruder? The answer became clear within moments of the arrival of our team of school psychologists. The whole school staff was so glad to see us; I wondered instead if we could live up to their expectations.

Because we were not a part of their close-knit community, we could stand in for them if they needed to step away and have a private moment, answer questions to assure them they were proceeding reasonably, and immediately provide resources such as handouts summarizing recommended procedures and information related to coping. As it turned out, my specialist paper was used temporarily as a training manual in my school psychology program because scholars had written so little that applied to school psychologists. The time had arrived when coping with death at school needed quite a bit more attention than the 15-minute lecture I had heard.

Teachers and Crisis Intervention

In school, the term used to describe school psychologists as well as other special education personnel is "support staff". We exist to lend support to teachers and to students, a critical role during crisis intervention. After participating in several crises in schools, I gained deep respect for how well teachers rose to the occasion. At the same time, I became aware of how little was being done to help teachers themselves cope with tragic events. We school psychologists listened to comments from teachers and other school employees and fielded questions the best we could, but we focused almost exclusively on the kids.

After witnessing the tremendous strain teachers and other school staff endured in the aftermath of a crisis—one that could last many months—I decided I wanted to understand their perspective better. I listened to the stories many had to tell, and eventually composed an essay entitled, "Empty Desks: Staff Reactions to Student Deaths". I found that disenfranchised grief, absent grief, compassion fatigue, and, if the death occurred by suicide, guilt, were common responses. Teachers were overwhelmed by the magnitude of the impact and reported feeling unprepared to respond. One theme that emerged from these conversations was shock at how widespread the grief was throughout the school community.

Rural communities are often closely knit, and how well everyone knew everyone else became vividly apparent after a death. By the time I had interviewed everyone, I wanted to tell their stories not just to analyze what we should do to improve our methods, but also to celebrate these unsung heroes (Ness, 2000).

Coping With the Death of an Adult

The death of a teacher or other staff member can have a tremendous impact on a school community, as teachers adjust to losing a colleague and children to losing a mentor. The death that affected me the most was that of a school librarian who had worked in her district for many years and knew practically all the students in middle school and high school. Because my office was near hers, we were well acquainted. Her name was Cindy, and she was the heart of the school. I used to tell her that I might be the school psychologist, but she was the school's psychologist.

It seemed everyone with a trouble to tell found their way to her office, where she would listen patiently. Many of our special education students had a daily habit of visiting her, so when she died, they felt an acute loss. To respond to everyone's grief, we turned the library into a quiet space for children to come and go. We handed out paper to write on or draw and supplied colored pencils and markers. Many students in addition to those in special education readily took to making cards for the family, so much so that I asked the language arts teachers if they would want to follow up with a similar activity in their classes over the next couple of days. I told them I would deliver the cards to the family at Cindy's funeral. I figured there would be at least 30 cards to deliver. As it turned out, there were almost ten times that many. In recognition of the outpouring of affection for their beloved librarian, my special education director gave me permission to use office equipment and supplies to make a book out of the cards as a memorial, as well as the tech support to do it. We scanned all the cards and created a hardbound book, copies of which were given to the middle school library where students could look at it, to the family, and to grieving colleagues.

Dealing With the Aftermath of Death

During the aftermath of a death, I was invariably impressed with the capacity of teachers to draw on reserves of strength to comfort students and one another, and at the same time, continue to teach. The wisest didn't stick too closely to the lesson plan of the day; they knew they had to adapt to their students' emotional needs first. Only then they could get on with the routine. Some teachers wanted to avoid even mentioning the death; they hoped that if no one said anything they could distract the children from thinking about their sadness. One teacher accused us of wanting to make the children cry, upon being told that support staff were available to accompany them to their classes to talk with students about the death. She learned very quickly once she entered her classroom that her students didn't need any prompting, and she came to appreciate our presence.

Time and again I witnessed teachers, counselors, and other school staff find the teachable moments within a tragedy. I particularly remember being in the classroom of the first grader whose parent, a teacher in the school, had died. I accompanied the teacher to her classroom to lend support if she felt she needed it, but as it turned out, I was not necessary. She rose to the occasion, as I was to witness time and again with other teachers over the years to follow. She had invited me there for moral support, and I was glad I could be there with her. But when the moment arrived to speak to the children, she found she could do it herself.

With quiet dignity, her deep concern and affection for her students were evident; her gentle manner conveyed as much as her words. The children asked questions, and it was soon clear that not all of them had a firm grasp of the finality of death. She realized this, and so asked the class if they thought their classmate's daddy could come back. Most solemnly shook their heads. But one little boy raised his hand and in a sweetly hopeful voice said, "Maybe? Just for a little while? To say goodbye?" No one agreed, and his teacher gently told him that no, his friend's daddy could not do that. I doubt I ever witnessed a more tender teachable moment.

Coping With Natural Disaster

In 1997 my long-time school psychologist partner in crisis and I gained experience facing a crisis that deeply affected one of the towns we served, as well as several others in our co-op. It came in the form of a natural disaster, what our community now commemorates as the Flood of 1997. The town where we both had our offices and its sister city across the river flooded to the extent that the event was covered on the national news. It was significant enough that the editor of the NASP *Communique* requested an article about it from us. This resulted in our article, "Respective on Disaster: One Year After in the Red River Valley" (Ness & Vanderpan, 1999).

The town of East Grand Forks was totally evacuated, and its sister city of Grand Forks across the Red River of the North evacuated 90% of its 52,500 residents. Schools closed April 18, not to resume until the beginning of the next academic year. Because of the crisis intervention we had undertaken in our schools after the deaths of children, my colleague and

I had experience to draw on. An important difference this time was that both of us were not only responders to the impact of the flood but were directly affected. Flood recovery can be very time-consuming, and it was a burden. But when school reopened in the fall, I appreciated the value of having gone through much the same experience as the kids I worked with. We all understood what it meant, and we were all in it together (Ness & Vanderpan, 1999).

In a nutshell, the flood created a huge mess to clean up and a lot of space was lost. Some schools were destroyed, so students were packed in together in the remaining buildings or temporary structures were provided until the new schools were built. Most everyone was anxious, and this was particularly evident among our special education population. Some became fearful there would be another flood. No one could promise there wouldn't be, but fortunately no lives were lost during the evacuation, so we tried to assure them that whatever happened, they would be safe (Ness & Vanderpan, 1999).

Our co-op and district staff had wonderful support in the form of a disaster intervention team out of our local mental health center. They remained with us for several months and provided activities for kids as well as debriefing sessions for teachers and therapy for individuals and families. The hardest hit were the families that lost their homes. Many parents also lost their jobs. While people were grateful to have a FEMA trailer to live in until they could find suitable housing, the cramped quarters could lead to stress. During the aftermath of the flood, we saw an increase in alcohol use, marital difficulties, and child abuse. The whole community needed to regain a sense of control, and it took time and effort to get there.

Two decades later, what especially remains with me is how the flood put us all, metaphorically speaking, in the same boat. (For most of us, it was a Humvee, piloted by a national guardsperson driving us through rising flood waters to safety.) At our special education cooperative, we had discussions among ourselves about how we are used to lending a hand when others are in need. It was a revelation to find ourselves also standing with our hands out.

Without the kindness of strangers, we would have been stranded in our homes, surrounded by flood water, and after the flood receded, many of us would not have had cars to drive or a safe place to stay, or even food to eat. After we moved back into our houses after the waters receded, everyone in my neighborhood had a hot meal once a day, compliments of the Salvation Army. For as long as we were without water and electricity, they came every day.

A few weeks later, a chartered bus from Minneapolis pulled up in front of my house, and a team of workers piled out and asked to help clean up our basement, which had been filled with flood water and so needed to be sterilized. Before they left, I asked what I could do to thank them.

They requested a tour of the neighborhood, so they could see what the river had done. I was happy to oblige, and as we walked through the abandoned neighborhood near the river, I listened to their stories of the floods they had witnessed themselves. It was apparent many of them were helping me because they, or some member of their family, had also been helped. Coming to Grand Forks was their way to pay forward their gratitude to the strangers who had helped them or their loved ones. The day became a fine lesson in shared humanity.

The Flood Did Not Take Everything

Of all my stories, Natasha's favorite concerns the flood's aftermath. Much of the town was devastated, and many buildings would be demolished. One was the junior high where a fellow school psychologist and I shared an office off the library. One Friday night the librarian called me in anguish, because she had just learned all the books were going to be destroyed along with the building, due to FEMA regulations. But not one page of one book had been touched by flood water. In fact, the library had not been flooded at all, because it was situated at a higher elevation than the rest of the first-floor rooms, so stayed dry when the water rose and ebbed. The librarian was beside herself. This was a well-stocked library, a portion of it funded out of her own generous pocket. I asked if she had a plan in mind, and she said she didn't know what to do. So, I said we had to steal the library.

We had to find a place to put it and we needed help moving the books. But we had Saturday to do it, so we had time. Within minutes the junior high librarian enlisted the enthusiastic support of the high school librarian who said she would happily store the books. And a couple of janitors volunteered to carry and transport. Another school psychologist, a middle school teacher, the librarian, and I boxed books, handing them off to the janitors for transport. It only took a few hours, and the collection was secure. We saved the district thousands of dollars, so our crime, if that is what it had been termed, was of the Robin Hood variety. I have to say, we did it joyfully. The flood had taken so much from the community; we just couldn't let it take the library, too.

Advances in Crisis Intervention

The twenty-first-century school psychologist must be even more adept than my generation at dealing with catastrophe. The increase in crises of both natural and human origin requires the school psychologist to have a firm grasp on crisis intervention. Fortunately, a great deal of understanding has developed over the past decades, and there is a fine body of literature available to learn from. Whether it's how to respond in the immediate moment or how to recover from the stress of dealing with a crisis, school psychologists have many resources at hand.

When I began as a school psychologist, we did not have a comprehensive approach to preventing crises, intervening as they occurred, or responding to them in the aftermath. Since then, the National Association of School Psychologists has developed a fund of resources that addresses the response not only to a crisis and what happens afterward but also to related topics. A cursory look at NASP's website shows a wide range of information, and all of it is available in translation into Spanish and other world languages. Their list is comprehensive. It includes systems-level prevention, school violence resources (including bullying), mental health resources, natural disaster resources, media and social media resources, and direct crisis support (National Association of School Psychologists, n.d.-a.).

I think of what it would have meant to me if I would have been part of a district level multidisciplinary team addressing systems-level prevention at the time a principal asked me to administer a violence test to a student who seemed a potential risk. There would have been a set of procedures already in place, with other team members beside me. A suicide risk assessment would have been conducted. All parents in the district already would have been informed about what steps the district would take to determine level of threat. We would have taken a close look at many aspects of the situation, instead of just relying on my impressions and wishing and hoping that all would turn out well in the end.

Had we had available to us then what is at everyone's fingertips now, my fellow school psychologists in our co-op and I would have had a guide to follow when we arrived at a school in the early morning the first time we had to respond to the death of a student by suicide. We were able to carry the day because of the expertise of one among us, but had he been out sick that day, my colleague and I, both inexperienced in crisis intervention, would have had to just make it up as we went along. Dealing with a crisis is never easy, but it is much less stressful if a school has a crisis plan and crisis team in place. By the end of the last century, people like Scott Poland, the chairperson of NASP's National Emergency Assistance Team, were giving crisis intervention workshops at state conferences.

Now school psychologists have access to comprehensive training through the PREPaRE Crisis Curriculum, so they can learn what to do during the five mission stages of a crisis: prevention, protection, mitigation, response, and recovery.

The letters in PREPaRE stand for:

- P—Prevent and prepare for crises.
- R—Reaffirm physical health and welfare, and perceptions of safety and security.

- E—Evaluate psychological trauma risk.
- P—Provide interventions.
- *a*—and
- R—Respond to mental health needs.
- E—Examine the effectiveness of crisis preparedness (National Association of School Psychologists).

What particularly impresses me is the information presented by NASP about prevention. The very best way to address crises is to do all one can to stop them from happening in the first place. NASP's "Responding to School Violence: Tips for Administrators" is succinct and comprehensive. It highlights prevention measures schools should take and suggestions about how to reinforce school safety. I especially appreciate the section on "What to Say to Students" (National Association of School Psychologists, n.d.-b). In my experience, one of the hardest tasks for many adults in school is finding words to talk to students about potentially frightening topics. NASP provides guidelines which make painful realities mentionable so they can become emotionally manageable.

Monitoring Yourself as You Respond to a Crisis

In the first few crises I faced I was fortunate to have school psychology colleagues at my side. I cannot say enough in favor of working as a team. Your partner(s) can offer support and reassurance as you make your way through the day and will be able to observe what condition you are in. A partner can remind us to step back and take needed breaks.

What I remember most is the intensity. I felt like my body was in overdrive, which of course it was. That was necessary to get through the first day, especially. But after that it is wise to temper one's reaction. We know that going full tilt without rest and time for detachment can lead to burnout. It can be soothing to express in writing what one has learned from the experience and plan a forward-looking response. I think of the example portrayed in an article published in the *Communique* (Mann et al., 2019).

Writing about dealing with the stress of working in schools with high levels of tragedy, one of the authors describes leaving for the weekend for a private time at a beach after a series of tragedies. While there, she begins writing the article about coping. She comments lightly about how she went to the beach, but what does she end up doing? Writing an article, which sounds like work, not self-care. But I suspect that was exactly what helped to restore her equilibrium, because in the face of events over which she had had no control, now she could take meaningful action. After doing crisis intervention a few times, I wrote some short articles for our cooperative and our state organization. It bolstered my morale because I felt I might be helping someone else manage better than I did when first confronted with a school tragedy.

We can also take heart that there are many organizations offering information and support for schools and students in crisis. For example, The National Education Association has "NEA's School Crisis Guide" available online (National Education Association, 2018). The "Model School District Policy on Suicide Prevention", a collaborative work by the American Foundation for Suicide Prevention, the American School Counselor Association, the National Association of School Psychologists, and The Trevor Project, was updated in 2019. They also have offered webinars on how to implement the policy. In 2019, 22 states required their schools to have a suicide prevention policy in place (American Foundation for Suicide Prevention, 2019). Clearly there is growing concern at the state level for such a policy.

There are also citizen groups devoted to promoting school safety. Safe and Sound Schools, for example, was founded by two mothers, Michelle Gay and Melissa Parker, who lost their daughters at the 2012 tragedy at Sandy Hook Elementary. Its website at safeandsoundschools.org shows a range of supports that they offer to schools throughout the country. It invests its resources in activities such as its post-crisis support network, which ranges from in-person visits to a community after a tragedy to phone calls and other long-distance guidance. They do not restrict intervention to the aftermath of school shootings; they can be summoned after a natural disaster or a violent act that did not result in death.

The role of the school psychologist in relation to crisis intervention has expanded dramatically over the past several decades. Fortunately, so has our knowledge base. I am optimistic that good can't help but come of having so many concerned professionals from several occupations collaborating to create guidelines and sharing information. That citizen activists are also participating gives me hope.

References

American Foundation for Suicide Prevention. (2019). *Four leading national organizations launch suicide prevention template plan for schools.* https://afsp.org/four-leading-national-organizations-launch-suicide-prevention-template-plan-for-schools

Mann, A., Zaheer, I., & Kelly-Vance, L. (2019). Self-care for school psychologists: Advancing social justice for youth. *Communiqué, 48*(4), 21–23.

National Association of School Psychologists. (n.d.-a.). *Direct crisis support.* www.nasponline.org/resources-and-publications/resources-and-podcasts/school-climate-safety-and-crisis/direct-crisis-support

National Association of School Psychologists. (n.d.-b.). *About PREPaRE.* www.nasponline.org/professional-development/prepare-training-curriculum/about-prepare

National Education Association. (2018). *NEA's school crisis guide.* www.nea.org/resource-library/neas-school-crisis-guide

Ness, K. (2000). Empty desks: Staff reactions to student deaths. *Communique, 28*(5), 8–9.

Ness, K., & Vanderpan, M. (1999). Retrospective on disaster: One year after in the Red River Valley. In A. Canter & S. Carroll (Eds.), *Crisis prevention and response: A collection of NASP resources* (pp. 197–199). The National Association of School Psychologists.

Chapter 18

Hand in Glove

Our Relationship With Teachers

I admire teachers. My experience as one taught me how difficult a role it is and how unaware people in general are of how hard it can be. Besides the skill required to do it well, one must also have a thick skin, almost limitless energy, and wholehearted dedication to students. They know they wouldn't get rich at their occupation; their reward is having a positive impact on the lives of kids by helping them to learn. I loved working alongside teachers, and, knowing what they were up against, I hoped I could serve as a strong support to them.

Mutual Support

We need to create time for teachers, so we can consult and collaborate with one another. Early on, I adopted a routine of making quick daily rounds among staff in my schools. At some point during my scheduled school visits, I would pop in for a few moments, just to check in with each teacher to see if anyone had any concerns. I did this on a regular basis with my special education teachers, school social workers, school counselors, and often with regular education teachers, too, if I was working with a child in their classroom. This way I could stay abreast of any escalating problems.

Sometimes the visit consisted of just a smile and a "thumbs up"; other times it led to a conversation or setting up a time for a conversation later. What I valued about these visits was that I was able to gain worthwhile information in a few, short moments, and at the same time, show my support. "Is anything gaining on us?" I would ask. A nod of the head told me a great deal.

I soon learned that teachers may view us in a wide variety of ways. We might be seen as a wise consultant who conveys necessary information that makes them feel more secure about whether they are proceeding in the right way on behalf of their students. But we might be seen as an interfering outsider who makes life more difficult with our attention to rules and regulations. Maybe we are someone who seems detached from the community, unencumbered with the intertwining relationships that

DOI:10.4324/9781003348344-18

are inevitable in closely knit groups. Or we might be seen as someone who can run interference for them with their administrator or a parent, precisely because we are more detached.

We might be seen as an interruption, or the annoying reason they must attend lots of meetings. Perhaps we are a trusted confidante, or a referral source, someone who knows the wider mental health community and can be trusted to recommend a professional outside of school. If we are itinerants, we may serve as their pony express for delivering school materials throughout the cooperative. Perhaps we are considered a strong support for the classroom teacher, or, on the other hand, we are seen as unaware of how hard their position is. We can also be viewed as a means to rid one's classroom of a particularly challenging child, or, as a trusted advisor who can help a child remain in a classroom.

Most of all, what I valued about this face-to-face contact, however brief, was that it was a way to reinforce our mutual support. I not only learned about how they were doing, I learned how what I was doing was affecting them. Had I overlooked something or failed them in any way? As convenient as email can be, I much preferred the briefest of conversations to something written. Email messages gave too many opportunities for misunderstanding, because the subtle emotional content of a face-to-face encounter was missing.

But times have changed. Beginning several years ago, much of Natasha's communication is conducted electronically. Because it's so easy to send and receive messages, she sometimes finds herself feeling too accessible and must set boundaries on how often she checks for new messages and how quickly she responds, so she won't be unnecessarily controlled by them. She reminds herself of the mantra she learned in internship: She must teach people how to treat her; otherwise, they will set the standard, and that might be to her disadvantage. Natasha has noticed how much pressure is brought to bear on teachers, in this regard. Now students can submit homework instantly, so shouldn't it be graded just as quickly? The pressures of the electronic age must be confronted so nobody is constantly at the mercy of someone else's agenda. Deciding how to handle email is a constant exercise in perspective taking.

Teachers were some of my best allies, and I sought and trusted their constructive criticism, something easier to elicit in person than in writing. I made it a practice, especially at the beginning of my career or when I was assigned a new school, to ask for feedback on my performance. I found people were pleased to tell me honestly what they thought, and I invariably found their comments instructive and reassuring, however frank they were. I think they liked knowing I cared what they thought of my work. I also came to see that my colleagues usually had great empathy for me. I almost always came to really like my teachers, so it was a pleasure to see them, if only for a brief exchange.

Student Support Teams and Multi-Tiered Systems of Support

Besides my informal encounters, I also worked with teachers in S.S.T. meetings. Each of my schools had a team of educators who met to gather information and make decisions about what the best way forward for a child who is struggling should be. At the beginning of my career, that meant I attended what were called pre-referral meetings. By its very name, it was a meeting where children were in the process of being considered for special education assessment. Often, testing was considered almost a foregone conclusion, unless the school psychologist, unofficial gatekeeper, did not agree that it was warranted. Essentially a deficit model, the focus was on the child, not the learning environment.

Over the last several years, the role of the school psychologist as gatekeeper for special education has broadened to intervention collaborator. In my era, we attended what were called school support teams or instructional support teams, to address student needs. We tried to identify a child's needs early in the hope of remedying whatever may be interfering with learning before an intervention as intensive as special education instruction becomes necessary. The emphasis shifted from addressing a limitation within the child to identifying what resources are available to foster the child's success in the regular classroom, that is, from a "waiting to fail" model to a proactive approach. At the end of my career, teams were just starting to adopt the Multi-Tiered Systems of Support, an integration of Response to Intervention and Positive Behavioral Interventions and Supports. M.T.S.S. is a structured method of designing both academic and behavioral strategies. It has several components: universal screening for all students, levels of intervention (tiers) adapted to the intensity of need, and continuous collection of data and assessment of progress. M.T.S.S. is a school-wide approach that can include parents, depending on the level of need. Natasha now participates in both the M.T.S.S. team and the mental health team in the main district she serves.

These teams are composed of regular education teachers, special education teachers, principals, school counselors, school social workers, school psychologists, E.L.L. teachers, reading specialists, and anyone else who might be able to lend expertise. Combining everyone's expertise made for collaboration at its best. Now technology adds another dimension to enhance collaboration, through the cloud sharing of documents, an advance Natasha appreciates.

Special Education Teams

Each student enrolled in a special education program has a team of school personnel who meet with parents on a regular basis, at least once a year, to review the individualized education plan (I.E.P.). In some instances, we meet far more frequently, such as in the example of a middle schooler whom I will call Nathan.

Nathan challenged his team's skills to the limit. Nathan had psychotic episodes during which he had delusions. He also would experience fits of rage, and he would verbally threaten people. He was tall and strong, and he had a quick temper, which led us to fear that he might do harm. He also had a penchant for running away. Consequently, he had never spent much time in the regular classroom.

He lived with a relative whom I met at a meeting in school where she complained forcefully that Nathan spent too little time in the regular classroom. The team tried to explain that he was such a high risk for flight and violence that we wanted to proceed with great caution in increasing his freedom of movement. But she was not convinced. Tensions ran so high in the home-school relationship that we decided to have a weekly Wednesday morning meeting with everyone together, including his social worker, so that we would be sure to hear immediate concerns and address them.

As a rule, I was pleased to encounter a parent/guardian who was a strong advocate for their child with disabilities. But this time I felt the school team was unfairly blamed. We made some progress after we presented a review of Nathan's entire school history, which revealed there had been incidents of violence, beginning in preschool.

Our Wednesday morning meetings were an opportunity for the special education teacher and his team to keep the guardian and social worker apprised of what interventions were undertaken educationally and behaviorally. As we became better acquainted, the social worker came to realize why we were so cautious, and she started to influence Nathan's caregiver. Our home-school relations improved as the guardian and social worker recognized how serious and sincere the teachers and support staff were in trying to help and protect Nathan. It was a relief to finally feel like we were working together, rather than being at odds. In the end I found my main contribution was to help improve communication by serving as a go-between with the social worker.

The strength required of Nathan's guardian in caring for him was brought home to me during one memorable meeting. Nathan's guardian commented that her day had started at 4:00 that morning, because Nathan had got up, so she had had to deal with him, and he was not easy to handle. She was many years older than I. My respect for her increased as I contemplated how fatigued she must be. There seemed to be no limit to what she was willing to do for Nathan, and I reflected on her initial hostility toward us, which, I realized, had been a sign of her devotion.

Another I.E.P. team I worked with was summoned one morning to meet with a mother and her attorney. The mother believed the special education program had created such stress in her son's life that he was even losing weight because of it, and she was intent on seeking legal recourse. We were mystified, because no one had observed he was distressed, and we thought he looked thinner because he had just gone through a growth spurt, as is typical of junior high age boys.

The I.E.P. team was gathered around a large table for the meeting, all of us anxiously wondering how it would unfold. The mother and her attorney joined us, and after introductions, the lawyer clicked open her briefcase, took out her legal pad, and began an interrogation. The case manager gave thorough, thoughtful answers, as did all others who were questioned. After several minutes of hearing what the team had to say, the attorney turned to the mother and said that the school was addressing her son's educational needs very well and there was no point in her retaining a lawyer. On that note, she snapped her briefcase shut. Case closed. After the two women left the room, we sat together in silence, exhaling in unison.

Better Together

Over the years I found it particularly gratifying to give in-services to teachers on critical topics, particularly concerning children's mental health. This took the form of lectures on A.D.H.D., crisis intervention, Positive Behavioral Interventions and Supports, pre-referral intervention, and various aspects of mental illness in children. Sometimes I partnered with colleagues to do this, but I also did it alone.

Teachers can feel beleaguered, even overwhelmed, because of the pressure to identify children with mental health problems. I was glad to impart what knowledge I had, which, as a side benefit, demonstrated the value of school psychology. Teachers are expected to deal with traumatized children every day. I was always glad to offer them what I could.

Our professions provide complementary knowledge, so they were able to offer me insight, in turn. School psychologists interact almost exclusively in an individual setting with children, which is an advantage in many respects. At the same time, it can be a narrow experience. Teachers work with children over the course of a school year and see them in several situations and relationships throughout their day. The demands of the teacher's busy day, however, may prevent them from interacting one on one. We can combine our perspectives to good advantage when designing plans to address a child's specific educational needs.

Behavior Intervention

Sometimes a teacher or parent would request that I counsel a student to address emotional/behavioral concerns. Children act out their feelings when they can't express them any other way, and in a classroom full of students, the actions of one unhappy child can be highly disruptive to everyone's learning, as well as taxing a teacher's nerves. Coming up with an effective behavioral intervention is one of the most satisfying aspects of being a school psychologist. Sometimes, even a simple intervention can work incredible change.

One of my most successful counseling sessions occurred with a first-grade girl whose behavior in school had deteriorated after the birth of a little sister. Before the new baby arrived, the girl had been a model student. She was at the top of her class academically and her teacher described her as an all-around, high-achieving, and considerate child. But her behavior over a two-week period became so problematic that I was called in to advise the teacher and meet with her individually. The parents were shocked and mystified. At home she was attentive to the new baby and eager to help take care of her. But at school she was rapidly becoming a terror, pushing, and hitting on the playground and rebelling in the classroom. It was as if a changeling had taken the place of the formerly delightful, cooperative child. So, what did I advise?

I didn't know what to suggest to the very capable teacher who had already done her best. But because I had had success using play with older kids, I figured it was worth a try with a little one. I brought a bag full of stuffed animals and in the corner of the room there also was a large doll (it was used as the school mascot) that, coincidentally, happened to be as large as the girl. Thus, we had plenty of characters to play whatever roles the girl wished. In my very first meeting she began by playing mama and baby, and in the middle of it, she went over to the mascot in the corner and started slapping it again and again. "Bad girl!" she cried and slapped the mascot across the face. "You want to hurt the baby! Bad, bad girl!" And she slapped it several more times. After beating the mascot soundly, she went back to mothering the baby.

I watched in amazement. I did not question her or comment on her burst of aggression. One principle of play therapy is to provide a permissive environment where any behavior that is not dangerous is allowed, so the child feels accepted, regardless of how aggressive their play may be. This allows for the full expression of their deepest feelings. When I spoke with the parents and the teacher, they were shocked at how she played, given the fact that the girl had shown only adoration for the baby. I made plans to meet with her again the next week, very curious about how she would respond in a second session.

When I returned a week later, the teacher greeted me smiling, as she asked what I had done in my session with her student. She explained that the girl had done a complete turnaround and was restored to her former self. I explained that all I had done was provide the toys and the setting—the child did her own work. Evidently all she needed was a safe place to play out—literally—her aggressive feelings. As Virginia Maxline, legendary play therapist, explains,

> Non-directive play therapy . . . may be described as an opportunity that is offered to the child to experience growth under the most favorable conditions. Since play is his natural medium for self-expression, the child is given the opportunity to play out his accumulated feelings of tension, frustration, insecurity, aggression, fear, bewilderment, confusion.
>
> (Axline, 1974, p. 16)

I was as amazed as the teacher. I never again had such dramatic results from one small intervention.

Mandated Reporting

Sometimes a school psychologist's action can look like something a social worker would typically do. A teacher approached me about the concern she had for a student who chronically fell asleep in class. His home room teacher came to me because he was sleeping in class so often that he was not completing his work. She said it was painfully evident he was simply too exhausted to stay awake, so of course he was unable to learn. He was irritable besides, an understandable consequence of his chronic fatigue. The boy confided to his teacher that he couldn't sleep much at night because it was too noisy at home.

We soon learned that he was being kept awake by late-night partying in the floor above and also in his apartment. His mother had a long history of addiction, and it appeared she needed intervention again. The school social worker I often partnered with, and I filed child protection reports with the county and recommended to his teachers that they do the same. They did, and soon the child was placed in foster care. His schoolwork and his behavior improved dramatically once he had regular sleep. This small act of cooperation among support staff and his teachers yielded immediate and dramatic positive results.

On another occasion, things didn't go as smoothly. I had arrived from a different school to attend an I.E.P. meeting after school. As soon as I entered the room, I noticed everyone looked glum. The meeting began immediately, so I didn't have a chance to inquire about the somber mood. There didn't seem to be anything in the course of the meeting to warrant how people were acting, so after the rest of the team left, I asked the case manager if something had happened. What she relayed was quite disturbing.

Evidently a substitute teacher had severely manhandled a student, and the teachers were upset. I asked if anyone had filed a complaint and she said no. I encouraged her to go ahead, but she hesitated. It looked like the incident was going to go unreported, so I told her that I would do it. My report would be weaker than hers because she had witnessed the incident, but I was also a mandated reporter, so I was duty-bound to file. The next time I entered the main office in that school no one greeted me. I surmised word of my reporting had spread.

Some days later in the grocery store a teacher from the school sidled up to me. In a half-whisper she said, "I want you to know you have many silent allies". Evidently the teachers had felt too intimidated to file a report. I wondered if they were even worried about being seen with me at school. But this teacher graciously took the opportunity to tell me of their silent support. It was a good lesson that sometimes we may not be as alone as we feel. After our encounter I was doubly glad I had made the report. When I realized how anxious the teachers felt, I was all the more grateful that I had the independence to act.

Our Partners

Special education teachers were typically true partners. I enjoyed the prospect of collaborating with them; drawing up assessment plans, doing the assessments, holding the meetings with parents to review results, and conferring about the needs of kids. I looked forward to these encounters because we were able to work well together.

Observing in their classrooms was a special treat because I was able to witness them in action as they guided children with disabilities through challenging task, while accepting them just as they are. The complete acceptance of their students as themselves, deserving the same devotion as everyone else, was an inspiration to witness. I think of a math teacher who gave his all every lesson to help his class learn each new concept, pacing his teaching to match their needs. His relentless encouragement brought forth whatever effort they could manage, and he celebrated whatever progress they made. However insecure they might have been about math, they could relax in his class because they were treated with compassion and respect amid doses of good-natured humor. Understandably, students adored him. He ended each year by teaching them how to walk on stilts, a skill he picked up while working as a clown in a circus. Whether or not it was the last day of school, he always did what he could to make their learning joyful.

I remember with gratitude a teacher who did me an enormous favor the last year of my career. The co-op was short-staffed, and so I was given an extra district to cover, as were some other school psychologists. I managed OK for a while but then I had an explosion of referrals, and the school psychologist who was assigned to be my backup was also deluged with work, so she couldn't bail me. The learning disabilities teacher with whom I shared the largest caseload volunteered to do all the classroom observations for the rest of our assessments that year, a task I usually did. She was not required to; she did it out of kindness. I will bless this teacher forever.

A Bow to Classroom Teachers

My encounters with regular education teachers usually occurred at I.E.P. meetings, in their own classrooms when I was asked to meet with them personally, or when I was observing a student in their class while they were teaching. They seemed to appreciate the fact that I had been a teacher, and I often found myself empathizing with them, remembering my own experiences in front of a class. What I had learned firsthand was that a well-run classroom depends on a myriad of factors, many of which are beyond the teacher's control. Teachers need to be well trained, of course, but the classroom environment has a great influence over how well they can teach.

There must be adequate supplies, including textbooks and other teaching aides, so students can be presented learning challenges at the level they are capable. Rules must be understood and evenly enforced throughout the school. Ideally, the children should be well rested and well nourished, and they must have adequate emotional support in life outside of school, so they are ready to learn. But in many schools, on many days, children come frightened, undernourished, burdened with trauma from various sources, and teachers have no choice but just to do the best they can.

I sometimes imagined how well I would be performing in their role should we have to change places, and it was a rare day that I wasn't impressed with what the teacher was achieving. I remembered what a balancing act it was to keep a wide range of students interested at the same time, and the amount of planning and preparation that went into a good lesson. Some teachers were so adept I felt like I was watching a symphony conductor directing an orchestra. These teachers were masters of the art of teaching, and I was filled with admiration, knowing as I did the range of ability and maturity within the class.

The good humor and affection shown to students by their master teachers was a pleasant subtheme to the lesson. These teachers were adept at guiding the whole class, all the while helping everyone to learn according to their ability. There were moments that to me felt sacred, as teachers encouraged anxious students to perform, and the kids surprised themselves with their own capabilities.

Our Professional Relatives

Besides classroom teachers, we work with an array of people in various specialties. Our first cousins in schools are other special education personnel. Early childhood special education teachers, school social workers, special education teachers dealing with specific learning disabilities, behavioral problems, and developmental delay, speech clinicians, and—although not special education—school counselors all overlap in some respects with our knowledge and point of view. I once heard a psychiatrist addressing special education teachers comment that they did him an enormous favor because they were usually the ones to first confront parents with the severity of their child's disability.

By the time the parents got to him, their anger was usually already dissipated; they had worked through a lot of their denial with the early childhood teacher and other special education people so by the time they were in his office, they were ready to hear the hard facts. What that process meant for the special education staff was often dealing with generalized anger, fear, grief—all the stuff that comes with having to give up the dream of having a normal child. School psychologists are also often a part of that process, but the teachers bear the brunt daily, and they deserve our respect. School psychologists and teachers work hand and glove with one another, so a high level of trust and respect is essential between us.

My Closest Allies

Employees at the rural cooperative served as my closest allies, even though I often didn't see much of them. Our paths would cross sporadically when we had business to tend to at the same school, but for the most part, I didn't see my co-op colleagues much except at meetings at co-op headquarters. That felt like coming home, because we were nearly all in the same situation, being itinerants and outsiders. A few were assigned to a particular school, but most were not. Early childhood special education teachers, for example, stayed put in a classroom in a district building, but the rest of us went from place to place. Itinerancy was part of our routine. I think back at what a pleasure it was to encounter another co-op person when she came to a school where I happened to be. We were able to compare our experiences within the district, often finding we had similar impressions, I suppose because we dealt with a lot of the same dynamics. Our relationship with the district administration was often strongly affected by how they felt about being affiliated with the co-op, and how well they liked our director.

A few years before I retired, I gave an in-service to my colleagues at our special education cooperative. It was the only time I addressed them, and the topic was urgent. We were all feeling a lot of job stress; it seemed like each year we were expected to handle more and more with less and less support. It was time to admit this to ourselves and come up with ways to address the situation. This resulted in a workshop entitled, "Circling In, Guidelines for Problem Solving".

The circle was our organization's main metaphor during much of the time I worked for our cooperative. Our director emphasized that he saw our structure as circular, rather than pyramidal. He of course was our boss, but he said he saw his role as a facilitator for us in our specialties to do the very best job possible. He told us he was not qualified to evaluate us within our areas of expertise; he assumed we were competent based on our credentials. So long as our schools were satisfied with our performance, he did not question our capabilities. He, as our director, was like the rest of us, having one seat around the circle and a particular role to play. He said he judged his success by how successful we were able to be. And so, our circle gathered to take a close look at our situation and share ideas, focusing on solutions, rather than just problems, to help us cope better with the conditions we faced.

Second Cousins

On the other side of the family, we are related to other psychologists, and like teachers, we have much in common with them but are different in important respects. The best way I've heard school psychologists described is that we know more about school than other psychologists do, and we know more about psychology than teachers do. Most of my dealings with clinical psychologists were with someone in private practice who was seeing a student attending one of my schools. Under the best circumstances, we were able to share information and work collaboratively. On some—fortunately rare—occasions we were at odds, and when we were it was always for the same reason: confusion caused by differing state laws.

A clinical psychologist from across the state border would give a child a medical diagnosis and then inform the parent that the child was eligible for special education services, not realizing that my state criteria would not necessarily support placement. We were both dedicated advocates for kids, so we would sort things out. It was unfortunate when confusion over laws gave rise to conflict between us.

Need for Mutual Support

Teachers and other colleagues are our partners; we need one another to accomplish our mutual goals. We need the benefit of each other's expertise to make wise decisions as we try to serve children well. School psychologists can make a difference in how well teachers can face the demands placed upon them, but we have to be good collaborators to do that. If we can help to boost a teacher's effectiveness, it will also serve to improve their morale. With all the challenges currently facing schools, they need all the support we can offer. We, in turn, need their support. I think of a comment a teacher made to me after a debriefing meeting when I had spent the day with students grieving the loss of a classmate. As she stood up to leave, she said, "Kathleen, some days your job is really hard". The fact is, she had been dealing with the same situation all day long too, but in a different setting, in a different way. Yes, some days my job was really hard. But so was hers.

Challenges for This Decade and Beyond

Madeline Will's article in *Education Week* from 2019 contrasted the challenges teachers faced ten years earlier with what they were dealing with ten years later, when teachers were adjusting to the effects of educational reforms in the first decade of the twenty-first century. In many schools across the country, it meant teachers were being evaluated for the first time based on their students' performance on standardized tests, and their pay and job security hung in the balance. Accountability and testing became overriding themes in the work lives of teachers (Will, 2019).

While teachers saw their role becoming more rigid, the rates of teen suicide and cyberbullying were increasing. During the earlier decade the nation experienced the tragedies of the school shootings at Sandy Hook Elementary School in Newtown, Connecticut, and Margory Stoneman High School in Parkland, Florida. Active shooter drills became part of school routine, and in some states, teachers were given the right to carry guns. The job of teaching was getting harder and harder, because of both top-down decisions from the federal government and societal pressures. This trend did not go unnoticed. One consequence was that fewer young people were choosing teaching as a career, so chronic teacher shortages were on the rise. Special education was particularly hard hit (Will, 2019).

Severe teacher stress had become so pervasive it became the topic of serious research. Teachers were reporting the same level of stress as nurses. The attrition rate among teachers during their first five years had risen to about 50%. Furthermore, about two-thirds of those who stayed reported feeling disconnected from their work, a sign they might be on their way to burnout. Such a high level of stress can have dangerous consequences for the health of the teacher and for the teacher's ability to perform in the classroom. Student performance also suffers when teachers suffer (Will, 2019).

And then came a pandemic. An article in *Education Week* from the autumn of 2020 asks the question, "Did Covid-19 Really Drive Teachers to Quit?" The short answer is that there was no identifiable pattern of retirements or resignations from the data that was analyzed. One teacher demographic factor that was mentioned is that our teacher population nationwide is becoming younger, and so less vulnerable to Covid-19 than older teachers are, because of their age. Also, some states have restrictive resignation policies, so it is not possible for someone to retire hastily once the school year begins. In addition, teachers need income, and that need does not go away during a pandemic. So even though a teacher might want to leave teaching, the financial cost would be prohibitive (Corbin et al., 2019).

Of particular interest to me was the attention in the article given to North Dakota, my home state. Evidently, the teacher retirement office received a greater number of calls than usual requesting information about what a teacher's benefits would be if the person retired immediately. Early in the fall they even received calls from teachers who had been back at school for only a couple of days, wanting to get out. Despite their distress, few chose retirement, because the financial benefits would be insufficient (Will & Schwartz, 2020).

As the pandemic stretched on over years, the toll on teachers became more and more apparent. In early 2022, Natasha commented that everyone at school was just surviving; no one had mental energy for anything beyond the routine. But there was little about life at school that was routine. Children had missed a lot of learning the year before, and there was no way that kindergarteners or first graders, for example, could be on track, as they could have been before the pandemic struck. Special education services could not make up the difference. Seasoned teachers were able to soldier on, but those with less experience were stretched to the limit and beyond. Natasha said she would not be at all surprised to hear that every teacher in a school resigned, overwhelmed by sheer exhaustion. When she compared the level of stress she felt during her internship with me, several years ago, to the current situation, she said, "Internship was trial by fire. Now we ARE on fire!" (N. Olson, personal communication, 2/17/2022).

Even before the pressure of the pandemic, there were places in our country in great need of teachers. Katharine Strunk, Michigan State University professor of education policy, has researched the situation over several years in the state where she teaches. She recommends raising financial compensation in the underserved communities, whether rural or urban, to improve retention. Schools have high turnover because teachers can be paid higher salaries in other communities. Interestingly, some teachers can be convinced to stay, despite lower pay, if they work in a school with a principal they like; a positive working environment is an incentive to continue. Rural areas also need teacher training located near hard-to-staff schools, according to Professor Strunk. That way, potential teachers in underserved rural and urban areas can find work close to home (Livengood, 2021).

Brandis and McPhee would agree that teachers need better working conditions, which can be accomplished through administrators and colleagues providing constructive, rather than punitive feedback. Teachers also need to have healthy interactions with students, so they must know how to use positive strategies to guide students, which will at the same time build friendly relationships. Finally, these authors emphasize the need for teachers to take good care of themselves. Like nurses, they cannot help those they serve if they are not in shape to perform their duties (Brandis & McPhee, 2018). As stressful as conditions were pre-pandemic, these comments, made before the pandemic, do not consider the severity of teacher stress created by Covid-19 and its mutations. My local newspaper, the *Grand Forks Herald*, devoted an editorial to the growing crisis in education, describing the alarming number of teachers in North Dakota interested in leaving their profession. They warn that industries eager to hire competent workers will be glad to welcome teachers, because they are skilled in many ways that transfer well into other occupations (Grand Forks Herald Editorial Board, 2022).

Schmidt and Jones-Fosu consider the stress levels in urban schools to have reached epidemic proportions, far higher than in rural schools. Frequently, disruptive student behavior was a leading cause, but a long list of other contributing factors makes teaching challenging to the point of exhaustion. Low pay, large classes, fear of violence, and not enough participation in decision-making are just some of the other reasons that teachers were being pushed to burnout. For teachers to understand their students better, the authors suggest that they need to study justice issues and critical reflection, recognizing that in our era 82% of people going into teaching are White females, and so are from a different demographic than most of their urban students (Schmidt & Jones-Fosu, 2019).

Jay Wamsted, a White teacher with several years of experience teaching in a majority Black high school, offers suggestions for how to perform on this interracial terrain. He recommends that White teachers think about what advantage their race gives them compared to their students of color, and that they learn about implicit biases and what effect they may have on their students and the parents of their students. Wamstad recommends that teachers assess how historically accurate and culturally valid course content is. He recommends studying the history of racism in our country and to gain a thorough understanding of the role of slavery and genocide in our history. He advises teachers to incorporate cultural diversity into their classrooms (Wamsted, 2020).

Opposition to speaking about systemic racism arose among several Red states in response to schools addressing racial issues directly. In 2021 the Texas state legislature, for example, passed a loosely written law forbidding discussion of racism beyond saying it is an aberration from America's founding ideals (Richman & Donaldson, 2021). This turn of events caused worry among educators who wondered whether they would be targeted for lawsuits or dismissal for something they said in their classroom. Matthew Hawn, a teacher in Blountville, Tennessee, was dismissed from his position after assigning Ta-Nehisi Coates's essay that considers how race affected Donald Trump's winning the presidency, and for playing "White Privilege", a spoken word poem that includes some vulgar language. The grounds for dismissal were violating the teacher's code of ethics. He appealed, supported by parents and teachers opposed to his dismissal, but he was not reinstated (McGee, 2021).

In another Red state, Amanda Curtis, president of the Montana Federation of Public Employees, which represents over 10,000 educators, said that teachers were confused by what was required of them. In several places, professional organizations mounted opposition to restrictions, saying the term "critical race theory" (C.R.T.) is being used as a buzzword to restrict racial discussions (Folley, 2021). Nick Archuleta, president of North Dakota United, a union representing public educators and employees in North Dakota, addressed the controversy in public media. He reviewed the origin of C.R.T., pointing out that it is a theory that emerged in the 1970s in academia, emphasizing that it is not a part of public school curriculum. Rather, it is being used to political purpose at this time of deep division, by claiming the theory is a method of teaching our students to hate our country. Archuleta assures the public that any concerns they have about what is being taught in school can be addressed directly with their child's teachers, administrators, and school boards. He takes umbrage at the insult to educators contained in the accusation (Archuleta, 2021). Because the federal government has no authority over school curricula, Secretary of Education Miguel Cardona did not make an official recommendation. He did, however, encourage school districts to trust the expertise of their teachers to handle sensitive discussions (Barnum, 2021).

Natasha commented that in one of her districts parents are objecting to social-emotional learning (S.E.L.) curricula, saying it's a way to insert critical race theory into school practice (Olson, N., personal communication, May 26, 2022). Such criticism ratchets up stress among well-intentioned personnel in schools. My hope is that this ongoing controversy can provide school psychologists an opportunity in their school communities to address underlying feelings such as fear and shame attached to racial issues and allow them to highlight the value of facing, rather than avoiding, difficult conversations. Learning how to participate in a sensitive discussion is a life skill worth practicing. The value of listening respectfully cannot be underestimated. Effective personal communication and constructive public discourse require it.

The goal would not be to instill guilt or shame about our history but to understand it, so students can recognize that facing injustice and overcoming it must be a mutual endeavor that all of us need to address, in our own thinking and in public policy. Then we can move forward as a nation, and everyone can feel valued. This would be a way to express our love of country. As Hannah Arendt said, we cannot "afford to take that which was good in the past and simply call it our heritage, to discard the bad and simply think of it as a dead load which by itself time will bury in oblivion" (Arendt, 1976, p. ix). Disowning our history does not free us from it.

There are examples from school districts around the country that show participatory democracy can occur, promoting healthy public discourse around issues within a school community. The Central Falls, Rhode Island school district, for example, engaged the community in what they named participatory budgeting, inviting the public to suggest ideas and create proposals which then can be voted on. The district put $100,000 of funds from the American Rescue Plan Act's Elementary and Secondary School Emergency Relief (E.S.S.E.R.) funds to this purpose. In this way, all interested parties can be heard, not just the loudest voices (Bessinger & Collins, 2022).

Besides contending with political issues, teachers also must continually improve their teaching skills. The need for teachers, especially those just beginning, to have time within their regular routine to learn from one another is of particular concern to veteran teacher Judith Harper. Collaborating with colleagues enriches teaching, allowing faculty within a school to improve instruction using a cohesive approach. Collective wisdom can be shared when teachers have time to work together. There are several high-income countries which support time for teacher collaboration in their schools to a much greater degree than does the United States, and it is time for us to raise our standard, Harper believes. She is adamant that increased funding for ongoing teacher training is necessary if we are to inspire new teachers to persist in their vocation (Rizga, 2019).

Evidently many teachers agree with her. In 2018, teachers formed the Red for Ed movement, through which teachers in several states and/or large cities went on strike to protest low wages and inadequate school funding. These were teachers who did not belong to a teachers' union but rebelled on their own, despite living in "right to work" states. This movement to improve conditions for teachers began in states controlled by Republicans, thus the "red" in their name. Beginning 2018, teachers struck in large numbers and continued to do so the following year (Blanc, 2020).

If schools are to retain teachers and attract idealistic youth to the teaching profession, they can no longer expect teachers to buy out of their own pockets the pencils, paper, and other classroom supplies their students must have to get through a day. The notion that it is reasonable for a teacher to have to work a second job to make ends meet, as is the case in some parts of our country, needs to be abandoned (Walker, 2019).

Besides a decent income, teachers deserve support staff such as school counselors, school social workers, and school psychologists in their buildings. The pandemic years brought added stress and grief associated with Covid-19 which must be addressed over the long term. The effects of the pandemic will be felt for a long time to come. Professionals who can help students deal with their loss and regain a sense of their own future are more necessary than ever before.

In so many ways, the fate of the teacher is also the fate of the school psychologist, so we are natural allies. Like teachers, school psychologists are affected by school climate, the threat of danger within a building, and the availability of services for kids. We know teachers can expect to encounter children who have or are experiencing physical, emotional, and sexual abuse; children who are affected by homelessness and malnutrition; children who have been traumatized in any number of ways.

Many of these situations have been exacerbated by the coronavirus, and the effects will linger for years to come. School psychologists have an important role to play by providing support on how to deal with children in distress. Systemic interventions designed to improve school climate in an entire school district can also be a powerful assist. In the public domain, school psychologists can join with teachers to lobby for improved working conditions, such as adequate salaries and funds for maintaining school buildings. When teachers are doing better, school psychologists will, too.

References

Archuleta, N. (2021, July 31). Critical race theory is a theory, not a curriculum. *The Grand Forks Herald*, A5.

Arendt, H. (1976). *The origins of totalitarianism.* Harcourt.

Axline, V. (1974). *Play therapy.* Ballantine Books.

Barnum, M. (2021, June 24). Cardona: I trust teachers to handle history 'we're not proud of'. *Chalkbeat.* www.chalkbeat.org/2021/6/24/22549078/miguel-cardona-critical-race-theory-schools-antiracism-house-hearing

Bessinger, J., & Collins, J. E. (2022, March 24). The case for participatory democracy. *Brookings.* www.brookings.edu/blog/brown-center-chalkboard/2022/03/24/the-case-for-participatory-democracy-during-educational-crisis/

Blanc, E. (2020, October). The red for ed movement, two years in. *New Labor Forum.* https://newlaborforum.cuny.edu/2020/10/03/the-red-for-ed-movement-two-years-in/

Brandis, A., Jeyers, J., & McPhee, K. (2018). The hidden threat of teacher stress. *The Conversation.* https://theconversation.com/the-hidden-threat-of-teacher-stress-92676

Corbin, C., Alamos, P., Lowenstein, A., Downer, J., & Brown, J. (2019). The role of teacher-student relationships in predicting teachers' personal accomplishment and emotional exhaustion. *Journal of School Psychology*, (77), 1–12. https://doi-org.proxy.lib.siu.edu/10.1016/j.jsp.2019.10.001

Folley, A. (2021, June 19). Teachers on edge over critical race theory debate. *The Hill.* https://thehill.com/homenews/state-watch/559242-teachers-on-edge-over-critical-race-theory-debate/

Grand Forks Herald Editorial Board. (2022, February 26). Warning signs point to crisis in education. *Grand Forks Herald*, A5.

Livengood, C. (2021, March 28). Q&A with MSU's Katharine Strunk: Teacher retention starts with compensation, school leadership. *Crain's Detroit Business.* www.crainsdetroit.com/crains-forum/qa-msus-katharine-strunk-teacher-retention-starts-compensation-school-leadership

McGee, K. (2021, June 15). Texas "critical race theory" bill limiting teaching of current events signed into law. *The Texas Tribune.* www.texastribune.org/2021/06/15/abbott-critical-race-theory-law/

Richman, T., & Donaldson, E. (2021, June 15). Gov. Abbott signs 'anti-critical race theory' bill into law over objections from educators and civic groups. *The Dallas Morning News.* www.dallasnews.com/news/education/2021/06/15/gov-abbott-signs-anti-critical-race-theory-bill-into-law-over-objections-from-educators-and-civic-groups/

Rizga, K. (2019, September 19). How to keep teachers from leaving the profession. *The Atlantic.* www.theatlantic.com/education/archive/2019/09/teachers-need-other-teachers-succeed/598330/

Schmidt, L., & Jones-Fosu, S. (2019). Teacher stress in urban classrooms: A growing epidemic. *Urban Education Research and Policy Annuals*, 6(2), 18–25. https://journals.uncc.edu/urbaned/article/view/907

Walker, T. (2019, July 25). Almost one-third of new teachers take on second jobs. *neaToday.* www.nea.org/advocating-for-change/new-from-nea/almost-one-third-new-teachers-take-second-jobs

Wamsted, J. (2020, January 6). 27 mistakes white teachers of Black students make and how to fix them. *Ed Post.* https://educationpost.org/27-mistakes-white-teachers-of-black-students-make-and-how-to-fix-them/

Will, M. (2019, December 10). Teaching in 2020 vs 2010: A look back at the decade. *Education Week.* www.edweek.org/teaching-learning/teaching-in-2020-vs-2010-a-look-back-at-the-decade/2019/12

Will, M., Gewertz, C., & Schwartz, S. (2020, November 17). Did COVID-19 really drive teachers to quit? *Education Week.* www.edweek.org/teaching-learning/did-covid-19-really-drive-teachers-to-quit/2020/11

Chapter 19

A Delicate Journey
Our Relationship With Parents

It can be a challenge for parents to accept their child's uniqueness. One of the tasks of the school psychologist is to assist parents in offering this gift to their child with a disability. It is a kindness, and in the context of having to accept the reality of a disability, it may be accompanied with suffering. And as the psychoanalyst Adam Phillips and his coauthor, historian Barbara Taylor, explain, practicing kindness is not necessarily easy, because to do so makes one vulnerable (Phillips & Taylor, 2010).

It may require special courage to accept a child's disability when it also entails the parents' grieving the loss of their dream of what they had hoped for their child—a life uncomplicated by disability. At its core, "Bearing other people's vulnerability—which means sharing in it imaginatively and practically without needing to get rid of it, to yank people out of it—entails being able to bear one's own" (Phillips & Taylor, 2010). This applies in the parents' relationship with their child and in our relationships with the parents and their child. And as Brene Brown contends, the reward of being able to accept one another's vulnerability is that it makes us more courageous (Brown, 2012).

We need to proceed with compassion, which means we do not judge their emotional response because we are aware they must navigate their own journey, in their own time. We are present to listen, to give useful, timely information, and to support them as they experience whatever they must face about their child's disability and their own reaction to it. We cannot hasten the process, but we can support them as they weather it. As we do, we must also maintain our professional boundaries, recognizing the constraints special education guidelines place on us as we participate in making decisions about services for the child.

It would be easier if our relationship with them was purely therapeutic, but it isn't. In each encounter, we walk a fine line; on the one hand, we sometimes fill the role of advocate for their child to receive special services, but on the other, we must follow state and federal regulations in determining eligibility, which, on occasion, may countermand what parents want. A parent's opinion, while highly valued, does not

DOI:10.4324/9781003348344-19

determine whether a child is placed in special education. Their input for their child's evaluation is a legal requirement, and they have the right to refuse services, but special education staff ultimately judge whether their child qualifies for services. Each state has its own criteria, and these criteria must be adhered to. For parents who live near a state border, this can be confusing when standards may differ significantly, depending on which side of the border one lives. Having served in border towns, I encountered this unfortunate situation more than once.

Many of us enter the field of school psychology with the intention of being advocates for children, so it can be tempting to want to align with parents. But the fact is—and I have heard more than one parent point this out—we work for the schools, and we follow state and federal law. We must be sure we do not mislead them into thinking we are working as an independent advocate.

What Is Unique to Us

School psychologists can be a strong link between the parent and the school, and, on the other hand, can be a buffer between them, also. Because the school psychologist is in a somewhat more neutral position, we sometimes have more leeway in our relationship with parents. And if we see that the school isn't responding to the parents' requests and concerns as they should, we can foster communication because we are perceived as a more neutral party. This is especially true if you are an itinerant and the parents know you work for an outside agency. Sometimes it is necessary to go toe-to-toe with a school over placement decisions, as, for example, in the case of the two brothers who spoke a twin language. Not to do so would have been unethical. On such occasions, the school psychologist can exert tremendous influence.

How Parents See Us

We might be seen as an advocate for their child, someone who has valuable expertise and is able to act on it. But we might be considered a meddler, someone who wants to impose an unnecessary and harmful label on their child which will follow them through life. We may be a "shrink", our very presence signaling there is something terribly mentally or emotionally wrong with their child. We might be seen as someone who lives such a different life from them that we cannot possibly understand how they feel. Conversely, we might be perceived as the only person who has really listened to them closely.

We might be seen as someone collaborating with social services to take their kids away, or, on the other hand, as someone who might testify on their behalf in a custody case. We might be seen as a liaison between them and the classroom teacher who can communicate their objections to the school if they cannot bear to talk to the classroom teacher themselves. We might be someone their child really likes, or, as someone their child doesn't want to see. We might be identified as a member of a racial or ethnic group that the parents identify with, or as a member of a group that the parents fear. We might be seen as a representative of a system that has done them, or their children, wrong. Or we might be seen as their child's main supporter at school.

Whatever preconceived notions parents may have about us, we can influence the relationship for the good if we pay close attention to a few realities. First, we must remember that the evaluation we have conducted with a child may be routine to us—maybe it's the 45th I.Q. test we've given so far in the school year—but it will not be routine to the parent, unless it is a re-evaluation with very little at stake. If it is the first time the child has been evaluated, the parent quite possibly may be a nervous wreck when s/he enters the meeting room. So, let's consider what this might feel like.

Empathizing With Parents

In her novel *The Book of Unknown Americans*, Christina Henriquez articulates the apprehensions and hopes of parents concerned for their child with disabilities. "We simply had to trust that . . . people would take care of her the way she needed to be cared for . . . What choice did we have?" (Henríquez, 2014, p. 32).

As Henriquez illustrates, parents have no choice but to trust us as they send their child with a disability off to school each day. And when we are making life-changing decisions about their child's future, most parents don't have the specialized knowledge necessary to challenge our choices. Let's imagine, then, what it might be like to enter a meeting room with us.

There may be as many as ten people sitting around a large conference table. Under the best circumstances, the parent is accompanied to the room by a staff member, preferably one s/he already has met, at least by phone. And then the parent is immediately introduced to each attendee, and everyone greets the parent warmly, perhaps some even commenting something positive about the child. After introductions, the case manager begins the meeting by addressing any questions and concerns the parent has in layman's language, free of jargon. The parent visibly relaxes, and a meeting full of constructive information sharing and discussion begins.

Here is another possible scenario. Staff may be talking among themselves and might not even acknowledge the presence of the parent until the meeting starts. The parent takes a seat alone and is ignored until the meeting starts. There's a computer for the case manager to sit in front of and a smart board for everyone to view. Instead of just providing visual reinforcement of the information presented, perhaps these tools will distract team members from looking at the parent, noting his/her reactions.

Now it's time for the meeting to begin. In the first instance, the person running the meeting is well acquainted with the parents, knows what the parent most wants to get out of the meeting, and so begins with their goals in mind. The best meetings typically begin by addressing the parent directly, asking if there are any immediate questions, answering them, and then stating in lay language whether the child is going to get help, who will deliver it, and how it will be delivered—all the while, framing these comments in terms of what these changes should and will mean for the child's education.

Less Is Sometimes More

I was once invited to sit in on an evaluation summary meeting with a beginning school psychologist because she wanted me to critique her performance. Her knowledge of this student's disability was praiseworthy. In a sincere effort to be thorough, however, she shared too much technical detail in her oral report. I could see the parents, and, most members of the team, were unable to follow much of what she said.

I encouraged her to make her future oral reports much shorter and simpler, avoiding jargon as much as possible, and to focus directly on the information that supported the team decision concerning special education placement for the child. Parents want to know whether the school is going to help their child, who is going to be in charge, and how the change in programming will affect their child's education and day-to-day life in school. They need to be told right away and in simple, easy to understand language. This will ease their anxieties and pave the way for an ongoing constructive relationship. She accepted my criticisms graciously, and soon learned to relax and speak unaffectedly when she translated technical language into ordinary English.

The example of a surgeon illustrates the point. After I had a tumor removed some years ago, the surgeon entered my hospital room the next morning announcing, "It's benign!", practically shouting his good news from the doorway. He did not show me any charts, pictures, or use medical jargon to discuss my life and death situation. He knew what I needed to know was whether I would recover.

We may not be removing tumors, but parents' worries for their children are serious. Whether a child gets needed help can affect the child's life and the family forever after. This is not a casual event, and it must be treated with the same respect and regard a medical condition is handled.

We should address the situation in terms of *need*. For my surgeon, that meant, deliver the critical news first. We should do the same. Parents have very likely already experienced enough suspense in their imagination. Every effort must be made to put them at ease as much as possible, as soon as possible.

I will extend the analogy one point further. The urgency with which my surgeon conveyed good news to me by not even delaying until he was at my bedside showed me that my fate mattered to him. He was on my side, 100%, and by his actions, I felt fully supported. We must do the same for parents, and the initial meeting provides a fine opportunity. One way is to sit next to them. Not one chair over—be right next to them, so if there is paperwork to go over, you can help, and they can easily turn to you with a question.

Watch to see if they understand what is said and pay attention to the impact of the information that is being conveyed. Interrupt the meeting to clarify anything that is confusing or delivered too quickly for them to absorb and understand. This is never a waste of time. The parents' comfort at the meeting will determine much about the ensuing relationship. Parents should never feel like the team is a closed club, speaking a foreign language. As Sharon Eicher, parent of a child with special needs, points out, parents typically do not know what acronyms and jargon like I.D.E.A., I.E.P., B.I.P., and 504 mean, and they need to have them explained in ordinary language (Eicher, 2018).

Then, when the meeting is over, linger. Parents may have unanswered questions. Be alert for "by the way", questions or comments. It is possible the most important information conveyed to the parent will occur in answer to their afterthought as they are walking out the door.

Parental Self-image

It is important to consider the impact of a child's disability on the self-esteem of the parent. Parents sometimes blame themselves for much that they can't or couldn't help and can be very unforgiving of themselves. Parents often need our compassion as much as their children do. It is our role to be a willing companion to them as they face the complicated and perhaps harsh reality of their child's disability. Bear in mind, too, that parents may not be in step with one another in their acceptance of their child's disability. They are each on a separate journey, and for many it is a painful one. If a school psychologist can speak to a parent's need, not only will the child be helped but the parent may also gain some comfort. As emphasized earlier, we are there to accompany them wherever they are, recognizing the parents themselves may be in very different places.

Providing Backup

Parents often are the true experts in the room. I once accompanied a mother who faced down a table full of teachers who did not believe in A.D.H.D. This was before neuroscience was able to show conclusively that it is an actual neurological condition, not a result of bad parenting. She bravely stood firm, trying to persuade the skeptics, and I was glad to offer what current scientific information I had. I don't think we changed any minds.

After the meeting we chatted for a while, and she uttered a statement that I never forgot. She said, "I wish there were a place where parents with a broken heart could go". At the time all I could do was share a piece of the sidewalk outside the school building to stand and listen. I have thought of her courage often. Not only was she dealing with her child's disability but she was being told her child's learning difficulties were her fault. It was hard enough for her to deal with her child's disability, but she also had to face hostility and skepticism when she advocated for him. Our role as ally is important, as is our ability to share accurate information with teachers so parents won't have to stand alone in the face of ignorance.

The Power of Denial

On another occasion I unintentionally shocked a parent into facing her daughter's disability. I was speaking by phone with the mother of a girl who was being reassessed for special education services. She had been served under the Mildly Mentally Impaired category of developmental disability since early elementary school, and she was now in junior high.

During our conversation, I alluded to the fact that her daughter was currently being reassessed for M.M.I. placement, and I had some questions I needed to ask. The phone went silent so long I thought the connection was broken. Finally, the mother replied by asking (in the language of the day), "Are you telling me that my daughter is retarded? Why didn't anyone tell me?"

I was left speechless, standing with a several inch-thick file which included not only school assessment reports but reports from outside agencies. The category under which she was served was mentioned again and again. I told her I would be more than happy to meet with her and show her the documentation which led me to understand her daughter was being served under the M.M.I. category. When we met in person, she again confronted me about the fact that she had never been given this information before.

Knowing that the school psychologist who had performed all the earlier assessments had indeed said the words again and again, I pondered how the mother could say she was hearing them for the first time. I suspect it was because my phone call caught her by surprise that the meaning of the words finally registered. I made a mental note to myself to never, ever, underestimate the power of denial.

The Value of Listening

I was given a lesson in the importance of deep listening by a man who was a single parent of a first-grade boy. His son was very bright, but he was so hyperactive he could scarcely settle down to learn. His very capable classroom teacher referred him for an evaluation after trying everything she could think of.

When the father received the request for evaluation, he asked that he be able to interview me before deciding whether to proceed. I often talked with parents about exactly what an evaluation entailed, but never had anyone asked to conduct a formal interview. As it turned out, the father wanted to put me through the process that he would perform with a prospective employee. I figured we had nothing to lose—except the time it would take for the interview—and everything to gain, because it looked like this child would not have an evaluation unless I submitted to his request. So, I did.

The father was formal and distant. The interrogation began with a set of questions which I answered as best I could. After several questions he stopped abruptly, saying that he had heard enough; that I was "OK". We then talked about what I and the special education teacher intended to do in our assessments. I did my best to assure him that we would do only what was listed on the request form and that he could withdraw his permission at any time. He remained suspicious, continuing our now less formal conversation with more than an edge of hostility. Finally, I decided I should not endure his disrespectful tone any longer, and said, "Your words are so hostile I cannot reply".

He stopped short, drew a breath, and then began the story of his own school experience 20 years earlier in a large city. He described being tested by a psychologist because he, like his son, was extremely hyperactive. Based solely on the score on one I.Q. test, he was placed in a special education program for the mildly mentally impaired and remained there for several years until the school realized he was incorrectly placed, and rather than being impaired, he was gifted.

But a great injustice was done, and he vowed he would protect his own son from such a fate. I realized he was terrified I would inflict on his son a repeat of his own suffering. I was glad I had the chance to explain how the laws had changed, and I was able to assure him that such a travesty was virtually impossible with all the safeguards now in place to protect the rights of the child, and the guarantees he had for recourse should the results of our evaluation contradict what he believed about his son. I repeated that the teacher did not for a moment believe that his son was cognitively deficient in any way. Rather, she was only seeking assistance to figure out how to help him learn.

By the end of our conversation, he gave me permission to meet with his child without his being present; at first, he acquiesced to testing only if he were allowed to witness it. We parted cordially, and unsurprisingly, when tested his son scored within the superior range. At the evaluation results meeting we developed a plan to help him focus in the classroom better.

The father's hostile treatment of me was borne out of fear that his son would be dealt a terrible injustice, as he had. But despite his fears, he was willing to give us a chance if we could prove our worth to him. Because I was patient with his demands, I was able to hear his whole story and give assurance that we had his child's best interest at heart.

The Consequence of Not Listening

The perceptions of others can impose constraints on our performance, particularly if we don't take them into consideration. I think of a situation with a child in elementary school who was acting out in the regular classroom. The special education teacher and the classroom teacher asked for my help, but there was just one thing—the mother refused to allow me to observe her son because my title was too intimidating. I would be invited to attend a meeting as a consultant, but I was not allowed to gather any direct impressions. I did not attempt to engage the mother privately in advance of the meeting, and a price was paid because of it.

At the meeting with the parent present, a staff member began by describing the child's behavioral difficulties. Then she turned to me and said, "You're the psychologist—show your stuff!" If I had had any savior fantasies, they evaporated at that moment. Sadly, I didn't have much stuff to show because I couldn't offer specific suggestions tailored to the needs of this child. It was a costly oversight that I did not request a meeting with the mother before the team meeting. Perhaps I could have played a useful role if we had got acquainted with each other. Maybe I could have shown her I was there to stand beside her and her son, not inflict anything on them.

Trying to Right a Wrong

Another father had a history of abuse toward his family, for which he had recently served time. He was out on parole when he and his former wife came to school one morning, carrying with them a suicide note their daughter had written the night before. She was emotionally fragile, but fortunately had not harmed herself. Evidently, the dad had again caused his daughter's trauma, and she was at a breaking point as a result. The school counselor and I met with the parents and then summoned social services as is required in an abuse situation. I invited the parents to sit with me in my office while we waited for the authorities to arrive.

The father sat quietly, waiting for the next step in seeing to the safety of his daughter. What was not spoken aloud but what we all knew was that a sheriff most likely would be accompanying the social worker, and the dad might be sent back to jail. I deeply respected his choice to come to school. He could have stayed away, but he cared enough to say so with his presence. What I saw before me was a father who loved his daughter, however imperfectly, and wanted desperately to save her from self-destruction.

Generational Trauma

I was assigned to assess a Native American preschooler who was already in a preschool special education program because of multiple difficulties. She carried a diagnosis of fetal alcohol syndrome, and her young life was replete with the consequences of the condition. She had suffered severe heart damage and consequently her growth was stunted. Her cognitive skills were far behind the average for her age. She was a delicate, sweet little girl who was a delight to be with, but the many strikes against her left me with a sense of foreboding. The little girl's heart was so damaged I wondered how much longer she would live.

Throughout our entire evaluation summary meeting, the mother sat with her eyes downcast, sometimes with tears escaping down her cheeks. She was attended by a social worker who would try to clarify what the implications of our findings were for her daughter. The mother's anguish hung so heavy in the air that the room felt saturated with it. Given the history of Indigenous people in our part of the world, it was likely that she and her daughter were both victims of intergenerational trauma. In the moment, it was our task to report our findings with compassion and respect and plan the best possible school placement for her daughter. That was the least we could do, and the most we could do.

Managing Our Role

Working effectively with parents requires us to take their perspective into account as much as possible, as I hope my stories illustrate. While we act to keep communication open with them, we also must maintain reasonable limits. In this age of social media, it is easy to blur boundaries. I decided not to engage with parents through social media at all, to avoid any inappropriate communications. I tried to make myself available at school and by phone and my work email to a limited degree. I preferred to communicate face to face, because I felt that was by far the most productive. I found my best tool was the ability to listen. If we do, parents will usually tell us what we need to know.

Wearing Two Hats

Knowing she has both the perspective of an occupational therapist who had worked with children with disabilities throughout her long career and the experience of raising her own son, who has a disability, I asked Jolene Mikkelson what advice she has for school psychologists. I wanted to hear how she coped with her son's challenges and dealt with crises along the way. What did she consider crucial for school psychologists to understand?

She began by stating that they ought to realize they are treating the whole family when they are working with a child at school. She advised the importance of understanding that the family may at times be overwhelmed with just getting through the day, so cautioned against scolding parents if they haven't followed through on something school related. She recommended being sensitive to where the parents are on the continuum from denial to acceptance of their child's disability because both parents may not be at the same point in that journey.

Jolene encourages parents of children with disabilities to trust their own observations and intuition, and she recommended that school psychologists listen closely to what they have to say about their child and respect their insights. In her own case, she recognized her son's developmental delays before anyone else. Her family physician was dismissive of her worry that her son was not developing normally until she was able to convince him that the boy could not figure out how to put simple shapes (triangle, block, circle) into matching holes when he was three years old. That was just one developmental milestone he had not attained. This caught the doctor's attention, and at last he agreed to refer her son for a comprehensive evaluation. Results of the evaluation qualified him for special education services, which meant he could start receiving the support he had needed all along. It was unfortunate she had to press to get it.

The doctor wasn't the only one overestimating the boy's abilities. She emphasized that school psychologists need to be alert to the degree to which parents can accept the reality of disability and recognize that the mother and father can be on different timelines. Jolene said her husband took much longer than she did to acknowledge their son's limitations, with one consequence that the evaluation results meeting was a horrible experience for him. His denial up to that point had been a protection against the pain of facing the extent of their son's disability.

Her husband loved sports and wanted his son to participate in team activities, so he signed their son up to play hockey when he was little, despite the boy's poor motor skills. Jolene said his lack of skill fortunately didn't matter much when he was young, but as time passed it became clear that he would not be welcome to join a competitive team. That was another milestone in her husband's understanding of their son's disability. He hadn't wanted to consider Special Olympics before but faced with no sports at all as the only other option for his son, he accepted that avenue for him. Thanks to Special Olympics, their son has been able to participate throughout his life, eventually attending an international competition, where he won a gold medal in his category.

As Jolene reflected on her son's early athletic experiences, she praised her husband for insisting their boy play team sports when he was little, because of the experience their son gained interacting with other kids. In retrospect, she feels she was too restrictive because she was so focused on his disability. Now it is commonly understood that it is wise to expose children with disabilities to a wide range of experiences, and she is glad her husband gave their son that opportunity. But there was no future for him in regular hockey or any other sport.

Most importantly, their son knew where he wanted to be. One day after going to Special Olympics practice, he told his mother, "These are my people, Mom". His parents fostered his self-esteem by encouraging him to strive and succeed within the limits of his abilities. As Beatrice Wright, the renowned expert on the psychosocial implications of disability, points out, "It makes all the difference in the world if painful facts about the self are first realized in a friendly and caring atmosphere" (Wright, 1983, p. 240).

Jolene's son's language development was quite delayed. In response, she became an astute listener out of the desire to gain all the insight she could from his utterances. For example, at about age 11, he was in the bathtub, and he slid underwater. When he sat up, he said, "Did you feel that?" She believes that his statement revealed that he still had not fully separated his identity from hers, since he assumed she would have simultaneously partaken of that experience. "They'll tell you who they are if you just listen", she said.

Besides having to advocate for her son with his doctor, she also had to with a teacher. Her son had his own para, and midday the para would escort him to a bus stop outside the school for a ride to another location. Unbeknownst to Jolene, the para would leave him there to wait for the bus. But one day the bus didn't come. She was amazed her son was able to find his way back into and through the school by himself. She called his teacher, who defended the practice, saying the para needed to go for lunch at that time, and so couldn't stand with him at the bus stop. Jolene was not satisfied with the answer and complained to the principal. The principal immediately tended to the scheduling problem, and her son never had to stand alone at the bus stop again.

From her vantage point now, Jolene wishes she had not been as angry with the teacher as she was when she called. She spoke out of fear for her son's safety, but she wishes she had kept a cooler tone and been more diplomatic. I think her reaction illustrates that anger often means fear. In such a circumstance, school personnel should not judge parents too harshly.

On another occasion she had to point out to a teacher that the behavior the teacher objected to was a sign of development. Jolene's son had started copying the behavior of other kids in the classroom, and his teacher tried to get him to stop. But Jolene recognized he had progressed to a new developmental stage, and so explained to the teacher they should be glad her son achieved the ability to imitate.

Jolene was very happy with her son's school experience and had particularly high praise for paras. She was impressed by the level of devotion they demonstrated; she found them to be unfailingly kind and open to understanding him.

I asked if her son ever attracted the attention of strangers when they were out in public. She laughed and replied, "All the time!" For example, the day before our conversation, a little girl at their Sunday church service turned around and gaped at him while they were singing a hymn. She said her son loves to sing and he sings very loud. He unfortunately cannot sing well. Once the hymn began, the little girl turned around and stared until her mother corrected her. But she couldn't resist turning around a second time, evidently both amazed and aghast at his singing. Her son was completely unaware of the attention he was getting, or its meaning. Jolene said she just laughs when such situations arise. "If it bothers him, only then does it bother me". She said this has become her mantra. She said she has had to learn to detach herself from reacting to small issues.

She also has become aware that how she interacts with her son in public affects how others feel about him. She had a vivid example one day when they were outside at a playground and a little girl saw them. The child later went home and told her mother that Jolene's son must not be a special needs kid, "because his mother loves him so much". Jolene has been pondering the implications of that statement for a long time.

It was evident throughout our conversation how supportive their extended families are toward their son. Jolene noticed he was calling one of his favorite cousins every day to say hi. Concerned he might be a nuisance, she asked her nephew if she should restrict the calls. He replied that they bring him a moment of joy every time, and he didn't want to miss out on them. It was a fine reminder of what her son brings to the lives of others, and how they appreciate him just the way he is.

At this point the family is adapting to a new normal. A few years ago, the young man became extremely ill with Lyme's Disease. He was bedridden and in extreme pain, and it took a while to achieve an accurate diagnosis. He started hallucinating and became delusional, frantically insisting he needed to go to a nearby town to join a team who was waiting for him to play. They would drive him over to the playing field to show him there was no one there, but he was not convinced. He eventually spent two weeks in a psychiatric ward. Fortunately, medication returned him, for the most part, to himself again. He suffers fatigue that he didn't experience before and there are other lingering changes. But he is much improved over what happened after the onset of the disease.

Jolene said that before this episode she was rather opposed to using psychiatric medication to treat someone with a disability. Their son had always been physically healthy, and they never had to worry about him being irrational. Their concern revolved around his developmental delays. But after seeing what can happen, she now welcomes the use of psychiatric medication, because she has seen the dramatic improvement it can bring.

Caring for her son has been a journey full of hard and unpredictable challenges. One of her favorite sayings is, "If you want to make God laugh, just make plans". What the experience has brought her is empathy for others as she sees them face situations that may be different in the specifics but are essentially the same in what is required in terms of strength, tolerance, and courage. Jolene said she has come to recognize that just about every family is dealing with something they wouldn't have chosen.

Disability is a challenge for many; it's a part of life. What helps, she said, is to be able to laugh in the face of it all. That, and having timely support. She has noticed that many parents of children with disabilities do not know that they qualify for services such as respite care. School psychologists and others dealing with parents of children with disabilities should be sure to tell them what community supports they are eligible for, as well as what can be done for their child at school.

It goes without saying that Jolene has endured severe stress because of her son's disability. What strikes me about her story is the perspective she takes. She has reframed the suffering in her own family by identifying with the suffering of the human family. She takes pride in being a listener to others walking a similar path and clearly enjoys being able to contribute what she has learned through her experience. She has been deliberate in helping other parents build confidence in their own observations. She learned how to advocate for her son, which built strength. She deliberately bolstered her son's morale every day; for example, at bedtime she would say to him, "You are the nicest boy I know". She accepts her son exactly as he is, and laughs readily, finding humor in awkward social situations and the comical circumstances she finds herself in because of his disability.

Jolene has learned to take care of herself and protect her own interests by accepting help from others. She has had to redefine what makes a good life, and she has developed deep humility, courage, and compassion in the face of it. Jolene participated in this interview with enthusiasm, glad to share her insights.

We've come a long way in our understanding of the needs of families who are raising children with disabilities. If their son had been born some decades earlier, Jolene and her husband would have been expected to leave him at an institution like the one my mother worked in. Rather than viewing a child with a disability as a threat to family life, now scholars are analyzing the positive effects that raising a child with a disability can have on parents.

Posttraumatic Growth

Jolene's story, it seems to me, exemplifies the posttraumatic growth that can arise from effectively meeting the stressful challenges of raising such a child. Janoff-Bulman discusses posttraumatic growth (P.T.G.) in terms of finding "strength through suffering", increasing "psychological preparedness", and doing an "existential reevaluation" (Janoff-Bulman, 2004). Scorgie and Sobsey explored transformations resulting from parenting children with disabilities, finding similarly that parents identified positive growth in terms of their "own personal growth, their relations with others, and changes in philosophical or spiritual values" (Scorgie & Sobsey, 2000). Gupta and Singhal also focus on the approach to coping that de-emphasizes the negative side of caring for a child with special needs and, instead, analyzes the way many parents with disabilities develop positive perceptions that are the foundation of healthy coping. Caring for their child's disability can bring parents both meaning and enrichment (Gupta & Singhal, 2004). School psychologists are positioned to aid in the process.

References

Brown, B. (2012). *Daring greatly: How the courage to be vulnerable transforms the way we live, love, parent, and lead.* Avery Publishing.

Eicher, S. (2018, June 21). Supporting parents of students with special needs. *Edutopia.* www.edutopia.org/article/supporting-parents-students-special-needs

Gupta, A., & Singhal, N. (2004). Positive perceptions in parents of children with disabilities. *Asia Pacific Disability Rehabilitation Journal, 15*(1), 22–35.

Henríquez, C. (2014). *The book of unknown Americans: A novel.* Knopf Doubleday Publishing Group.

Janoff-Bulman, R. (2004). Posttraumatic growth: Three explanatory models. *Psychological Inquiry, 15*(1), 30–34.

Phillips, A., & Taylor, B. (2010). *On kindness.* Picador.

Scorgie, K., & Sobsey, D. (2000). Transformational outcomes associated with parenting children who have disabilities. *Mental Retardation, 38*(3), 195–206. https://doi.org/10.1352/0047-6765(2000)038<0195:TOAWPC>2.0.CO;2

Wright, B. A. (1983). *Physical disability: A psychosocial approach* (2nd ed.). Harper Collins. https://doi.org/10.1037/10589-000

Chapter 20

Entering Their World
Our Relationship With Children

As we seek to enter the minds and hearts of the children we serve, we must acknowledge them as individuals seeking meaning and acceptance. Part of that responsibility is to recognize that they often need adults to reassure them that they are ok just as they are. With a host of insecurities roiling around inside, the prospect of having to go to visit the school psychologist can be intimidating.

I once had a child become convinced that he was going to be sent to a mental hospital merely because his parents had him meet with me. Nothing during our meeting suggested such a fate; he just assumed the worst. By the end of the day, he had broken down in tears, terrified he would be sent away. When I returned to his school a week later, his principal demanded to know what I had said to frighten him like that. So far as I knew, I had said nothing to inspire such fear. We may see ourselves as kindly and seeking only to help, but to children we are authority figures. Our title can even strike terror into their hearts.

On another occasion an E/BD teacher asked me to interview one of her students because she feared he was suicidal. I did and determined to the best of my ability that he was not. But shortly thereafter the boy walked by my office in the company of his teacher and, to her shock and mine, stormed into my room, pointed his finger at me, and said, "You want to send me to the psych ward!" I assured him that was not what I had in mind, but he was not convinced. Thereafter he glowered at me whenever I entered his classroom. It required the passage of time to convince him I was not his enemy.

Because children don't want to be coerced, school psychologists must be adept at conveying we are not there to force them to do anything. On a few occasions I caught children by surprise. This typically happened because their parents had not addressed testing with them at home. I didn't blame them for not wanting to work with a stranger who was asking them to do things they had never done before and didn't understand the purpose of. I would explain how it was decided that they should undergo an evaluation, and I would tell them that we could reschedule

DOI:10.4324/9781003348344-20

if they would be better able to do it another time, but once we had talked it over, they almost invariably accepted the process without delay. If they can see we are their ally, most kids want to be tested once they understand it is a step along the way to getting the help they need.

Some of the children we see have been to different kinds of psychologists or counselors, and so they have their own preconceived notions of what we will be like. Sometimes these preconceptions don't work in our favor. An eighth-grade boy who was seeing a therapist outside of school was also scheduled to meet with me by parent request. He made it clear he opposed additionally meeting with anyone at school, but his mother would not relent. I made a deal with him. I told him that I was there to help him do better in school, but if he could improve his performance on his own each week, I would just do a quick check-in and he could scoot right back to class. Our meeting wouldn't be any longer than a trip to the bathroom. I promised him I would also check with his teachers to see what his progress was like, and if he faltered, he would have to see me for longer than just a check-in. He accepted the compromise.

A Safe Place

On the other hand, to some children we are a haven where they can safely reveal how they feel. Sometimes in the middle of talking about something else, a student would interrupt our conversation to interject, "You have any kids?" One day a high school girl asked me that out of the blue, and I said I had a son. She replied, "I bet you talk to him". "Yes", I said. "We talk". "My mom never talks with me. She just yells", she said. We went on to examine why that might be and what she might do to deal with her mother's treatment of her.

I have never forgotten the wistful expression on her face when she asked about my own family. She yearned for intimacy with her mother, and I felt her nose pressed to the glass, imaginatively looking in on people doing what she knew she wanted but so far was helpless to get.

Sometimes We Mean More Than We Know

Sometimes children may need to imagine we are their own, at least while we are together. I once heard Garry Landreth, a play therapy expert, advise that those of us who work with children should not have pictures of our own children in our offices, so that the child we are with does not have to feel in competition with them for our attention and affection. I took his advice to heart, and ever after I was careful to restrict what images I had on display.

Even without emphasizing my personal life, I noticed kids were attuned to it. A boy I had been meeting with regularly happened to catch a glimpse of me entering my house on a weekend. The next time he saw me he made a point to tell me. Then he asked, "Does just your family live there?" I realized with dismay that he was probably comparing his family's living situation to mine, and he was feeling the distance between our lives.

You may remember Sarah, the fifth-grade girl who told me about dreaming I took her shopping and what pretty things I bought for her. I don't believe she was hinting for presents; I think she was imagining what it would be like to be the daughter of a teacher, and she imagined it to be an abundant life.

The same year my schools were faced with multiple violent deaths I ended up taking in a student, for fear he would kill himself otherwise. He had left his foster home because he wanted to be independent, an understandable desire at his age of 19. He was warned by his social worker that because of his age he could not return to foster care if he couldn't make it on his own, so he ran the risk of becoming homeless. He was nearing graduation and was unemployed. As it turned out, he ended up sleeping on the couches of friends until one by one he wore out his welcome and found he had nowhere to go.

He sought me out at school one morning and exposed a wrist for me to see. He had made a very visible longitudinal scratch, evidence that he knew what direction to cut if he wanted to end his life. I suggested he seek outside help, but he refused; nor did he want to go to the local mission. After we exhausted all my suggestions, he asked if he could come and live with me. He had been seeing me for counseling for a long while, so we knew each other well. He had no family he could turn to.

I knew a school counselor in a neighboring town who took students in regularly. She took it in stride as part of her contribution to her community. I suspect she saved more than one life. I had never been in a position before where I felt I should offer shelter, but this young man seemed on the verge of despair. I asked my director if there was any reason that I shouldn't take him in temporarily until we found something more permanent. I had just dealt with too many suicides to turn him away with no place to go when he was desperate. I was painfully aware that the research on boys and suicide is chilling; all too often boys carry through on a suicidal threat, and I had ample evidence of this tragic fact from working in my schools. As it turned out, my director gave me his blessing. My husband agreed that we should offer a room, and I told the young man he could stay.

I couldn't help but notice how at peace the young man seemed that evening when we ate supper together. As the days passed, however, he was gone a lot and I started suspecting drug abuse. Despite being in a supportive environment, he couldn't seem to discipline himself to finish the few assignments he was required to satisfy his I.E.P. and earn his diploma. Finally, I had a frank talk with him, and he admitted his addiction problems. I suggested that he voluntarily commit to treatment. He agreed immediately and packed his bag, and I took him to the treatment center.

After a while he hated it there, and he came to resent me for encouraging him to go. He particularly disliked the fact that the counselors there insisted he give up his friends. He told me that they were all he had; he couldn't just cut his ties with them. He ended up leaving treatment, and he did not graduate. I wondered what would become of him.

Years later my son ran into him on a trip home. The young man, by then in his early thirties, was gainfully employed. They sat down together for a visit. During their conversation he confessed that he was still on this earth because of two people: one of his high school teachers and me. When my son relayed the comment, I was stunned. I was convinced the young man thought I had failed him. Evidently over time he had forgiven me and had arrived at a point where he could appreciate my efforts.

His story ever after illustrated for me how we often do not know what impact we have on a student's life. Our efforts, however ineffectual they seem at the time, just might be enough. It's not for us to judge; time will tell.

Students can't or don't always express their gratitude to us directly. An encounter with a high school boy with a severe hearing impairment brought me up short. I met with him on a weekly basis for counseling and he also saw an occupational therapist, and a teacher of the deaf and hard of hearing. I literally stood in line behind them for our session one day. When it was my turn to see him, I commented that he might be getting tired of us middle-aged women coming to see him all the time. He looked me right in the eye and said, "Oh, no. You are my best friends". And of course, he was right. Thoughtlessly, I had denigrated our relationship, and I felt ashamed. I knew he didn't have friends among his peers; of course, his strongest bonds at school were with us. We were his social lifeline.

What Our Aging Means to Them

Over the course of my career, I couldn't help but notice what impact my age had on my relationship with kids. I enjoyed the easy rapport I had when I was young; children just naturally take to someone who looks youthful. Because of my small stature, at the beginning of my career I could even be mistaken at a distance for a high school student. To my great surprise and their deep embarrassment, on one occasion a couple of senior boys sidled up to me in the hallway between classes, evidently thinking I was a new girl in town, until they saw my face up close. One melted away so fast he was almost invisible, but the other graciously welcomed me to their school, minding his manners in the presence of an elder.

Inevitably as time passed, I gradually morphed into a mother figure. I found this role also suited my position; kids seemed to like that I was also a mom, and with some at least, I gained credibility if they happened to know my son. They were aware of signs of aging, as illustrated by one boy's recommendation to me that I really ought to start dyeing my hair, now that it was showing signs of gray. "You're too young to have gray hair, Mrs. Ness", he announced. "Oh, I don't know about that", I replied. I'm over 40, so it's normal for my hair to gray. I'm getting wrinkles, too, and they sort of match the gray in my hair". He was not convinced. "You need to dye your hair, Mrs. Ness". That was his final word.

Over the next two decades my hair grew whiter and more wrinkles did indeed appear on my face, so it came as no surprise the day a kinder-gartner looked up at me and chirped, "Whose gwamma are you?" I was delighted to be cast in that role, knowing there is scarcely anyone on this earth better trusted than a "gwamma". Another child asked me if I liked Abraham Lincoln. He had become quite obsessed with the president and wanted my opinion. I told him that yes, I did like President Lincoln. He went on to ask if I thought Lincoln was a good dad. I replied that I supposed he was. Then he asked, "Mrs. Ness, were you born yet when Lincoln was president?"

When we are young, kids can identify with our youth; in middle age we are parental figures and can perhaps signify protection and safety, and finally we become elders, able to represent the patience and wisdom advancing age can bring. What is the best role? I would say, any of them, so long as we accept the stage we are in and recognize its meaning to children.

Their Need Determines Our Role

We must also keep in mind that children cast us in the role they need us to be. I am reminded of a high school girl who was half desperate to see me each week and upon entering my office would greet me warmly. Working with her was very reinforcing; it had been extremely easy to establish rapport, she was eager to learn and grow, and she made rapid progress and soon was able to function without my support. We were both pleased with how she had worked her way through a serious per-sonal crisis that had been undermining her school performance.

A few weeks after we completed our sessions, I encountered her in the hall between classes, and she didn't seem to recognize me. I was always very discreet about acknowledging students publicly out of respect for their privacy. Typically, students would give me a little smile in recogni-tion, or I'd hear a quick "Hi!" Because she had been so enthusiastic in our sessions, I was a bit mystified when she looked right through me when we passed in the hall. It happened again soon after.

Then I realized what was happening. I was playing my role, and my purpose in her life had ended. My role had been to see her through her crisis, which I did. Now she had moved on and very appropriately left me behind along with the troubling time in her life she had just weathered. I thought about a physician whose patient I had been some years before, and how I now never thought of him or had any inclination to see him. I appreciated him deeply when I was his patient, but that time was over, and so was our relationship. I believe the same was true for me and this student.

Overcoming a Professional Crisis

We cannot always communicate effectively with children through words alone because of developmental or emotional reasons. Talking works for those who can express themselves well verbally, but many children can't. Information gained through medical and school records, classroom observation, parent report and testing can't get to the heart of how a child feels, either. Because we often encounter children who suffer limitations which impede their ability to communicate in words, we need other means. Fortunately, there are methods available to us to use in our quest to enter their world that enable us to gain a deep understanding of them.

After I had been a school psychologist for several years, I faced a professional crisis because of my failure to communicate well with some very angry boys. I typically counseled students on a regular basis and had usually felt successful in that role. But one year I was faced with some junior high-aged boys who nearly convinced me I was not fit for the job. They had no use for a counselor of any stripe, having seen way too many of them over the years. My only value, if I had any, was to get out of class for a little while, at best.

These boys were very uncomfortable in a conversation where feelings were addressed, and they were also prone to getting into trouble, so to them I suspect I was just one more adult who would inspire guilt. I used drawings and other nonverbal approaches with some minimal effect, but I was driven to my wit's end. I felt ineffectual and, sometimes, even despised. Then an opportunity arose that changed my work life for the better.

Sand Tray World Play

In 1992 I received a notice for the ninth annual international play therapy conference, "The Many Colors of Play Therapy", to be held in

Nashua, New Hampshire. The agenda included presenters on sand tray therapy, including an approach to working junior high and high school students as well as adults. I was intrigued. I figured I had nothing to lose and everything to gain, so I requested to attend the conference. Luckily for me, my director liked the idea, and he immediately approved my request.

At the conference I was introduced to sand tray world play, and I brought the notion back to my junior high office. I had a sand tray filled with sand and a set of figures (not to be referred to as toys) that the students would use to create scenes. In short order, I had students who resisted seeing me begging for extra sessions. When a middle school boy made a scene in the tray and then turned to me to show me his "little world", I knew I had found what I was looking for (Ness, 1997).

The sand tray seemed to have a calming effect in part because it inspires deep concentration. For several minutes, the student's normal frustrations, worries, and other distractions are put on hold, and the student becomes an artist, creating a world. Within it, the child has the freedom to play out traumatic events and relationships, expressing intense feelings safely. Because they are forming a design with miniature figures within the rectangle of the sand tray, they often create what looks like a tiny stage set. As a student set out figures to depict a scene, I was alert to the visual story that was unfolding. I usually didn't ask that it be told aloud, but sometimes the student wanted to narrate it (Ness, 1997).

Often the figures in the tray became symbols of meaning that they didn't have words for or couldn't bring themselves to express. For example, I witnessed this when a student for weeks repeatedly enacted the death of his beloved grandfather. He had had a heart attack while driving a tractor, and the sand tray became the chaotic scene of a tractor out of control. But gradually, the boy depicted the scene more gently, and after many weeks, the scene in the sand tray was again calm, with farm buildings, animals, and the tractor at peace, no longer careening over a field. As play therapists are quick to point out, play is the language of childhood, and children can use it to tell what in words is inexpressible (Ness, 1997).

I was meeting with a boy who had a failing kidney. He was on his second transplant and would likely face another surgery in the not-too-distant future. With such a serious medical condition to deal with day to day, I was concerned he might be feeling extremely vulnerable, but I was reassured when I saw his sand tray. He created a complicated display, with half of the tray devoted to a family with a house and many trees. The other half showed a war going on.

He placed the figure of a child among the trees. He pointed to it and said, "That's me". I asked if it was a safe place, and he replied that yes, the child was in a safe place. His response was consistent with what I had already learned about him. Despite his serious medical condition, he exuded an air of happy confidence, secure in his identity and excited about life. He pointed to the bride and groom he had placed near the house and said that they had a son, but he died. A father was off in the area where the war was being fought, and he got killed. It was evident that the possibility of death was very real to him, but his scene didn't seem to express an immediate threat to himself.

Another boy created his scene using a row of armed figures lined up like executioners with their weapons aimed at a lone figure at the opposite end of the tray. He pointed to the unarmed figure. "This is what school is like for me", he said. Once he had illustrated it, we could talk about it.

And those angry boys? I think of one young man who had all but refused to come to see me before his teacher of the Emotionally/Behaviorally Disordered (E/BD) was finally able to persuade him to go to my office. As soon as I showed him the sand tray, he became entranced. When it was time for him to return to his classroom, I thought I would have to summon help to get him to leave. He couldn't wait to return for his next session. Another student who had just returned from seeing me was asked by a classmate in the E/BD room if he had been down "with that lady". He replied, "Yup". The other student said she'd seen a sand box in my office and asked if he played in it. He said, "Sure do!" To which she replied, "That's cool!"

The sand tray can illuminate one's feelings without confronting them directly. Time and again I saw children depict their reality without feeling the pain of it, as might have happened if the story were spoken. Through the placement of figures and the movement of sand, they were able to express what was beneath the surface without any threat of exposure. In representing an experience symbolically, they gained objectivity and were able to comment on it with reduced emotionality. Also, they had created something that they could look at, reflect on, and admire, a gratifying accomplishment.

A Social Story

Another therapeutic use of imagination is the social story, now commonly used by school psychologists. At the time I used one I hadn't heard of the term; I just knew I had to find a way to help a girl cope with her anxiety, and she happened to like books. I was asked to meet with this special education student to help her adapt to making transitions. The task we focused on was how to endure the ride in the car to the lake after school on Friday. Her family frequently went to the lake, where this student, whom I will call Kary, loved to be. We knew her anxiety about the trip was not about the destination; it was about the ride in the car.

The car ride had become almost unbearable for the mother. Kary would melt down every few miles and it ended up taking forever to make a normally two-hour journey. It was getting so extreme the mother wondered if she could stand to continue making the trip. I decided to try a social story, an approach that has since come into favor among therapists who work with children.

Kary and I made a little book together of her going to the lake. The text was drawn from her own words about what she had to look forward to when she got there, and what she could say to herself when she started feeling upset as she rode in the car. This little social story proved to be quite helpful after we practiced for a while.

When she would start to become agitated in the car her mother would encourage her to use her book. It helped her relax to be reminded of all the wonderful experiences she could expect at the lake. To encourage her, I would check in with her early in the week to find out how the trip went, and so reinforce her taking control of her anxiety. Having her very own story engaged her imagination and spoke to her heart, so she was receptive to the instruction contained within it.

One day, when I checked in with her to find out how the trip went, she told me about an early memory. Kary was a normal little girl until one spring day when at age two or three she was playing outside and fell into a small stream that was swollen with water from melting snow. Her mother discovered her almost immediately and an ambulance was called. She was not breathing, and her mother told me that she was technically dead for about two minutes. The rescue team brought her back, but she sustained severe brain damage. Her cognition, ability to walk, and her speech were impaired to quite an extent. It was no surprise she needed intensive special education intervention to learn. Our conversation, however, brought home to me that a person's self-awareness cannot be predicted by an I.Q. score.

We were talking about her trip to the lake as was our habit, but this time she told me about a friend of hers at the lake who had sustained a severe head injury and whom she visited in the hospital several times. Her mother had made a point to tell me how obsessed she had become about this boy and his injury. Kary would go to see him at every opportunity. The moment she entered the room for our visit, she was eager to tell me about the boy and her time by his bedside. As I listened to her tell me about the accident and his hospitalization, it became clear that she understood very well what had happened to him. As she came to the end of her story, she said in her halting, palsied voice, "I remember the day when my life changed forever. He is just like me".

After that conversation I never saw her in the same way again. From that day forward I realized she carried a sorrow for the person she used to be and had a strong inkling of what she had lost. She taught me not to assume her limited thinking skills reflected her ability to remember and to feel. Kary's compassion for her friend increased my compassion for her. She affirmed what my mother said countless times about the people with developmental disabilities she had worked with: They so often understand far more than they are given credit for.

Groups

Like most school psychologists, I met with groups of children, as well as individuals. On one occasion, crisis intervention provided me with such an opportunity. A fifth-grade teacher asked me to talk with students about death after a teacher in their school died, feeling they would be less inhibited in their questioning with me than they would be with her. I was happy to do it. The teacher introduced me to her class as someone they could feel free to ask whatever questions they had, and then she departed. After she left, I assured the students I was willing to talk about whatever aspect of death they had questions about.

The students were especially curious about what a funeral was like (many had never attended one), what happens to the human body at the moment of death and immediately afterward, how deep a body had to be buried, and what funeral and burial practices are used throughout the world. Does everybody do what we do? They were deeply interested.

When they saw I was comfortable with whatever they asked, they started to ask questions that might be viewed as silly or flippant. For example, one student really wanted to know if one's eyes rolled back in one's head at the point of death and if hair continued to grow. One student confessed that she tried to question her parents, but they became offended; they thought she was being cheeky. I took all their questions at face value and answered them as completely as I could. The students listened with rapt attention, and they thanked me for being willing to speak with them. I was glad I could give them a chance to express their curiosity about death and get their questions answered.

An ongoing group consisted of several boys, all of whom were on the autism spectrum. One task I focused on with them was perspective taking. Because they all liked to build things out of Legos, I had them do some group projects which would require their considering what their fellow participants wanted to do and to cooperate with them to achieve it. I sometimes began the exercise by asking one to choose a project they thought someone else in the group would especially enjoy. The first time I made this request, it was met with stunned silence. The student I asked to choose argued with me, fiercely insisting that he knew best what the group should do. I gently persisted as he resisted coming up with an idea that another boy might like, an extremely difficult concept for him to grasp.

Sometime later this same child told me proudly of an insight he achieved on his own that required him to imagine someone else's perspective. He came to realize that one reason he kept getting into trouble in class was that he interrupted his teachers while they were presenting a lesson. He realized he might get along with his teachers better if he stopped blurting out what he considered to be corrections while they were presenting the lesson. For him, this was an important step forward in understanding his impact on others and what it meant in his relationship with them. Now his time in class could be devoted to learning, rather than arguing with his teachers.

The Risk of Being a Boy

I was working with two boys, Jake and Nate, who happened to be frenemies. I needed to do an assessment with Jake, so I went to his classroom to get him. Jake sat in his desk with an ice pack on top of his head. "Your head hurts?" I asked, noting the obvious. He replied that it did but insisted he wanted to come along with me anyway, so we went down the hall to the testing room, ice pack positioned in place. When we were settled, I asked Jake how he got hurt. He replied, "I told on Nate, and he got mad and picked me up and dropped me on my head". I hesitated, wondering if I should test under these circumstances. When I voiced my concern, Jake replied, "Ah, my head is a rock. I don't need this anymore". He flung away the ice pack and pulled his chair up to my table, ready to begin. I have rarely tested anyone who enjoyed it as much as he did. I met him in the hall later, and he hollered out, "Thanks for testing me!" and waved.

Coincidentally, my next session was with Nate. Right away he confessed he was having a bad day. When I asked why, he replied in a voice barely above a whisper, "I hurt Jake". And then he unburdened himself by telling me all about how he accidentally dropped Jake on his head. He needed to make amends.

It is tempting to dismiss this anecdote as a "boys will be boys" story. But all too often, boys deal with their conflicts through violence, and they suffer because of it. Besides the fact that I was raising one myself, I developed a particular interest in the emotional needs of boys because my caseload was heavily skewed toward them. When I went through my graduate training, I assumed that I would be dealing with about the same number of boys as girls, but once I was on the job, I found the reality was far different.

At the time I was finishing my training, how best to educate girls was the focus of a lot of attention, and justifiably so. How to reduce discrimination based on gender was a frequently addressed topic, as well as how to raise the self-esteem of girls. But once I started working as a school psychologist, I couldn't help but notice I seemed to be meeting a whole lot more boys than girls who weren't thriving. My counseling and assessment caseloads flew in the face of the notion that boys had it better and easier, in school and in life. Whenever I was assigned to help a school deal with the aftermath of a suicide, it was almost invariably because a boy had died. I often wondered about the disparity between my experience and the assumptions of the day.

I think of a high school boy referred to me by an assistant principal because of the trouble he was in. The specific event that precipitated the referral was an incident in the school parking lot. Jeremy (not his real name) had smashed his fist through the side window of another boy's car in an attempt to hit him. Fortunately, neither boy was seriously hurt, but the one referred to me was now under probation with the law because of the attempted assault.

During our first session, I learned how little sleep Jeremy was getting. As it turned out, he was attending school during the day and then working an eight-hour shift at a fast-food place and was responsible for closing. Consequently, with such long, demanding days, Jeremy never got a decent night's sleep. His schoolwork was suffering, and he readily admitted he had become moody and short-tempered. He was working so hard because he really wanted to have his own car, and his family couldn't afford to buy him one, so he had to earn it himself. He didn't need the car; it was something he just wanted very badly.

Jeremy had no history of getting into trouble. After reviewing his history, it looked to me like he was suffering the consequences of chronic sleep deprivation. He had taken on so much responsibility that he was pushed over the edge, and unsurprisingly for an adolescent male, he responded with physical aggression. After educating him about how much sleep adolescents need and the consequences of not having enough (such as bad moods, temper outbursts, inability to concentrate), he concluded he shouldn't be working so much. It would take longer to save for the car, but he could cut back on his hours during the week and maybe work more on the weekends.

Within a couple of weeks, I saw a new Jeremy. Once he wasn't sleep deprived, he became an altogether pleasant person to be around. He was remorseful about his reckless aggressive behavior, and he didn't want to ever repeat what happened. So far as I know, he never did. An Army recruiter called me several months later. Jeremy wanted to enlist after graduation, and the recruiter wanted my opinion about how fit he would be to serve. I told him I believed Jeremy would make a good soldier. He faced up to his mistake, changed his behavior for the better and made amends to the best of his ability.

Just before I retired, I attended a meeting with a Somali adolescent boy who was having difficulty in school. I remember none of the bureaucratic details of the meeting. I don't know if the meeting was called to plan an assessment or review his progress or anything else. What I do remember is how trapped he looked. He sat at the head of the table, slumped in his chair, smoldering with anger. His face was tense, on the edge of fear and rage. Rather than charting a path to his future, I believe he saw us as holding him captive.

As I recall, he was also involved with the law, or was about to be. He had moved with his family from Minneapolis, and it was not unusual for Somali families to head north from the city when their sons got mixed up with a gang. Maybe his family came here hoping the move would separate him from harm. But the comments I heard after the meeting made me fear that this young Black male would end up incarcerated. I left the meeting feeling that his chance for a good life in this country was slipping away, and the school's efforts to change the course of his life for the better would be of little effect. We offered too little, too late.

In 1999, when *Lost Boys: Why Our Sons Turn Violent and How We Can Save Them* by James Garbarino was published, I felt the author was expressing what every school psychologist working with boys needed to understand. At the time, school shootings were becoming chillingly routine. Our nation finally paid attention because White kids, not just children of color, were becoming murderers and were being murdered. As I reread the text now, I am struck by how timely it has remained. He refers to "socially toxic environments" which can lead to horrific acts of violence (Gaborino, 1999, p. 19).

Garbarino's deep compassion for the "child inside the killer" led him to study in depth the lives of boys who killed so he could understand what risk factors in early childhood can set their demise in motion. Unsurprisingly, damaging, traumatic experiences early on pave the way for disaster. Combined with the way many males are socialized to accept violence to address conflict or gain control, the outcome can be lethal when boys are old enough to plan a murder or suicide. To reduce violence in schools, the psychological and societal underpinnings of masculinity and violence must be faced (Gaborino, 1999, p. 21).

For boys of color, the intersection of their race and masculinity puts them at great risk in another respect because it can lead to more severe punishment when engaging in stereotypical actions, thus the "school-to-prison-pipeline" (Price, 2009).

Reeves and Smith report results from the *American Family Survey* that indicate American parents are currently more worried about their sons than their daughters having the personal resources to become successful adults. In general, daughters are viewed as being better able to cope with setbacks and so are believed to be more resilient. Parents continue to express concern over the challenges girls face but believe they are less vulnerable than boys (Reeves & Smith, 2020).

The alarming rise in child and adolescent anxiety disorder in recent years combined with double the number children and adolescents admitted to hospitals because of suicidal risk indicates that life has become more threatening for both boys and girls over the past few years. Experts say this is the consequence of young people facing a world that seems frightening, the stress of social media, and the pressure of high expectations for success (McCarthy, 2019).

The Risk of Being a Girl

Now we are well aware that being a girl also carries risk, but in different ways from what boys face. Boys often landed on my caseload because they expressed their distress by acting out physically, against themselves or someone else. Girls, on the other hand, are much more prone to suffer internally, their misery made manifest through anxiety and depression, at double or more the rate boys experience (Anxiety and Depression Association of America, n.d.). At the beginning of my career, they often didn't appear on my caseload because they were suffering quietly. If they acted out physically, it was likely to be through cutting themselves, which they could conceal under their clothing.

In general, up to 10% of adolescents suffer significant depression. By adolescence, girls are two to three times more vulnerable to developing mood disorders than boys are. Experts report many causes, including "hormonal differences, impact of different social stressors, variations in gender expectations, and coping methods". Depression can last from weeks to years. It may occur in response to a particular trauma, or it may result from no directly observable cause. It may co-occur with other conditions, such as anxiety, attention deficit hyperactivity disorder, and substance abuse problems. Also, poor academic performance puts students at risk. Because of the seriousness of depression and its impact on school achievement, it is important to have mental health services available at school (Huberty, 2010).

As the years passed, I saw more and more adolescent girls suffering from depression and anxiety. All too often, their symptoms included cutting. At one point, I realized one girl was teaching a friend how to do it; it appeared they bonded over this shared secret. I saw girls suffering from severe body image anxiety, which may or may not have been related to overweight. I encountered others who were under intolerable stress from a destructive home life, as well as depression related to gender-imposed expectations for their future. Some acted out with substance abuse. The possibility of pregnancy was a stressor that sexually active girls also faced, and when that occurred, it severely escalated the anxiety, to the point where suicide could become a concern. By the end of my career, suicide prevention was emphasized enough in my schools that sometimes students would bring a friend who was in danger directly to a school social worker or school psychologist, as mentioned in the chapter on crisis intervention.

I encountered girls, as well as boys, who were victims of violence. My most memorable example is of an 18-year-old girl whom I had met with for quite some time because of emotional difficulties which affected her school performance. She was very bright and was described to me by her English teacher as perhaps one of the most promising students in the senior class. She was steadily overcoming her personal challenges, and it was a joy to watch her gain confidence in herself and her future. It was looking more and more like she would be college bound, a goal she was excited about.

Then one Monday morning she came to me in a desperate state. Trembling, she revealed that over the weekend she had been raped by a friend of her parents, who was visiting in their home. I asked if she had told her parents. She confessed she had not because she felt they wouldn't believe her; they would blame her and wouldn't want to make trouble for their friend. I offered to accompany her to the police, but she refused. Because she was over 18, it was not my right to call child protection. I could only offer support by helping her sort out her options. In the end, she decided there was nothing she could do. As it turned out, she never went to the police. The girl's plans for her future took an abrupt change shortly thereafter, also, with her dropping out of school.

Race adds another dimension of risk for girls. An article noting a federal lawsuit brought by the NAACP Legal Defense and Educational Fund addresses disparate school discipline policies for Black and White girls. We are already aware of the much higher discipline rates of Black boys compared to Whites. Now, attention is being focused on the differences between girls. The *New York Times* reports that the rate of receiving multiple out-of-school suspensions for Black girls is sevenfold that of White girls, and the differences between Black and White girls are greater than between Black and White boys. According to studies that have been conducted, this disproportion occurs not because Black girls are behaving worse than Whites; it's because their behavior is judged more harshly (Green et al., 2020).

A study addressing how to address low-income urban African-American girls' mental health needs stated that participating mental health professionals reported strong resilience among the girls they worked with, even though the girls often lacked access to mental health support. Girls reported "exposure to violence, limited trusting relationships, depression, and low self-esteem" as problematic for them. The need for training for those providing mental health services to this population at school was highlighted. Interventions for African-American girls should be sensitive to the need for these girls to develop positive gender and racial/ethnic identities, the authors said, particularly because "higher levels of racial ethnic identity have been positively correlated with higher self-esteem and less risky sexual and substance abuse attitudes" (Harper et al., 2016).

The Risk of Being LGBTQ

According to Paul C. McCabe, author of "The R(ally) Cry: School Psychologists as Allies and Advocates for the LGBTQ Community", the treatment of LGBTQ students has been improving nationwide, but there is unquestionably much that still needs to be done within school communities to safeguard and affirm LGBTQ youth. McCabe explains that schools with explicit policies forbidding bias and harassment against LGBTQ students have the lowest incidence of victimization. Also, the presence of a Gay-Straight Alliance club contributes to a safer environment (McCabe, 2014).

Particularly vulnerable are LGBTQ students of color. Their plight is compounded by their likelihood of attending a poorly financed school and so do not have access to adequate educational resources with highly qualified teachers. Special education services and English Language Learner classes are in short supply as well. They are also more likely to suffer harassment and assault because of their identity (Fondas, 2013).

Because of their expertise on topics relating to mental health and school climate, school psychologists are positioned to promote positive attitudes, help staff adapt curriculum to reflect such attitudes, and address LGBTQ needs when working to improve school climate. Acceptance of difference within school culture will result in improved perceptions of diversity and reduce the likelihood that LGBT students will suffer insults, social exclusion, and violence. Schools need to be funded at a level so that all students have access to the support they need, which should include the services of a school psychologist.

In a letter to the editor in 2020, Faye Seidler, clinic administrator, Harbor Health Clinic, Fargo, North Dakota, reported that queer students in our state "are nearly twice as likely to experience bullying on and off school property" as others and are at double the risk of running away from home, or being required to leave because their family chooses to abandon them (Seidler, 2020). The need for increasing intervention at school to reduce bullying is urgent.

A press release from the U.S. Department of Education's Office of Civil Rights on June 16, 2021, indicated that the Title IX prohibition against discrimination on the basis of sex will be enforced to include discrimination based on sexual orientation and gender identity. The Title IX Education Amendments of 1972 forbids discrimination on the basis of sex if the educational program receives federal funding (U.S. Department of Education, 2021).

The Risk of Being a School Psychologist

We usually perceive ourselves as protectors of children, but I must also note that sometimes we may need protection from them. I think of an incident that occurred when I was middle-aged. A new student who had to have a re-evaluation immediately for his I.E.P. to stay in compliance moved into one of my districts. I knew almost nothing about him except that he had come with his parents to the little community from a large city where he was being served through special education. His special education file had not yet arrived, so I didn't have access to any background information.

Almost immediately upon beginning to administer the I.Q. test I felt the hair on the back of my neck start to stand up. I could not identify anything specific that he said or did—was it how he looked at me—his tone of voice—I couldn't really say, but the truth was I felt like a sexual target, and that impression remained the full 90 minutes it took to complete the evaluation. By the end of the test, I was rattled. I don't think I was ever so glad to see a student leave a testing room as I was on that occasion.

After he left, I questioned my reaction. Could I have misinterpreted? He was a young teenager, and I was old enough to be his grandmother. I felt foolish at the thought of mentioning it. But despite my misgivings, I decided I should talk with his special education teacher, and I was glad I did. I said I could not point to any particular action on his part, but to me he seemed predatory, even though he hadn't done anything I could accuse him of. She listened with rapt attention, and when I had spoken my piece, she replied, "You, too?"

A week later I returned to the school and the special education teacher couldn't wait to hand me his file from his previous school. Contained within was mention of incidents of sexual harassment. I was glad I had confessed my concern when I did, rather than dismissing it as a possible over-reaction. In so doing, I affirmed the special education teacher's impression, which increased her resolve to be watchful of his behavior in her classroom and not be dismissive of his effect on her.

My experience was mild compared to that of another school psychologist I know who had to deal with a sexually excited adolescent. She was able to get him to exit the room where she was working with him, but only after several commands from her to leave. This experience of sexual harassment brought fear and trauma. Her awareness of the need to position herself physically in as safe a location as possible when working with a child was one lesson she took from the encounter. Over the course of my career, I made it a habit of being sure I was as close as possible to the door, so if I needed to escape, I would not be hemmed in by a desk or table. While school psychologists are knowledgeable about child and adolescent psychopathology, we are not well equipped to deal with it in a school setting, where children are expected to behave according to accepted social norms. How difficult it is for schools to prevent lethal violence stands as the ultimate example of the risk school personnel face.

We Are a Part of Their Community

School psychologists are often in the background, concealed from view, working to influence constructive change in the lives of children. This is often deliberate, to protect students' privacy. But however unobtrusive we try to be, sometimes we can't avoid being highly visible, such as while conducting a classroom observation. Even though I tried not to be disruptive, kids often would try to interact, regardless of how quietly I took a seat in the back of the room. Over time I came to expect to encounter kids I already knew, and some would greet me with a "Hi, Mrs. Ness! Who are you here to watch?" or "Who did you come to test today?" or a playful, "Can I come?"

I particularly remember a little boy who sat in the next row and a few seats ahead of me during an observation. He turned around and grinned disarmingly, so I couldn't help but grin back. We remained smiling at each other for some moments and perhaps would have indefinitely, except that his teacher called his name and twirled her finger at him, gesturing to get him to turn around so he could pay attention to her. He did, but reluctantly, and he couldn't resist quickly looking back for one last grin. I hadn't intended to be a distraction; I just couldn't refuse his friendliness.

I think of another class where I knew so many students that before the lesson officially began, I received a little round of greetings, some from across the room. What these encounters did to the objectivity of my classroom observation, I can't say, but, in retrospect, I think the sense of community their welcoming attention created was good for all of us. I am grateful for those magical moments when I was treated as a welcome member of their world. They made me trust that my role in their lives was a positive one, and I felt glad to be there. Perhaps that is why I looked forward to my encounters with students as much on my final days as a school psychologist as I did decades earlier when I first stepped inside a school as a teacher or school psychologist.

Moving Forward

Through our relationships with children, we help them build relationships with others and with themselves. Through our observations of, and interactions with them, we are often able to come to understand the underlying causes of their distress and consequent poor school performance. By being present in their classrooms and through individual or small group encounters, we observe firsthand aspects of their physical, social, and emotional health that might be undermining their ability to succeed in school. Working with them individually and in small groups gives us insight into what needs to change for them to progress in school and in life. Our goal always is to help children reach the highest academic performance they possibly can, by addressing whatever barriers are in the way, whether they be educational, social, emotional, behavioral, or societal. Our interventions with individuals, groups, a whole class, or a whole school community can make a critical difference.

Conspicuous by its absence from my narratives are whole group interventions in classrooms and school systems. I occasionally met with an entire class, but these were rare occasions. For most of my era, school psychologists addressed issues one child at a time or in small groups pulled out of the classroom. We had an indirect impact through consultation and in-services with teachers and administration, but my schools did not have a comprehensive approach in place to guide a whole school system. Positive Behavioral Interventions and Supports with its three-tiered framework was just starting to be instituted in my schools at the time of my retirement. Now, Natasha serves on P.B.I.S. teams and is a leader in data collection and analysis. This enables her to influence children more broadly, whether they are enrolled in a special education program. She continues to see students in small groups and individually, but she has a much stronger role in prevention for the whole school community. Natasha also has the option of telehealth meetings with students over the Internet, as when schools closed in the face of the pandemic. She found this not to be an ideal substitute for in-person counseling, but it was better than no counseling at all.

Another current focus that was only beginning to get attention in my day is the impact of trauma on children, including intergenerational trauma experienced particularly by children of African-American and Native American heritage. Dauphinais et al. address the complexities and subtleties of accurate assessment of ability and achievement with Native American students. Cultural aspects such as the role of sovereignty in identity are discussed, as well as the effect of the local way of speaking on English verbal expression (Dauphinais et al., 2018).

DeAngelis points out that the historical effects of slavery have not been studied as directly as has the impact of oppression on other groups, such as Jews and aboriginal peoples. However, the related topic of racial discrimination is being studied, and recently a measure to assess anxiety related to such discrimination has been developed (DeAngelis, 2019).

The trauma created by exposure to violence is another topic gaining more attention. Ridgard et al. posit that the prevalence of violence children suffer is so high that it has become, as a portion of their title states, "A Social Justice Imperative" for schools to deliver trauma-informed care. They cite statistics from the National Survey of Children's Exposure to Violence from 2011, which covered 50 separate categories of victimization, indicating 57.7% of youth had some exposure to violence. Of them, 4.9% had been exposed to ten or more categories. Children living in predominantly racial/ethnic minority communities in low-income urban neighborhoods have the highest exposure. They report that recent immigrant children are at especially high risk for exposure to violence. Their rates for P.T.S.D. symptoms are 32%, and for clinically significant symptoms of depression, 16%, respectively (Ridgard et al., 2015).

There is another population of children that requires our particular attention, and that is children placed in foster care for whom there are no homes, and so they are held in other settings, including detention centers. The U.S. Department of Health and Human Services, 2018 AFCARS Report, listed that more than 690,000 children spent time in foster care in 2017, with 443,000 in foster care on any given day. One-third were children of color. More than 69,000 children were waiting to be adopted because of their parent's parental rights being terminated.

More than 17,000 aged out of foster care without a family to go to (Children's Bureau, 2018).

These youngsters have a higher rate of homelessness as adults. Hopefully this is now a preventable outcome if help is accessed through the Family First Prevention Services Act, a law signed into effect in 2018. The overriding purpose of the law is to safely keep children with their families (Dworsky et al., 2019).

The population of children school psychologists encounter most frequently are those served through special education. Besides needing academic intervention, they also need emotional support. Children with learning and attentional difficulties are more likely than their school peers to be bullied and, in turn, to bully others. Those with disabilities were bullied at higher rates than students not identified with disabilities Students with specific learning disabilities had a dropout rate of 18%, almost three times as high as the rate for all students (6.5%). Leaving school without a diploma increases the risk of unemployment and involvement with the criminal justice system (National Center for Learning Disabilities, 2017).

The need for help at the level of prevention is obvious. Our children's problems are becoming more serious; the stakes are very high. The value of the school psychologist's role is evident when one considers that timely intervention can change the course of a child's life from a path leading to disappointment and despair to self-sufficiency and healthy survival. Rectifying injustice in the world of children is a worthy commitment.

References

Anxiety and Depression Association of America. (n.d.). *Girls and teens.* https://adaa.org/find-help/by-demographics/women-and-young-girls/girls-and-teens

Children's Bureau. (2018). *The AFCARS report.* www.acf.hhs.gov/cb/report/afcars-report-25

Dauphinais, P., Robinson-Zañartu, C., Charley, E., Melroe, O., & Bass, S. A. (2018, October). Using the indigenous conceptual framework in assessment—part 2: A Native American perspective. *Communiqué, 47*(2), 27–29. www.nasponline.org/publications/periodicals/communique/issues/volume-47-issue-2/using-the-indigenous-conceptual-framework-in-assessment%E2%80%94part-2-a-native-american-perspective

DeAngelis, T. (2019, February). The legacy of trauma. *APA Monitor on Psychology, 50*(2), 36. www.apa.org/monitor/2019/02/legacy-trauma

Dworsky, A., Gitlow, E., & Horwitz, B. (2019). *Interrupting the pathway from foster care to homelessness.* Chapin Hall at the University of Chicago. www.chapinhall.org/research/interrupting-the-pathway-from-foster-care-to-homelessness/

Fondas, N. (2013, November 18). Schools are failing minority LGBT students. *The Atlantic.* www.theatlantic.com/education/archive/2013/11/schools-are-failing-minority-lgbt-students/281600/

Gaborino, J. (1999). *Lost boys: Why our sons turn violent and how we can save them.* Free Press.

Green, E. L., Walker, M., & Shapiro, E. (2020, October 2). A battle for the souls of Black girls. *The New York Times.* www.nytimes.com/2020/10/01/us/politics/black-girls-school-discipline.html

Harper, E., Kruger, A. C., Hamilton, C., Meyers, J., Truscott, S. D., & Varjas, K. (2016, January). Practitioners' perceptions of culturally responsive school-based mental health services for low-income African American girls. *School Psychology Forum, 10*(1), 16–28. www.nasponline.org/publications/periodicals/spf/volume-10/volume-10-issue-1-(spring-2016)/practitioners-perceptions-of-culturally-responsive-school-based-mental-health-services-for-low-income-african-american-girls

Huberty, T. (2010). Depression: Supporting students at school. In A. Canter (Ed.), *Helping children at home and school III: Handouts for families and educators.* National Association of School Psychologists. www.nasponline.org/Documents/Resources%20and%20Publications/Handouts/Families%20and%20Educators/Depression_Supporting_Students_at_School.pdf

McCabe, P. C. (2014, January). The r(ally) cry: School psychologists as allies and advocates for the LGBTQ community. *School Psychology Forum, 8*(1), 1–9. www.nasponline.org/publications/periodicals/spf/volume-8/volume-8-issue-1-(spring-2014)/the-r(ally)-cry-school-psychologists-as-allies-and-advocates-for-the-lgbtq-community

McCarthy, C. (2019, November 20). Anxiety in teens is rising: What's going on? *Healthychildren.org.* www.healthychildren.org/English/health-issues/conditions/emotional-problems/Pages/Anxiety-Disorders.aspx

National Center for Learning Disabilities. (2017). *Social, emotional and behavioral challenges.* www.ncld.org/research/state-of-learning-disabilities/social-emotional-and-behavioral-challenges/

Ness, K. (1997). This is my little world: Counseling middle school students through sand tray world play. *Communique, 25*(6), 34, 36.

Price, P. (2009). When is a police officer an officer of the law: The status of police officers in schools. *Journal of Criminal Law and Criminology, 99*(2). https://scholarlycommons.law.northwestern.edu/jclc/vol99/iss2/6

Reeves, R., & Smith, E. (2020, October 7). Americans are more worried about their sons than their daughters. *Brookings.* www.brookings.edu/blog/up-front/2020/10/07/americans-are-more-worried-about-their-sons-than-their-daughters/

Ridgard, T., Laracy, S. D., DuPaul, G. J., Shapiro, E. S., & Power, T. J. (2015, October). Trauma-informed care in schools: A social justice imperative. *Communiqué, 44*(2). www.nasponline.org/publications/periodicals/communique/issues/volume-44-issue-2/trauma-informed-care-in-schools-a-social-justice-imperative

Seidler, F. (2020, July 10). Letter: The next focus for LGBTQ+. *Grand Forks Herald.* www.grandforksherald.com/opinion/letters/letter-the-next-focus-for-lgbtq

U.S. Department of Education. (2021, June 16). *U.S. Department of Education confirms Title IX protects students from discrimination based on sexual orientation and gender identity* [Press release]. www.ed.gov/news/press-releases/us-department-education-confirms-title-ix-protects-students-discrimination-based-sexual-orientation-and-gender-identity

Chapter 21

Rolling With Our Roles

From the time I became a school psychologist over three decades ago, my roles, like that of many school psychologists, kept expanding from almost strictly assessment to counseling, behavioral intervention, crisis intervention, and giving in-services to staff on special education and mental health topics. At the end of my career, districts were beginning to study how to develop school-wide discipline approaches based on current behavioral science principles and wanted assistance from their school psychologist. Our profession has not stood still in the face of societal and educational changes that affect children. I welcomed the increasing responsibilities, as does Natasha now, but at the same time, they brought additional potential sources of stress, since they provided so many more opportunities to fail. One particularly demanding role is that of an unofficial leader.

Leading From the Outside

By its very nature, our leadership role is a paradox. We are not designated as a leader in our title, but we are often perceived as such. We are highly trained and often viewed as authority figures, but we are not supervisory; consequently, there is scarcely any power inherent in our position. Our role is mainly consultative and collaborative, and while we can often wield great influence, what we can achieve depends ultimately on how willing others are to trust our expertise. This underlying reality of being an unofficial leader has several important implications for us to consider. First, we need to look at how we view ourselves.

Former NASP president Leslie Paige's comment that school psychologists are perceived as leaders held true in my experience. As she said, "Even if we do not think of ourselves as leaders, other people believe that we are" (Paige, 2019). Early on, I thought of myself solely as a member of child study teams who brought a particular perspective, thanks to my school psychology background. Natasha expressed the same sentiment. When she first began, she saw herself as "an equal among peers—period".

DOI:10.4324/9781003348344-21

I thought of the director of special education and high school principals and superintendents as the leaders in my school world, because of course they were. They had the authority to hire and fire, they controlled the budget, and they represented their entities before the public and the state legislature. Their positions carried enormous responsibility. But what I came to realize was that in my schools I became the face of my cooperative, because I was the person who showed up every week at least once, and I had unique expertise. As a matter of fact, one day one of my special education teachers said to me that he was aware our co-op employed lots of people, but as far as he was concerned, *I was the co-op*. One day when I was in his classroom one of his students asked him what I did. He replied, "She solves problems".

I was given another vivid example of how a colleague viewed me the day I returned to school after a long absence. A special education teacher with whom I worked very closely happened to be standing at her open classroom door when I came down the hall toward her. I had been gone for some weeks recovering from surgery, and this was my first day in her building again. She waited as I made my way slowly down the hall. When I reached her, she smiled and said, "Our leader is back".

Natasha has experienced the same response after being in her position for just a few years. One of her teachers jokingly refers to her as "the boss", expressing a felt truth. So please take it as a fact that if you are ever named as their leader, then you probably are. Acknowledge it as a part of your professional identity, and do not protest. Instead, reflect on what leadership qualities are built into the role of a school psychologist.

Here are some to consider. School psychologists have to know how to collaborate, because much of our work at school occurs in cooperation with interdisciplinary teams. Also, individual teachers often call upon us to join with them to solve problems with behavior in their classroom and to consult about academic interventions. Beyond the schoolhouse door, we welcome partnerships with families and know how to develop them effectively to support the academic and emotional needs of children.

Perspective taking is central to our role. We know how to express our own point of view, but we are keenly aware of the importance of listening, so others will be encouraged to contribute their ideas. School psychologists cultivate empathy and gain practice at it daily. As Nichols and Straus point out, "empathy requires an effort at openness" and "restraint; it takes work". "Effective listening requires suspending our own "memory, desire, and judgment" (Nichols & Straus, 2021, pp. 188-189). We get constant practice setting our own wishes and needs aside to attend to those of others.

Our vocation compels us to be innovative. It is our duty to share new, research-based ideas that have been shown to benefit students. We support, and sometimes provide, continuous training about topics pertinent to improving schools and educational practice. Our role does not give us the authority to insist teachers accept what we recommend, but we can offer, inform, and guide, trusting them to judge for themselves.

We seek to act out of compassion and kindness, knowing we will achieve the best results by showing respect. When we speak, we want to clarify, not make points to win or to put someone in their place, and so oppose using fear or punishment to motivate others to change.

Unlike administrators, we can't give orders, but we usually neither need nor want to. Especially if we are itinerants, we lead informally from the outside. Our schools have their own internal formal structure, and we are not a part of it. Even if we are hired by a school district, school psychologists typically are not a member of the administrative staff. Our authority rests on the timeliness and quality of our advice. To be effective, we must tap into underlying needs and address them. Our power abides in how applicable our expertise is and how effective we are at sharing it at the right moment. The best ideas usually develop organically, in concert with others. It is not our purpose to seek credit for a good idea. What counts is, do our colleagues trust us, and is the knowledge we have useful and timely, or not?

Our professional standards guide us toward behaving in ways that encourage trust. These standards address our responsibility to protect the privacy of others, to maintain confidentiality in communicating with fellow professionals, and to observe appropriate restraint with family members of the students we serve. We are duty-bound to use methods and instruments that are designed to avoid biased conclusions. School psychologists are also trained to interpret data accurately to effectively analyze a child's progress and performance as a basis for recommendations. Our goal is to address problems in concert with others using the best information available.

A delicate situation that fortunately arises infrequently is the need to criticize someone else's work because it is substandard or unethical. The school psychologist usually knows the rules and regulations quite well and so notices when things are amiss. Sometimes we can offer guidance to help our colleague recognize the error and remedy it. In more serious situations, we must follow the chain of command and complain to the teacher's supervisor. On occasion we might need to alert the administration that the school district is being placed in legal jeopardy.

The special education cooperative I served in for most of my career was large; the director could attend only a select number of meetings. Consequently, the school psychologist was very often the conduit through which special education legal information was conveyed and policies were explained. And so, it was not uncommon to have heads turn my way when a decision had to be made. If necessary, I would consult with my director to make sure I was on track. But I was so often placed in the position of saying "yay" or "nay" that it became normal for me—as it was for my fellow co-op school psychologists—to perform a leadership role.

The Perils of Gatekeeping

Our leadership role places us in the position of sometimes having to stand firm on principle. Sometimes the systems within which we work exert pressure on us to perform in a way contrary to our professional standards. Teachers are trying to do right by students by referring them for special education services when they can't keep pace in the regular classroom. However, they may not understand the legal and ethical restrictions we are required to operate within. Special education services, particularly within the category of specific learning disabilities, can be seen as the best, and in some circumstances, may be the only available avenue to provide help to kids who need assistance. If we determine that the child does not meet the criteria for placement, we can be seen as a barrier to getting the child the help he or she needs.

Particularly in states that still use a discrepancy formula between an academic achievement test score and an I.Q. test score as one requirement, the school psychologist can be under pressure to place the child based on numbers, rather than looking at a complete picture of how the child functions academically. Unfortunately, what can quickly become an ethical question for the school psychologist can appear to be resistance to serving the child. We can look like we're splitting hairs to teachers who are overwhelmed and acting out of genuine concern for their students.

This circumstance points to two necessities. First, schools need more resources so special education doesn't become the only way to address a child's learning problem. Ideally, the M.T.S.S. model can provide an avenue to cope with this situation. M.T.S.S. provides a structure of three levels of prevention, from the first tier of universal supports to all students, to the second tier which addresses improving student skill deficits, and then to the third tier, intensive, individualized supports. If teachers join the school psychologist to address the child's needs outside of special education before pressing for special education intervention, learning and behavioral problems often can be addressed to everyone's satisfaction. Growing evidence indicates that the achievement/I.Q. discrepancy formula is not a valid method to determine special education eligibility, so states are gradually dropping it in favor of a more equitable approach. Several states have already eliminated the discrepancy model altogether, and it appears this is the way of the future.

Second, teachers and administrators need to have a better grounding on the finer points of the law that schools are duty-bound to uphold. Otherwise, unfair pressure is put on the school psychologist to go ahead and place a child despite scant evidence it's the right placement. When there is no other alternative available to address the child's needs, what is one to do? The rest of the child study team can override the school psychologist's judgment. At that point, going on record by writing a dissenting opinion becomes an ethical imperative for the practitioner.

Such action does not make one popular. I was on the verge of writing one when I was under pressure to place the child who spoke a twin language in special education. Fortunately, there was a better alternative available for me. But when there isn't a viable alternative, school psychologists shouldn't have to suffer the fate of being on the losing end of "kill the messenger". If the educational needs of kids were fully supported in our schools, this would not become an issue.

We Can't Always Know as Much as We Would Like

Even under the best of circumstances, our ability to speak with full confidence can be hindered, because in the moment we fall short of having all the knowledge that we would like. This is part of being cast in the role of leader; one must make decisions based on the information at hand. To cope with this reality, I learned over time to preface my remarks with the following phrasing: "Based on the information available at this time, I suggest . . .". Besides stating the limits of my ideas to colleagues and parents, this was a good reminder to myself that there might be other information which would turn my thoughts in a different direction, but deadlines are a fact of life in special education, and decisions must be made. We must be willing to change our decisions when we have better information, admit when we are wrong, and proceed with humility.

The Long Haul

I once supervised an intern who came to tears over the fact that a judge had ignored a letter she had written on behalf of a child. Her letter was a model of professionalism, but the judge disregarded what she had to say. In commiseration, another school psychologist and I listed off changes we had hoped for and had been working on but that hadn't yet come to pass during our careers. By then our combined years of experience added up to about half a century, and on many issues, we were still waiting. One might say we had failed.

For example, the year I retired some of my schools were, at last, starting to institute Positive Behavioral Interventions and Supports as their approach to discipline. Fifteen years had elapsed between my first informational lectures to staff about P.B.I.S. and its acceptance. I would never have wanted to impose anything unilaterally on my schools; I say this just to emphasize that we are not in charge. Often cast in the role of resident expert, we must take care not to take offense when not consulted and instead be grateful when invited to share expertise, because no one is duty-bound to take our suggestions. We are expected to have a wealth of knowledge to share, but others are free to disregard it. Perhaps in time they might recognize what we are saying has merit. In the meantime, we must exercise patience and persistence and not blame ourselves when our recommendations don't gain traction as quickly as we would like. How we adapt to that basic truth will determine a lot about the state of our mental health.

The key is to remember that we are in for the long haul when we are disappointed in the short run. Like Sisyphus in the Greek myth, each morning we must brace our shoulder against our boulder and attempt to heave it up our proverbial mountain. But we are more fortunate than him, because our rocks don't always slide all the way back down to the bottom. If we are determined, we usually do make incremental progress. The fact that it took 15 years from the first time I gave a lecture in my schools about P.B.I.S. until it was instituted is an example of this reality.

Taking the long view, I like to believe my efforts nudged the process along. In special education, we are accustomed to measuring success in baby steps, whether that means the progress of an individual child or progress toward institutional change in a school system. It is a character-istic of good leadership to persist toward a goal, even when the chance of realizing it immediately is unlikely.

Noting progress, however far it falls short of our goal, is always worth-while, because it helps us to stay hopeful. I like the story a friend of mine tells about a trip to Iowa to view the tulip fields. She stopped for direc-tions at a place near the fields, and there happened to be someone there who had just seen the tulips. "Well", he said, "Spring came earlier than usual this year, so the tulips are past their prime already". But then he added, "They can still look pretty good—if you stand back far enough". On some days at school, we might have to stand back so far that we need binoculars, but let's remember it's all a matter of perspective. Just the fact that one hasn't given up counts as a victory, however small.

Building Courage

Assuming the responsibilities of leadership requires courage. School psy-chologists are often promoting change, and that can provoke resistance, so we must be brave. Jim Detert, the author of *Choosing Courage: The Everyday Guide to Being Brave at Work*, reports that building courage is like developing any other skill; it does not require a particularly daring per-sonality. What it does require is practice developing the ability to over-come fear. His text offers actionable steps to take to become courageous at work, which can help us change how we think, how we behave, and how we manage our own physiological response (Detert, 2021).

Detert recommends mentally rehearsing what we need to say or do if we run into a difficult situation. That way we are emotionally prepared for uncomfortable encounters. We must identify the self-talk that results in self-defeating attitudes, so we are aware that we are undermining ourselves, and we need to substitute language that builds strength. In interactions with others, we need to learn how to advocate for our position and how to inquire effectively to learn what the basis for the opposition is. It is wise to reframe the situation to get people to move from their current position by restating the discussion in terms of the problem that can be solved mutually. Additionally, he warns against polarizing language such as "always" and "never" in summarizing someone else's point of view. Finally, we need to commit to action and reinforce our commitment by stating our intention to someone else. To do so publicly is particularly effective. The process of gaining in courage isn't easy, but the alternative is to live with the regret of not attempting to live up to one's potential (Detert, 2021).

Need for Deeper Training in Leadership

Training programs are recognizing that the time has come to recognize the importance of leadership for the school psychologist. Practitioners need some instruction, so they won't be caught unprepared when they are called on to perform a leadership role. That school psychologists should understand leadership theory has been encouraged by our profession in recent years as one way to become more adept at collaborating with principals and others in power. Burns et al. conclude that because school psychologists are often involved with system-level change, it is fitting that they grasp what approach to leadership best fits the schools they serve. They delineate instructional, relational, servant, and transformational leadership theories and describe how they apply within school settings (Phillips & Taylor, 2010).

On another level, perhaps school psychology training should also emphasize how to develop the courage that it takes to incorporate leadership into one's daily habit. Committing to Brene Brown's exhortation to dare greatly by embracing vulnerability so we can feel free to pursue a worthy idea might deserve attention, too (Burns et al., 2017).

The Role of Itinerant

An aspect of working for a cooperative is that itinerancy is a fact of life. All our roles are affected by the basic reality that we are never anywhere all the time. I soon realized that how I was received was a function of how my work week was structured and who my boss was, and my boss's relationship with the superintendents and principals our co-op served. Sometimes my identity or what I did was rather unimportant; what and who I represented was what mattered. The role of itinerant to an important extent shaped my identity.

There were distinct advantages to itinerancy. Sometimes somebody had to voice a position that would contradict someone in authority or state something that was considered too sensitive to address. The itinerant school psychologist role lends itself to carrying out such tasks. It was easier for me than those within a school district because I was able to get in my car and drive away after the meeting, and I wouldn't return until my next scheduled day, which gave people time to think about what I had said before I showed up again. My colleagues appreciated my willingness to say what needed to be said and were relieved they didn't have to be put on the spot. I always kept in mind that the cost to them would have been much higher, since it often meant telling an administrator something they didn't want to hear. This was less threatening for me because I was not challenging my boss. Not true for the teachers I worked alongside.

On one occasion a special education teacher took advantage of my itinerant role to protect herself. There was a student who we agreed should be evaluated for possible special education placement, but unbeknownst to me, she told her administrator that it was my idea, once he expressed disapproval. The next week he met with me behind closed doors to tell me how dissatisfied he was with my action. I already had the support of my special education director, so I was able to reply that my director approved, and he backed down.

When I told the teacher what her administrator said, she lifted her chin and replied, "People have been angry with me sometimes, too"— no acknowledgment that we had developed the plan together after she requested it. I believe she acted out of fear. Although I didn't appreciate her using me as a foil, I did not tell her administrator that I had a partner in his school. I forgave her because she was under far more pressure than I was. That the administrator was not my boss gave me more freedom to act.

Itinerancy also enhanced my ability to keep secrets. The nature of my work meant that I was continually being given information in confidence. The necessity of always having to move on to the next school protected me from getting too enmeshed in each school's social world, which helped to limit any temptation to reveal anything I shouldn't. One paradox of the school psychologist's role is that it makes one an insider in some respects, while being an outsider in others.

As an itinerant, I invariably would miss out on significant events, and so I wouldn't know the whole narrative of what had happened between visits. My special education teachers were very good at bringing me up to date, but that could never be as complete as being present in the first place. In this respect I was an outsider, albeit a well-treated one.

At the end of my interview for the school psychology position I held for almost 30 years, the director offered me a salary which I found acceptable. After I agreed, he paused, and then added an additional $500.00, he said, to compensate "for loneliness". Because of our role, we cannot expect to develop the same kinds of relationships people who work side by side do; being an itinerant can impose a certain degree of social isolation. What I came to see, however, was that I was no lonelier than many of the teachers I encountered, and in some cases, much less so. Sadly, I met teachers who felt isolated from their peers who worked right beside them. Unlike me, they couldn't get in their car and drive away to a different setting where they perhaps would have found a better fit.

School Psychologists as Allies

Over the course of my career, some of the best support came from fellow school psychologists who worked under conditions like mine. I benefited a great deal from a regional group of school psychologists in northwest Minnesota who met regularly, albeit infrequently. The quality of these encounters with kindred spirits facing similar challenges was so worthwhile that I came to look forward to them and depend on them for emotional support as well as professional sustenance.

Our meetings struck exactly the right note because we took them seriously—but in a light spirit. Our loose agenda allowed us to get straight to the heart of what mattered most to us. We were able to expose our deepest concerns and fears; it was a real boon to meet with other school psychologists who, to use the cliché, knew one another's pain and who shared one another's concerns for kids at school. To be among those who could accurately finish my sentences and with whom I could laugh until my sides hurt was a catharsis.

These encounters were valuable because we all faced the same sorts of challenges. Thanks to our northern winters and rural environment, most of us had to drive far distances under adverse conditions, and we all worked in schools dependent on the rural economy, which meant budgets were often stretched too far. We couldn't count on support that might be taken for granted in more prosperous districts.

Our meetings unfolded naturally in what amounted to a roundtable discussion, intently listening to one another, our conversation often punctuated with bursts of laughter while we did our best to address problems. Most of us shared a common rural background, so we didn't have to explain why we would choose to live in such a remote place. Many of us had family attachments which kept us where we were. Several even enjoyed the prairie landscape, finding a special beauty in its stark vastness under the dome of the huge, ever-changing sky, viewing it as more than just empty space to speed through on the way to somewhere else.

But we also knew, living where we did, that we constituted a minority within our profession. Sometimes this status did not gain us respect. I once had a big city school psychologist tell me that my life sounded to him like a B movie. I had left rural life in my youth and seen the big world, and I had chosen to return. He shook his head in disbelief. I prefer the attitude of writer Eudora Welty, a person from the rural South who sympathized with those living in out-of-the-way places. She expressed the belief that where one lives does not determine whether one can have deep emotional experience or have a well-developed mind (Welty, 2002).

Now school psychologists have the advantage of being able to hold virtual get-togethers online, so distance doesn't have to be a barrier. Many state organizations help their members connect online through their webpage, and, on the national level, NASP provides online discussions in the NASP Member Exchange, where school psychologists can discuss topics of concern and get advice about handling tough situations in their schools. Whatever form it takes, communicating with other school psychologists can boost morale and reduce stress. I believe this is the best kindness we can give to one another. We are strengthened by wearing our vulnerability on our collective sleeve, which allows returning to our schools better able to bear the vulnerability of others.

Merging Our Interests With Our Roles

Within the constraints of performing our day-to-day tasks, it is often possible to merge our own interests with our professional roles. At least part of the time, we can focus on what personally excites us and so draw on our strengths, which, ultimately, can make us more effective. It's worthwhile to compare what one does on the job with what one would like to do. The next step is to work to bring the answer to these two questions closer together. If a desired role is a legitimate aspect of the profession and one is qualified to perform it, then steps can be taken to absorb the role into one's work.

As I have mentioned, I enjoyed giving in-services to teachers, sometimes sharing information with them that I wanted to learn myself. For example, after doing a lot of crisis intervention, I became more and more interested in compassion fatigue and burnout, because I was becoming increasingly aware that I could fall victim to them. In my self-study I gained knowledge useful to share with colleagues and so gave a presentation to them. By addressing my own needs, I was also able to contribute to their well-being.

Whether or not it resulted in a workshop, I often selected a theme to learn more about over the course of the year. This gave me a wider perspective by shifting me away from concentrating only on day-to-day tasks. One year it was self-esteem, another it was childhood anxiety, for example. With the demands on my time that my daily routine imposed, I didn't have much left to do anything extra. But having a specific focus helped me to take small steps in a direction I purposefully chose.

We don't get to concentrate on our specific interests all the time, of course, but we can let our schools know what those interests are, and opportunities may arise. Natasha has a strong focus in behavioral management, and she has developed this in her relations with her schools. For example, she served on a team at one of her schools to get P.B.I.S. off the ground. Her expertise in analyzing data to be used in determining interventions for students makes her a key member of such a team. Every school she is in may not allow her as large a leadership role in her strongest area of interest, but whenever the opportunity arises, she is ready.

Natasha appreciates the ease of accessing and sharing documents through off-site data storage in cloud-based services which make it possible for her to work in collaboration with others from any location with an Internet connection. She can contribute to special education reports and edit files whether she is in the same building as the student who was assessed or not. This flexibility allows her to be more efficient and flexible than my generation was. Her expertise with technology is a strong step forward from the norm in school psychology practice when I was her supervisor.

Setting Boundaries to Preserve Oneself

Setting and maintaining personal boundaries is also essential and can be difficult, at least for those who are by temperament caregivers, as many school psychologists are. We must train others how to treat us; otherwise, they will treat us as they wish, which can result in being taken advantage of, however unintentionally. Therefore, learning to say "no" is a skill that needs to be developed early on. It came as a relief when I finally realized I not only had a right but an obligation to decline unreasonable requests, because taking on too much was self-destructive. This is not always easy, however, as Natasha indicated in describing her challenge of handling email in a way that would allow her to be in charge of her time and not feel obligated to respond instantly whenever she receives a message.

As the resident listener, we each must decide how much time and energy to devote to those who want us to absorb the angst of their lives. It's a delicate balance to know how much of other people's personal grief or complaints to accept over the course of a day; how much of our own energy should we contribute to meeting someone else's needs? Once a school psychologist becomes a familiar member of the school community, it is likely s/he will become a keeper of secrets. Staff will confess to us their personal trials, which can mean sharing their interpersonal strife with other staff. It is a bit of a tightrope to remain impartial and yet show empathy. One must keep any personal revelations confidential, both as a matter of professional ethics and also to avoid becoming in any way a contributor to the school rumor mill. It's worthwhile to reflect on what our limit for keeping other people's secrets should be.

After all, we may have our own secret sorrows in our personal life. Besides personal losses beyond our control that descend on us, participating in crisis intervention after death(s) or natural disaster will provide baggage to unpack from our professional experience, also. Like teachers, we are vulnerable to disenfranchised grief, and because of our role as caregivers, we may delay expressing our own feelings far too long. But our body will experience our distress, whether we are acknowledging it. Just admitting to ourselves that we deserve the same consideration we would offer to others supports healing.

Most of the time, school psychology can be an intensely rewarding profession. Tending to the educational and emotional needs of children is gratifying work; that's why many of us choose to dedicate our lives to it. But one potential pitfall is that it's easy to minimize one's own distress when confronted with the serious challenges and intense suffering in the lives of children who come to us. Constant exposure over time can be very wearing, ultimately resulting in severe fatigue, even burnout. Consequently, we must allow ourselves to admit our own anguish without comparing our needs to that of those we serve. Then we can take steps to address our distress constructively.

The ambivalence we feel toward expressing our own need for support can be dealt with by being clear about what relationships and circumstances are appropriate for expressing grief. A guideline to follow is to share grief with others in a similar situation to our own; avoid sharing with those who are more deeply affected. For example, unless one already has a very close relationship with the parents of a child who died by suicide, we shouldn't draw attention to our own grief in their presence but rather express it with members of the crisis team we served with. Regardless of the cause, school psychologists must address their own suffering in a timely manner and treat it as the serious need it is.

Because we may have more expertise in certain realms, like report writing, we also can be shaped into doing a lot of other people's work for them, just to save time. Sometimes the sacrifice is worth it to get a job done, but if it results in unreasonable expectations ever after, the price paid can be quite high. I fell into a situation for a while where I all but did a teacher's writing for her. In retrospect, I should have clarified early on what I was willing to do and not do, rather than having to back off after feeling taken advantage of. Plan how to protect yourself from the teacher who demands too much.

Besides setting limits with others, we need to set some with ourselves. Some days everything can feel like an emergency—and may just be. While addressing a group of college students about school psychology as a career, I was asked what I liked best about the profession and what was the hardest aspect of it. The answer to both questions was the same: the variety. There is always a new challenge ahead, always fascinating new people to meet. As soon as I would think I'd seen everything, an unexpected circumstance would arise. When what I was facing seemed reasonable, the variety was richly stimulating and interesting. But sometimes situations that felt overwhelming arose, requiring high-stakes decisions for a child, a family, a teacher, or a school. It didn't take long for me to realize being a school psychologist can be stimulating to the point of exhaustion.

Consequently, I had to take steps to preserve myself. The fact that I almost always was part of a team when dealing with a challenge helped tremendously; we could garner strength from one another. My fellow school psychologists filled that role often, especially my colleague Marti, who was assigned to the elementary and preschools in the same town where I was assigned the middle and high schools. We made a regular practice of consulting with one another about tough situations. When I faced a serious concern, it helped to double-check with a colleague to make sure I had done all I could.

Best Practice as Antidote to Anxiety

Staying abreast of best practice made it easier for me to cope. I attended workshops, read professional literature, and did my best to stay current. Perfection is not attainable, but we can expect to perform at a level commensurate with the present standard of the profession. When it comes right down to it, that is the least that can be demanded, and the most; and it is what a judge will expect, should one ever be taken to court. I knew it would be the best defense if my performance was ever called into question.

To rein in constant fretting, I made a small sign that I hung on the wall above my desk so it would be the first thing I would see when I sat down each morning. It said: DO THE POSSIBLE. Following best practice was both just and possible. This reminder offered some protection from chronic worry. If I knew I had followed my profession's recommended standard, I could keep anxiety about the consequences of my actions to a minimum.

I found following best practice got me off the hook with my inner impostor. I would never disparage a colleague who followed best practice, so I could quiet my negative inner voice by reminding myself that the fact that I kept to that standard meant I was not a failure; I was good enough to do the job. Of course, it is important for us to always keep learning and improving, but we don't have to be worthy of the Nobel Prize to be adequate. I like to imagine our impostor identity as the tiniest doll in a set of Russian nesting dolls. It is the tiniest because it is the least capable. But it is enclosed by ever-enlarging dolls, who can symbolize our ever-increasing abilities and confidence.

Current research on impostor syndrome indicates there can be a silver lining to the condition. If we are motivated to work harder and learn more because of our feelings of inadequacy, we can gain in confidence while maintaining humility. As psychologist Adam Grant emphasizes, confident humility is a prerequisite for future learning (Grant, 2021). Isn't it interesting that, done right, fearing we are a failure can make us less of a failure?

And speaking of dolls, I found a fine use for an imaginary doll house one night as I lay awake, ruminating about someone who I felt was unkind to me. Suddenly, an image of a charming little house appeared, and I gently eased this person, who had shrunk down to fit, in through the front door. I did no harm, and I voiced no insult. It was a comfortable little dwelling, where I trust she felt safe and protected. In the blink of an eye, she was where I needed her to be, which was out of earshot, away from me. I had, imaginatively speaking, put her in her place. I must confess I have used this image more than once since, and it always makes me smile. We can't control anyone else, but we can use our sense of humor and imagination to gain control of our own emotions.

It's easy to fall victim to cognitive distortions from time to time, especially when tired and feeling chronically stressed. As we ruminate, we need to watch our language. Even when we are talking to ourselves, we must mind our manners—and our grammar. It can mean the difference between creating a self-destructive loop that undermines our confidence and sense of self-worth and a self-affirming experience that acknowledges our right to be the ever-evolving, living, and growing human being that we are.

Otherwise, our language can entrap us, as scholar Lawrence Weinstein points out. He says to watch out for forms of the infinitive "to be", because it can box you up unfairly. For example, if someone says to you or you say to yourself that you *are* incompetent, that quality is now set as a feature of your identity. Imagine if, instead, you or the other person says that how you scored a test last week indicated you were reading across the wrong line on the chart and you need to correct your error, redemption is at hand. Correct your error, and you get to be competent again (Weinstein, 2020).

We also get to be forgiving of ourselves when we engage in faulty thinking, because being human means we are prone to making unconscious inferences, or as Banaji and Greenwald call them, "mindbugs—ingrained habits of thought that lead to errors in how we perceive, remember, reason, and make decisions". These mindbugs account for our unconscious biases, the stereotypes we may unknowingly hold toward race, gender, sexual orientation, disability, nationality, social class, age, and any other identifiable aspect of human beings (Banaji & Greenwald, 2016, p. 10). When we discover we have applied a stereotype, we must acknowledge it, perhaps apologize, correct our action, and try to do better next time. To err is human. We are no exception. So, let's stumble on to our next mistake, and do it with enthusiasm.

The Challenge of Leaving Work at Work

Balancing our work and our private life can present a huge challenge. Probably the toughest part for me daily was figuring out how not to bring the trauma of the day home. I often described my occupation of school psychologist as looking up at the under-belly of the communities where I worked. What I meant was I was privy to the quiet tragedies being suffered by children, often on an ongoing basis, and sometimes these children felt like sand through my fingers.

It helped to develop good exercise and eating habits, as well as maintaining an active artistic, intellectual, and spiritual life so that I could become absorbed in outside activities to the point I could not think about work. I enjoyed my friends and cultivated a happy home life. Still, I would dream about kids when I was worried, and all too often I did some of my best thinking in the wee hours of the morning.

Moment to moment, what helped the most was to determine what action I could take to improve a situation. Performing one small act would help me move forward, with the happy side effect of also reducing my anxiety. But there is only so much we can influence in the lives of the children we serve, and so I had to develop the humility to acknowledge that sometimes, despite our highest hopes and best efforts, bad things happen anyway. I could help in the ways I was able at the time, but I was not a one-person rescue service, and I was not equipped with a magic wand.

Like most school psychologists, I performed to the best of my ability and did my best to err on the side of kindness. The trick was to extend that kindness to myself and forgive myself for not being able to do more than what I could. This required that my hopes be realistic. So sometimes the one small act I performed to move forward had to be for myself. That was a tough one, because school psychologists are in the business of hope, and we don't like to give up. Sooner or later, each of us will probably work with a child who has a terminal condition, a true test of how realistic we can be.

I am reminded of a child I worked with over a span of several years who was gradually succumbing to a degenerative condition that ultimately killed her. When we met, she was still ambulatory, but because her soft tissue was calcifying, her gait was precarious. The temptation was to want to slow her down and wish her into a wheelchair, rather than allow her to barrel down the hall, looking like she was about to ricochet off a wall and crash. Her parents wisely said to let her move on her own, for as long as she could.

Consequently, I had to override my anxiety for her (and for myself) and allow her to live out her life in her own way. Doing this had the side effect of making me more courageous, as I witnessed her determination and grit. Also, she proved my fears groundless. She never did collide with anything when we were together. The only collision occurred within my head, between my desire to be overprotective at times and my responsibility to allow her to take charge of her own action. This experience prompted me to reflect on what my function was. Besides being there to possibly soften a fall, I mainly served to listen, witness, and support, so far as I was able. At the time I never felt like I was contributing very much, but I now see that being there, reliably, and predictably at her side, demonstrating my confidence in her ability to make her own choices, was enough.

How Play Can Make Us Stronger

I had always enjoyed drawing and wanted to learn to paint someday. The first year I was earning a real paycheck, I signed up for a workshop on watercolor painting. As I stood in line to pay, I overheard a conversation between two women, both several decades older than me. One asked the other how many supplies she intended to purchase. The other replied, "I am going to buy one of everything, and I don't care how much it costs. I have spent my whole life looking after others, and now it's my turn". I followed her fine example and bought one of everything, too.

I vowed that I would not take my painting so seriously that it would become a burden. It had to be an antidote to my daily stress, not another source. I'm pleased to say that now that I am the age of the women I mentioned, painting is an important aspect of my life. What matters most about what I have learned and continue to learn through painting is not so much about art—although that is immensely rewarding, but about my own limits and desires.

Karen Rinaldi's book about courage and resilience, *It's Great to Suck at Something*, expresses a perspective which I embrace. Her subtitle, *The Unexpected Joy of Wiping Out and What It Can Teach Us about Patience, Resilience, and the Stuff That Really Matters* sums up what my painting efforts have meant to me. Basically, it provides an activity that I love, but whose stakes are so low that I can fail again and again, without serious penalty. Rinaldi's outside interest was surfboarding, and she started in middle age. The likelihood of becoming a star was remote, and she didn't. Fortunately, she didn't care about impressing anyone else. Surfing helped her to keep the rest of her life in perspective, and for her that included a bout with breast cancer (Rinaldi, 2019).

Perhaps not coincidently, I became more expressive through art and writing when I endured a similar health challenge. What a life-threatening illness can do is teach us there is no point in putting off doing something worthy because of our insecurities about our abilities, because time is running out and maybe faster than we thought. That's why Karen Renaldi is telling us to just do it and fail all over the place. And then pick yourself up and get on that surfboard another time. Eventually, we'll improve and our capacity to act with courage will grow.

Or crochet. My mother, Nettie Johnson, said crocheting "helped to settle" her nerves. We should do whatever can get us focused on something meaningful and enjoyable outside of work and do it repeatedly, because what it can do is bring us back to our serious work refreshed and more deeply connected to ourselves. And that will make us stronger, which just might carry over to our high stakes' endeavors. At the very least, it will give us a reason to look forward to our weekends.

Survival as a School Psychologist

Life at school has become more and more complicated, and stress within the profession of school psychology has risen to the point that experienced practitioners wonder if they can survive until retirement age. As I mentioned earlier, a woman about 20 years younger than I asked me point blank, "How did you do it? How did you survive?" This led to a conversation about all the stress she—and all the school psychologists she and I knew—endured. How did I make it to my mid-sixties without having to quit out of sheer exhaustion?

I confessed that summers saved me, regular exercise helped enormously, having strong interests outside of school psychology provided a mental vacation when I needed one, and my husband and friends were supportive. On the job I had terrific colleagues and I found kids to be unfailingly fascinating, so I didn't want to give up. Besides, I believed in my profession. Yet I had points along the way when I wondered if I could stay within the field until retirement age.

During my era, I don't recall self-care being emphasized much at all, whether in my school psychology training program or, later, at professional conferences or in school psychology literature. If it was mentioned, it was in an aside, a brief reminder to take care of ourselves, particularly when dealing with acute crises, in the unlikely event we would ever have to deal with any. Like many other school psychologists, I all too frequently used my weekends to catch up on report writing, because my weekdays were filled with other duties. There was never a firm limit on what was asked of us if it could somehow be crammed into the day.

Add on a pandemic, and the situation can become intolerable. During the pandemic, leaving work at work became even more difficult. Natasha described her impossibly long workdays, leaving scant time for anything else in her life except basic chores at home and rest so she would have the strength to go back another day. Being highly organized kept her stress in check, but she admitted freely that the pressure promoted workaholism. School psychs traditionally have adopted much the same attitude as health care workers: no hours too long, no cases too many. Cope with the needs of others and ignore your own until summer. Then collapse.

When we are healthy and young, this can work for a while, if we're lucky. The pace caught up with me one year when I came down with mononucleosis at the beginning of summer. My doctor said he had seen a rash of cases, mostly early-middle-aged mothers who worked full time. Like me. My strength did not return until the last week of summer break, so I was ready to return to school that fall, no one the wiser, except for me. This jolt of reality made me realize I had better take care of myself because otherwise I might not last.

I told my younger counterpart I thought it was unfortunate that as a profession we didn't emphasize the need to take care of ourselves very much. We agreed that the work never seemed to be getting any easier, and how important it is to acknowledge our limits. In this way, we admired the problem together, and I wished her well for the future. I hope she has been able to persist in her chosen profession. The odds of her doing so may be increasing, with NASP stepping up and naming self-care as a high priority for best practice. School psychologists must tend to their own needs first, a difficult concept for many to accept, until one understands the consequences of not doing do.

NASP now designates self-care as an ethical principle, necessary to avoid doing harm. The pandemic has raised this issue like nothing else could. When I reflect on my own career, I wish I had been more deliberate in tending to my own self-preservation along the way. If I could turn back the clock and encounter myself when I first stepped into a school to begin my life as a school psychologist, this is what I would tell myself:

Taking care of oneself is not a selfish act; it is a self-sustaining act. To be of use to others, one must be physically, mentally, and emotionally fit. Consequently, we must offer ourselves the same level of care we would extend to someone else. Furthermore, it is also an ethical responsibility. We must be able to perform well so we can behave responsibly in our interactions with others (Moore et al., 2019).

Get Enough Sleep

Short of illness, the quickest way to be brought low is through lack of sleep. Evening needs to be a prelude to sleep instead of a continuation of the workday. One way to do that is to have realistic expectations of what can be accomplished during the day. My sleep was disrupted all too frequently because I was ruminating over a child. It would have been better for me to just get up and write down my thoughts or read something gentle so I could relax and complete my night.

Move That Body

When I became a teacher, I learned to prevent exhaustion by going for a run in the morning several times a week before I went to school. Thereafter, I built a habit of regular exercising that I keep to this day. I doubt I would have had the physical stamina to make it to retirement age a practitioner had I not.

Stay Home When You Are Sick

For your own sake as well as everyone else's, take care of yourself when you are ill and don't expose others to infections. At the time of the S1N1 epidemic, the nurse administering my flu shot told me she felt school personnel should be considered at the same level of risk as health workers, because of the exposure to disease that occurs in schools. Covid-19 provided a crash course in that reality.

Play Hard

Another important way to prevent becoming over-stressed is to devote yourself to a pleasurable activity outside of work. I became a watercolorist. Natasha rescues abandoned pets. Within the rural cooperative for which I worked, there is a school psychologist who directs school plays on the side, another hikes and kayaks regularly, and one who helps organize an enormous community musical festival every summer. It doesn't matter what the activity is, so long as it can be a great escape.

Feed Your Strengths

No one can be an expert on everything, so focus on your strongest interests and take advantage of your natural abilities. Address any weaknesses that might undermine your effectiveness but make the very most of your strengths. If you respect and develop them, chances are others will notice and you will find yourself doing more and more of what you like.

Know You Can't Push the River

Have faith in your own creativity and work ethic. There is a dynamic within yourself that governs your rate of learning and gaining insight. It cannot be forced or hurried. And when you follow in harmony with it, the experience will bring joy.

Simplify Your Work

Maximize your efficiency day to day by streamlining how you approach your work. My co-op made a template for evaluation summary reports with introductory standard phrases for each section of data to save writing time and as cues so we wouldn't omit any required information. Everyone's life got a little bit easier.

Plan

At the end of each day, take a moment to get a plan in mind for the following day. As you begin each year, set some goals for yourself. Then, at the end of each day and at the end of each year, forgive yourself for not achieving everything you set out to learn or do. Plan your recreation, a necessity of survival.

Problem-solve With a Trusted Colleague on a Regular Basis

Getting a second opinion from someone you respect will keep you from second-guessing yourself.

Accept Your Best as Good Enough

Be satisfied to do what is possible under the circumstances. When we step away, we must let go so we can move on to the next challenge and start afresh. We can cultivate compassion satisfaction, rather than succumbing to compassion fatigue. Natasha gained an insight into burnout while observing in a language arts class. She had an epiphany while the teacher was explaining the difference between internal and external conflicts in literature, realizing we can set ourselves up for burnout if we allow self-imposed internal conflicts about performance to combine with the impact of external factors that press on us (N. Olson, personal communication, November 11, 2019). On the other hand, if we can take satisfaction from our performance, we will maintain hope, develop strength, and build resilience (Hueber, 2019).

Consciously Build Emotional Strength

Make a daily habit of reflecting on the ways you are moving forward, what is satisfying in your work life, and reasons to be hopeful. Do not be afraid of your compassion for others; our profession guides us in how best to apply it. Take comfort that you are part of a much larger community working on behalf of children.

Learn to Interrupt Thoughts That Create Negative Stress

Cognitive distortions undermine self-confidence and make life harder than it needs to be. We especially need to watch our language when we ruminate, because it can weaken our confidence and sense of self-worth. Best practice requires good enough, not perfect. Perfectionism is a self-defeating trap.

Acknowledge Disenfranchised Grief

When immersed in the grief of others, you can't help but be affected. After assisting in crisis intervention, be sure to take time to express your own sad feelings.

Complain When the Demands of Your Position Have Become Unreasonable

If possible, join with others who are also becoming overwhelmed. Document your actions so you have a record of your efforts to improve the situation.

Celebrate Often

Whatever you achieve, however small it seems, matters. So, when you achieve something you're glad to have done or pass an important milestone, celebrate. Practically every day brings something to appreciate, even if it's just being glad that you survived what the day required of you.

Preserve Your Stories

One of the great privileges of being a school psychologist is the opportunity to work so closely with children that we catch them being themselves. Also, the more complete the record, the better you will recognize what themes threaded through your days and years.

Advocate for Yourself, Schools, Children, and Families

School psychologists can be effective advocates because of our unique experience. Our state and federal legislators need to hear from us regularly and with purpose in mind.

Be as Helpless as a Rattlesnake

Like psychologists, rattlesnakes sometimes get a bad rep. Contrary to the stereotype, some rattlesnakes have an unaggressive temperament. The first choice of a timber rattlesnake is to escape a threat, not attack. So only confront when there is no other choice. Even then, be kind and fair.

Cultivate Gratitude

Gratitude can help us to appreciate both the long view and the short run. At school there is usually something to appreciate or someone we are pleased to have encountered. I can say that having ended my career with a grateful heart brings me peace.

References

Banaji, M. R., & Greenwald, A. G. (2016). *Blind spot: Hidden biases of good people.* Random House Publishing Group.

Burns, M. K., Preast, J. L., Kilpatrick, K. D., Taylor, C. N., Young, H., Aguilar, L., Allen, A., Copeland, C., Haider, A., & Henry, L. (2017, September). Leadership theory for school psychologists: Leading for systems change. *Communiqué, 46*(2), 30–31.

Detert, J. (2021). *Choosing courage: The everyday guide to being brave at work.* Harvard Business Review Press.

Grant, A. (2021). *Think again: The power of knowing what you don't know.* Viking.

Hueber, S. (2019). Measuring the triad of positive emotional strengths: Gratitude, life satisfaction, and hope. *Communiqué, 47*(5), 25.

Moore, E. C., Jeglum, S., Young, K., & Campbell, S. M. (2019). Self-care in supervision: How do we teach others to care for themselves? *Communiqué, 47*(8), 30–31.

Nichols, M. P., & Straus, M. B. (2021). *The lost art of listening: How learning to listen can improve relationships* (3rd ed.). The Guilford Press.

Paige, L. (2019, October). Has this ever happened to you? *Communiqué, 48*(2), 2.

Phillips, A., & Taylor, B. (2010). *On kindness.* Picador.

Rinaldi, K. (2019). *It's great to suck at something: The unexpected joy of wiping out and what it can teach us about patience, resilience, and the stuff that really matters.* Atria Books.

Weinstein, L. (2020). *Grammar for a full life: How the ways we shape a sentence can limit or enlarge us.* Lexigraphic Publishing.

Welty, E. (2002). *On writing.* Modern Library.

Chapter 22

Looking Back, Facing Forward

I hope the preceding chapters have illustrated what the vocation of school psychology contributes to the lives of children. I used examples from my own career to illustrate how the profession melds idealism with hard realities. I wanted to show what is required of a practitioner day to day, emphasizing the skills and knowledge that have become fundamental to the job of supporting the academic, behavioral, and emotional needs of students, and how our roles have expanded.

I also felt it was important to feature legal, historical, and political events that have had, and continue to have, a significant effect on disability and civil rights, because they form the backbone of policies affecting educational rights. Because laws matter, how to advocate on behalf of schools, children, and families deserved prime attention.

Woven throughout are insights from Dr. Natasha Olson, the practitioner who succeeded me in the position I vacated through retirement and who was my final school psychology intern. Her perspective as a young school psychologist helped to bring the account into the present with an immediacy that it otherwise could not have had. Her presence also represents the future of the profession, now burdened with enormous challenges while, at the same time, gifted with better insights based on research than ever before.

I began the book with my mother's story, because it set the stage both for my own narrative and for the much larger story of the history of disability rights. In the first chapter, I emphasized the high standard my mother set in her care of people with severe disabilities. The deep respect she demonstrated for their basic humanity exemplified the same attitude the profession of school psychology cultivates. Her example served as a guide for me as a practitioner throughout my career.

The next several chapters span my early teaching experiences within diverse cultures. I found that what I learned about language acquisition, immigration, and racial equity issues transferred easily to my practice of school psychology. Although decades have passed since I taught in an all-Black school in the American South, in an American school with

DOI:10.4324/9781003348344-22

an international student body in a majority Muslim country, and in a migrant program for Hispanic students, the lessons I learned still apply, verified by scholarly research. The need for advocacy on behalf of marginalized groups also remains. Understanding has broadened and deepened, but variations of the same problems continue to confront each new generation of school psychologists.

Learning how to intervene in a crisis at school from the ground up was the greatest challenge I dealt with over the course of my career. Because meeting the needs of children in crisis at school is a grave responsibility, I devoted attention to crisis intervention after deaths and following natural disasters, including a brief summary of evidence-based practices now available.

In the twenty-first century, pandemic has added yet another dimension of responsibility. An overview of the history of handling health in schools places the most recent pandemic within a larger context. The economic security of schools is an ongoing concern and has become increasingly so. A chapter is devoted to explaining why many public schools are underfunded and emphasizing the need to advocate on their behalf.

Practitioners work in close cooperation with others throughout the school community, so our relationship with fellow travelers is the focus of several chapters. How we relate to other adults such as teachers, paraprofessionals, administrators, parents, and other specialists often determines how effective we can be. They are our best allies, and I emphasize the need to listen to them. I give an overview of the contribution we can make to them through sharing our specialized knowledge of disability, children's mental health issues, and the legalities involved in addressing special education placement. Central to our practice are our individual relationships with children. A chapter is devoted to an in-depth look at how we communicate with them, highlighting the value of play.

Finally, describing the breadth and depth of the roles we perform in our schools as we carry out the tasks required of us day to day illustrates what school psychology requires of its practitioners. I emphasize the importance of unofficial leadership because school psychologists are being called upon to stand at the forefront of current movements in schools, such as championing educational equity. Rural school psychology deserved attention, so I devoted space to itinerancy and other aspects of working in special education cooperatives.

Because our profession can be intensely demanding, it seemed fitting to end the book with a look at the impact our responsibilities can have on our health. Coping strategies and building courage were highlighted. I ended by offering a list of suggestions I would give myself if I could address the young teacher, later school psychologist, who I was when I began my adventure in serving the educational needs of children.

My intention in writing this book was to illustrate the ways in which school psychologists help children to thrive. I present my own experience as a window through which the reader can have a glimpse of what was required of one school psychology practitioner. My purpose was to inform others, but unintentionally, I also informed myself. As I recounted incident after incident from my years of work with children, I found myself reflecting on my own childhood, discovering meaningful connections between the child I was and those I served in school. Through this review, I gained a deeper understanding of why school psychology was so compelling to me. The reason, I believe, is rooted in my own childhood, in moments when I needed a supportive adult to cope with difficult circumstances. I suspect this may be true for many others who have found a life's work in serving the needs of children.

Valuing Our Own Childhood

Charles Schultz, the creator of the beloved "Peanuts" cartoon, based his illustrated narratives on disappointments and challenges from his childhood experiences, transforming his little boy hurts into touching vignettes (Michaelis, 2007). Likewise, it is useful for us to reflect on the value and meaning of our own story to deepen our understanding of why school psychology attracted us. I must confess, before undertaking this project, I did not fully grasp how important my mother's or father's example was. Nor did I contemplate what meaning a serious childhood illness probably had on my choice of career.

Because we were once children ourselves, most of us eventually meet children whose circumstance strikes a chord within us. Even if this recognition may not be fully conscious, it can deepen our commitment to helping them cope. My most relevant childhood memory involved temporary disability caused by physical illness. I seldom thought of that time, but decades later, what happened in a ballet class reminded me of the impact of that childhood experience.

At age 50, I signed up for adult ballet lessons. I was a total beginner, so even hoisting my leg up on the bar felt like an accomplishment. But our teacher was welcoming and glad to teach anyone, regardless of their level of experience, so I didn't feel self-conscious. Then my delightful teacher left to take another job and the class for adults evaporated. I was shifted to another class, but this time, my fellow students would be junior high age girls. The teacher, focused on training the girls to become excellent performers, barely acknowledged my presence, and my fellow students didn't either, except for one. There was one girl who always greeted me at the beginning of every class, and at other moments quietly acknowledged my presence with an encouraging smile. Her classmates, like the teacher, looked right through me.

I realized that this is like having a physical disability. Everyone else is performing at a level you have no chance of matching, and because you can't, you become invisible to those who are able to compete. Except to those who are aware that you are a person, too, even if you are obviously different. This experience prompted me to think about the students with disabilities I knew, who faced rejecting indifference as a part of their daily life. The uncomfortable atmosphere also jogged a memory from when I was just a few years younger than were the girls in this class.

When I was about ten, I had a bout of rheumatic fever, an infection of the heart that causes joint inflammation, pain, and life-threatening fever spikes. My dad had to interrupt harvesting one hot August day to rush me to the doctor for a shot of penicillin. Spikes were so dangerous that my temperature had to be taken every morning, and I was allowed to go to school only if it was normal. I was forbidden to run; I had to avoid doing anything that might stress my heart.

Rheumatic fever meant my school attendance was unpredictable, and I missed so many days that if I had missed just one more, I would have been retained, under North Dakota state law. My attendance at events outside of school was sketchy, also. At a 4-H meeting one evening, someone suggested to me that I should quit because my inconsistent attendance would ruin the club's chance of getting a perfect attendance ribbon at the state fair.

I stood there trying with all my might not to cry in front of everyone, as I realized she wanted to banish me. It was hard enough to have rheumatic fever; to be told I didn't belong added insult to injury. Our club's leader spoke up immediately, saying that wasn't a concern, and I should just continue to come when I was able. Perhaps to my 4-H leader it seemed a small gesture, but to me it was the greatest kindness, and she became my hero.

Over the months before I healed, I had a taste of what it felt like to have a disability, although we didn't frame it in those terms in the 1950s. Beatrice Wright, in a chapter entitled, "Disability and Self-Esteem", describes the emotional toll of humiliating experiences related to being under-valued because of difference. "Idolizing normal standards relegates the person to an inferior position, not only objectively, in terms of a particular characteristic, but may also do so morally, as a total person" (Wright, 1983). This can result in shame and feelings of inferiority, such as I felt when I feared I was no longer welcome at 4-H.

My 4-H leader accepted me exactly as I was, and that response had tremendous power. With one sentence, she validated me. As we know from research on resilience and children, the influence of supportive adults can mitigate negative effects of trauma (Weir, 2017). A school psychologist is often able to offer this level of wholehearted acceptance to children, and help to counter self-deprecating, negative feelings that could undermine a strong sense of self. My personal experience taught me how important this is.

Memories Matter

Learning to be a school psychologist in so many respects requires that we work to understand who we really are. We bring much more of ourselves to our day at school than our knowledge and interests. We each have our own genetic, physical, and neurological make-up and gender, our own family history, ethnic background, and personal beliefs which bring with them the implications of linguistic, racial, and cultural heritage. We also have our personal memories, which create a receptive heart in us and so can deepen connections with the children we serve. It is worth reflecting on one's memories to identify moments that helped us to develop empathy for others and set us on course for a career in school psychology.

The meaning of our life events isn't always readily apparent. The renowned writer Eudora Welty described it as "stumbling upon cause and effect in the happenings" of one's experiences. Subjective time, she says, offers "the continuous thread of revelation" (Welty, 2020, p. 121). It is a lifelong task to become aware of our own assumptions and history and recognize that others may—or may not—share them. Our personal memories can be a bridge to others within the school community, enriching our interactions with them. Working with the wide range of children, their parents, and all the staff and students at school that we encounter gives us plenty of practice to reflect on how our unique identity matches or contrasts with this whole cast of characters, all of whom have their own unique identities and backgrounds. It is a fascinating life, figuring out where we fit and how we belong. Our own deepest, pivotal, experiences form meaning that, if articulated, can help us to understand ourselves and can serve to enlighten others who are following a similar path. Natasha encouraged me to write my stories with this thought in mind.

The Sustaining Power of Meaning

As mentioned in the previous chapter, my personal health history would not inspire anyone to follow in my footsteps. It is true that I adopted healthful habits early on, which no doubt helped me manage negative stress and possibly was even the reason I was able to persevere. I must emphasize, however, that when I made time to go to the gym, hike, cook healthful food, and do all the other things I did to protect my health, I was just trying to survive. I had enough hints along the way that the consequences of not doing so could be dire.

So why didn't I throw up my hands and find something easier to do? Because school psychology meant so much more to me than just a way to earn a decent living. That moment in Delhi, India, when I heard the school psychologist describe his work with children with disabilities and emotional problems, I easily imagined myself in the role. Once I became one, I felt I had found what I had been looking for. I recognized that it could sustain me with meaning throughout my life.

I loved engaging with children of all ages, meeting with their parents, working alongside their teachers, and joining with my colleagues at all levels to support the educational needs of kids. Mentoring and encouraging school psychology students in their practica and internships enhanced my sense of purpose. The motto of the special education cooperative where I spent most of my career was "Resources Invested in Children". This phrase aligned with my deepest beliefs. I was wholeheartedly behind the notion that all our children deserve to be invested in; every single one should have an opportunity to thrive.

I was where I wanted to be, and I considered it a privilege and a stroke of good luck to be there. However pessimistic I might be feeling about the specific events of any given day, I seldom felt my time had been wasted. Studies over the years confirm my opinion. There is a wealth of research indicating the sorts of interventions school psychologists conduct reduce the likelihood of students dropping out, increase academic performance, and reduce behavior problems. Mental health interventions decrease discipline referrals and lead to improved test scores. It is well documented that supporting the social, emotional, and behavioral health of students leads to higher academic achievement in school (National Association of School Psychologists, 2010). Joining hands with others to invest in children, which for each of us meant investing our very selves, brought meaning that sustained us. Survival strategies certainly helped, but what brought us strength was the knowledge that what we did mattered.

That meaning carries us through is not a new concept. As contemporary philosopher Ella Estafan Smith remarks, the ancient Greek philosophers wrote about it, as did giants in psychology such as Victor Frankl, a Nazi death camp survivor. Smith identifies what she considers to be the four pillars of meaning: belonging, purpose, storytelling, and transcendence. I believe school psychology and other vocations within education are imbued with all four (Smith, 2017).

Our school communities and the children we serve within them often claim us, so school psychologists regularly experience belonging. Being a part of the profession of school psychology also offers this connection. Our profession is full of purpose, which we seek to make manifest each day. Although it is painful to witness the suffering of children, we can support their resilience, which strengthens us as well as them. It only takes a short time for a school psychologist to have a repertoire of stories, which can illuminate one's path by showing what one has learned and accomplished. And, like everyone touching children's lives, we continuously enjoy the transcendent experience of creating the future through supporting the young in their education. There is scarcely anything in this life that can matter more.

Conclusion

To meet the challenges of their profession, school psychologists need to know themselves and their limits well. It takes strength to deal with controversial and serious issues while at the same time carrying out daily duties, duties which have expanded significantly in number and complexity since our profession was in its infancy. Today practitioners like Natasha and her cohorts must be equipped to deal with the individual academic, behavioral, and emotional needs of children, but also must have the skill to guide a school district to improve school climate through behavior management approaches that take advantage of current insights from behavioral science and trauma therapy. They must be ready to help schools face tragedy, and they must know how to proceed in a rolling crisis, such as a pandemic. Their assessment and counseling practices must be sensitive to racial, cultural, and linguistic diversity to avoid discriminatory placements. Recommendations for academic interventions must be research based. Furthermore, school psychologists now must be well informed about the larger political scene and increasingly need to take an active role in influencing it. Their work requires a commitment of body, mind, and soul. Not a small order, but a worthy one. I trust that the next generation of school psychologists will be a strong force, working together with their allies to counter the injustices children face, through supporting educational justice in school. May they grow in number and exemplify the best of what school psychology can offer.

References

Michaelis, D. (2007). *Schulz and peanuts: A biography.* HarperCollins.

National Association of School Psychologists. (2010, January). *Evidence for the positive impact of school psychological services.* www.casponline.org/pdfs/pdfs/positiveimpactsp.pdf

Smith, E. E. (2017). *The power of meaning: Finding fulfillment in a world obsessed with happiness.* Broadway Books.

Weir, K. (2017, September). Maximizing children's resilience. *APA Monitor on Psychology, 48*(8), 40. www.apa.org/monitor/2017/09/cover-resilience?gclid=Cj0KCQjwntCVBhDdARIsAMEwACkv2oLz3fTPTRn-UJMZmmLuK6tOznp-5jxpKdmvcMklsrI14vc5YjJYaAlhPEALw_wcB

Welty, E. (2020). *One writer's beginnings.* Scribner.

Wright, B. A. (1983). *Physical disability: A psychosocial approach* (2nd ed.). HarperCollins. https://doi.org/10.1037/10589-000

Discussion Questions

What is the significance of the Fourteenth Amendment for schools and special education? How are civil rights and disability rights linked?

It may require special courage to accept a child's disability when it also entails grieving the loss of the dream of what parents had hoped for their child—a life uncomplicated by disability. What is the relationship between vulnerability and courage? What role does listening play? How do you develop your own courage?

Describe how your own cultural background relates to your working with children. How would you reply to the student asking, "Why can't we all just get along? Why can't we all just be American? That's who we are, aren't we?"

What are the necessary features of collaboration and cooperation with others in the school? With entities beyond the school setting?

Philosopher Ella Estafan Smith considers belonging, purpose, storytelling, and transcendence to be the four pillars of meaning. Where do you find belonging, purpose, and transcendence?

What stories, strategies, and facts can you draw from as you advocate for the needs of children and schools? What themes thread through your stories? How do they connect to a larger purpose?

Index

For Product Safety Concerns and Information please contact our EU
representative GPSR@taylorandfrancis.com
Taylor & Francis Verlag GmbH, Kaufingerstraße 24, 80331 München, Germany